THE OFFICIAL HANDBOOK

MARVEL UNIVERSE

VOLUME ONE: ABOMINATION TO CIRCUS OF CRIME

Presented by
STAN LEE

MARK GRUENWALD
Writer/Packager

PETER SANDERSON
Writer/Researcher

ELIOT R. BROWN
Technical Illustrator

JOSEF RUBINSTEIN
Inker/Embellisher

ANDY YANCHUS
Colorist

PAUL RYAN
Cover Penciler

BOB SHAREN
Cover Colorist

BRENDA MINGS
Typesetter

**BARRY SHAPIRO
DAWN GEIGER**
Paste–Up/Mechanicals

GREGORY WRIGHT
Associate Editor

HOWARD MACKIE
Assistant Editor

JIM SHOOTER
Editor in Chief

Published by Marvel Comics Group,
A Division of Cadence Industries Corporation.
387 Park Avenue South, New York,
New York 10016

Manufactured in the United States of America

ISBN 0-87135-208-7

2nd Printing

CONTENTS AND ARTISTS

PREFACE

Stan Lee had an idea. It was an idea that would soon take on universal proportions. The year was 1961, and Stan was the editor and chief writer of what would soon be called the Marvel Comics Group. The germ of the idea was first implanted in a comic book that premiered in late 1961 called *Fantastic Four*. The book was about four people who went up in a rocket and returned to earth with fantastic powers derived from cosmic rays. Although descended from both the big monster books Marvel was publishing at the time (featuring such colorfully named misanthropes as Googam, Groot, and Fin Fang Foom) and the super hero books Marvel (then known as Timely-Atlas) had published in the 40's and 50's (notably Captain America, the Human Torch, and Sub-Mariner), the Fantastic Four was at once different from anything that had gone before in the comics medium. Despite their wild superhuman powers, the Fantastic Four were more lifelike and realistic than anyone expected "comic book characters" (a term often used as a synonym for two-dimensional stereotyped characters) could ever be.

But it was not until Stan and his small crew of talented collaborators came out with other imaginative characters in their own titles (such as the mighty Thor, the invincible Iron Man, the incredible Hulk, and of course, the amazing Spider–Man) that Stan's idea would have the space to unfold. That idea was to provide a common context, a sense of continuity, a consistent *universe* for all of the characters in all of the Marvel titles. "Crossovers"—heroes from one series "crossing over" into another hero's series—had been done before, sometimes even on a regular basis. But never before was there a concerted effort to create a consistent backdrop for so many series at once, so that the depiction of New York, or Mars, or Atlantis, would be the same from one series to the next. It is hard to document when the term "Marvel Universe" was first used (I believe it *was* some time within Marvel's first five years), but it was indeed a *universe* of marvels that Stan Lee and his gifted collaborators had created and bequeathed to the reading public. For twenty years, the Marvel Universe flourished and expanded, and new characters and concepts grew upon the sturdy foundation Stan and company had built.

Then Jim Shooter had an idea. The year was 1981, and Jim was the editor in chief of the entire Marvel line which had grown from the ten or so titles published when Stan was editor to over sixty monthly titles. Jim got his idea while listening to the collective voice of Marvel's almost fanatical readership who constantly bombarded Marvel with such earnest queries as "Just how strong is the Hulk?", "How does the Invisible Girl turn invisible?", "What kind of energy shoots out of Cyclops' eyes?", "Where does Ant-Man's mass go when he shrinks?", and "What's the maximum limit Mr. Fantastic can stretch?" Jim realized that readers' concern about questions like these was testimony that the Marvel heroes were so believable that the readers felt questions like those above had concrete answers. Furthermore, he realized that providing answers to those questions would enhance the Marvel reader's reading enjoyment, not detract from it (as the conventional "wisdom" went). So Jim's idea was to publish a series where these questions and more could be addressed in detail. He thought of it as a Specifications Handbook with detailed information describing the precise nature and limits of the Marvel characters' powers and weaponry, to be done in the manner of specifications books for military hardware. Jim figured that such a package done in comic book format would have immense appeal to Marvel's legions of readers.

The next step was finding someone to get the job done. Jim came to me. I had a good working knowledge of the length and breadth of the Marvel Universe, having had the good fortune to have begun reading Marvel Comics the year the first *Fantastic Four* came out, and having the good sense to have never given up reading them in all the intervening years. Jim told me his idea, and I immediately took to it since I had long felt that someone should do an encyclopedia to the Marvel Universe. Jim's emphasis on the specifications of powers gave such an enormous undertaking a workable approach. All I had to do is come up with the specific format and get it all written and drawn. *All!* We published the orginal edition of the *Official Handbook of the Marvel Universe* from the fall of 1982 to mid-1983. I now look at the original edition as practice, since we worked out many of the design bugs in the course of publishing it on a monthly basis. The comics reading public was a bit puzzled by the *Handbook* at first, so different was it from what had been published in comics form before. But even with the first issue, it became one of Marvel's top sellers.

The Marvel Universe is a constantly expanding, evolving entity, with events occurring in almost sixty titles every month. By the time we finished the original edition, certain information in the earlier volumes was already outdated. So Jim and I immediately made plans to not only revise the entire series, but also to expand it to include all the information we could not fit in our original one-entry-per-page format. The Deluxe Edition of the *Official Handbook* commenced publishing in the summer of 1985, still in comics form although with twice as many pages per issue. Our dream, however, was to get the series published in book form, and with this trade paperback edition, we have realized that dream. The information published herein, like all information, is subject to change in the future. But for a concise overall picture of the scope of the wondrous Marvel Universe, this is the best source that currently exists.

So get comfortable, take a deep breath, and start reading. A universe awaits you.

Mark Gruenwald
New York City
September 1986

ABOMINATION

Real Name: Emil Blonsky
Occupation: Former spy, former first mate of the starship *Andromeda*, former agent of the Galaxy Master, criminal
Identity: Secret
Legal status: Citizen of Yugoslavia with no criminal record
Former aliases: Agent R-7, the Ravager of Worlds
Place of birth: Zagreb, Yugoslavia
Marital status: Single
Known relatives: None
Group affiliation: Former partner of the Rhino, former member of the crew of the starship *Andromeda*, former agent of the Galaxy Master, former agent of Modok
Base of operations: Mobile
First appearance: TALES TO ASTONISH #90
Origin: TALES TO ASTONISH #90
History: Almost nothing is known about the life of Emil Blonsky before he infiltrated the U.S. Air Force base in New Mexico that was commanded by General T.E. "Thunderbolt" Ross and which was where Dr. Robert Bruce Banner, the nuclear physicist who became the Hulk, conducted many of his experiments with gamma radiation. (See *Hulk*). Blonsky made various attempts to sabotage missiles at the base that were vital to United States defense. Although each attempt was narrowly thwarted, the Air Force still did not know who the saboteur was.

At this time the enigmatic alien being known as the Stranger had decided that the people of Earth were not responsible enough to use their nuclear weaponry wisely and therefore presented a threat to the other civilizations of the universe (see *Stranger*). The Stranger put the Hulk under his control and intended to use him to destroy humanity. However, the Stranger's control did not extend to Bruce Banner's persona, and, when the Hulk next changed back into Banner, the scientist decided to commit suicide in order to save the world from a Stranger-controlled Hulk. Banner

made his way into his laboratory on the Air Force base and prepared to activate a machine that would bombard him with enough gamma radiation to kill him.

Unknown to Banner, Blonsky was hiding in the laboratory, where he had been photographing Banner's gamma radiation equipment. Security officers burst in and carried Banner off. Unaware of the nature of the machine that Banner was about to use on himself, Blonsky stood in front of the machine and activated it. It bombarded him with a more concentrated and intense dosage of gamma radiation than Banner himself had received from the nuclear explosion that had first turned him into the Hulk. Like Banner, Blonsky had some unknown genetic factor in his body that saved him from being killed by a great dose of gamma radiation. Instead, the radiation had an immediate mutagenic effect upon Blonsky, transforming him into the monster whom General Ross's daughter dubbed the Abomination.

The Abomination gained greater strength than the Hulk at the latter's "normal" level of strength, and, unlike the Hulk, Abomination retained his full human intelligence, and could not transform back into a normal human form. Infatuated with his newfound power, the Abomination beat the Hulk (into whom Banner had again changed) nearly to death, and kidnapped Betty Ross. General Ross was so fearful for his daughter's safety that he ordered that the Hulk be revived so the latter could pursue the Abomination. When Banner's confidant Rick Jones pleaded with the Hulk for help, the Hulk broke free from the Stranger's mental control and reverted once more to Banner. Acting with General Ross's cooperation, Banner activated a powerful gamma radiation generating device he had invented directly upon the Abomination, thereby causing the latter's strength to diminish rapidly.

However, Banner grew so excited that he became the Hulk and smashed the weapon's controls, causing it to shut down before the Abomination's strength had been reduced below superhuman levels. The Abomination's strength was left at the level he has possessed since, which is greater than that normally possessed by the Hulk, but which the Hulk can exceed upon becoming sufficiently enraged. The angry Hulk attacked and defeated the Abomination. The Stranger, watching from afar, was so impressed by the heroism of Banner / Hulk that he decided that there

might indeed be hope for humanity. The Stranger transported the Abomination to his base on another planet, intending to use him as an agent in future endeavors.

However, the Stranger came up with few missions for the Abomination. Eventually, the Abomination was rescued from the Stranger's world and taken aboard an alien starship, the *Andromeda*, where he became first mate. After many months, he was returned to Earth. He battled the Hulk several more times, being soundly beaten each time.

After one of these battles, the Abomination was saved from death by the Galaxy Master (see *Appendix: Galaxy Master*), a powerful non-humanoid being which enslaved civilizations and forced them to produce the energy it required to exist. The Galaxy Master employed the Abomination to precede it in attacking civilizations that might offer particular resistance to conquest. Empress Daydra of the Sagittarian race recruited the Hulk to defeat the Abomination, who had become known as the "Ravager of Worlds" (see *Alien Races: Sagittarians*). The Hulk succeeded in defeating both the Galaxy Master and the Abomination.

Somehow, the Abomination made his way back to normal space in Earth's vicinity. A U.S. space shuttle found the Abomination frozen in ice, once again in suspended animation, in orbit around Earth. He was brought to the attention of General Ross, and revived by former AIM leader Modok, with whom Ross had formed a treasonous alliance (see *AIM, Modok*). The Hulk now possessed Banner's intelligence (although this state was to prove temporary) and had been granted a presidential pardon. Ross, disagreeing with the pardon, made a deal with Modok that the latter would revive the Abomination and take him as a servant in exchange for having the Abomination kill the Hulk. But the revived Abomination, as a result of having been defeated by the Hulk so many times, had a pathological fear of facing the Hulk. Modok subjected the Abomination to painful psychological conditioning to make him more afraid of Modok than of the Hulk, and sent him against the Hulk. The Abomination failed to defeat the Hulk, however, and so Modok used his mental powers to disintegrate the Abomination. Despite his seeming destruction, it is believed the Abomination will in some way be resurrected.

Height: 6' 8"
Weight: 980 lbs.

Eyes: Green
Hair: None
Skin: Green
Unusual features: The Abomination has two toes on each foot, webbed ears, and a ridged brow.
Strength level: The Abomination possesses vast superhuman strength, enabling him to lift (press) approximately 100 tons. He is not on the "Class 100" strength level since he cannot routinely lift (press) in excess of 100 tons.
Known superhuman powers: The Abomination possesses superhuman strength that surpasses that of the Hulk at the Hulk's normal "calm" functional level. But whereas the Hulk has a specially adapted adrenal gland whose secretions trigger the release of far greater amounts of physical strength than that of the Hulk's normal level to correspond to his heightened emotional states, the Abomination does not. Hence, the Abomination's strength does not fluctuate like the Hulk's.

The gamma radiation that mutated the Abomination's body fortified his cellular structure and added, from some as yet unknown source, over 800 pounds of bone marrow and muscle tissue to his body. Unlike the Hulk's, the Abomination's transformation has proved stable: he cannot change back and forth between his human state and his superhuman state.

In addition to great strength, the Abomination's body possesses a high degree of resistance to injury, pain, and disease. The Abomination's skin is capable of withstanding great heat without blistering (up to 3,500° Fahrenheit), great cold without freezing (down to −175° F), and great impacts without injury (he can survive direct hits by field artillery cannon shells). It is possible to injure him, however: for example, the Abomination could not survive the detonation of a nuclear warhead from ten feet away. The Abomination's highly efficient physiology renders him immune to all terrestrial disease.

The Abomination can hold his breath for long periods whose limits have yet to be defined. Extreme pain or cold (beneath the limit mentioned above) or extended lack of oxygen can cause him to enter a coma-like state of suspended animation, in which he can survive, perhaps indefinitely.

Like the Hulk, the Abomination can use his superhumanly strong leg muscles to leap great distances. The Abomination has been observed to cover 2 miles in a single bound. ∎

ABSORBING MAN

Real Name: Carl "Crusher" Creel
Occupation: Professional criminal
Identity: Publicly known
Legal status: United States citizen with a
criminal record
Former aliases: None
Place of birth: New York City
Marital status: Single
Known relatives: None
Group affiliation: Former agent of Loki and
of They Who Wield Power
Base of operations: Mobile
First appearance and origin: JOURNEY
INTO MYSTERY #114

History: While serving time in prison for
aggravated assault committed while a
member of an extortion racket, Carl
"Crusher" Creel was selected by Loki, the
Asgardian god of mischief, as his unwitting
agent in a scheme against Thor, god of
thunder (see *Loki, Thor*). By adding an enchanted potion composed of rare Asgardian herbs to Creel's drinking water in the
prison commisary, Loki granted the brutal
convict a bizarre power he hoped would enable him to defeat Thor, the power to absorb the physical properties of anything
with which he came in contact. Creel used
his new-found power to break free from
prison and soon became engaged in battle
with Thor. Due to his ability to absorb the
properties of Thor's hammer and Thor himself, Creel, now called the Absorbing Man,
became one of the strongest mortal foes
Thor ever combatted.

After his first defeat, the Absorbing Man
returned to plague Thor again, and Loki
transported him to Asgard where the criminal could be used in his scheme to take
over Asgard. But when the Absorbing Man
dared to challenge Odin, lord of the Asgardians, Odin summarily dispatched him into
space (see *Asgard, Odin*). Creel eventually
managed to return to Earth by hitching a
ride on a comet. He soon encountered the
Hulk, however, and was defeated while in
the process of absorbing the Hulk's power
during his transformation to the human
Bruce Banner. The Absorbing Man then
challenged Thor again and was defeated
when he was tricked into turning into water.
A short time later, Thor defeated him again
by tricking him into absorbing the properties
of a cardboard replica of Thor's hammer.
Serving a short prison sentence, Creel
managed to escape and was contacted by
They Who Wield Power, a cabal of power-
seekers from El Dorado, who hired him to
destroy the Hulk. He failed and inadvertently absorbed the properties of glass
while falling.

Eventually reassembling the shards of
his body, the Absorbing Man decided that
he was tired of fighting against and losing to
superhuman champions. Seeking to flee
the country, Creel foolishly took a hostage,
thereby bringing the Avengers after him. To
escape them, he jumped into the ocean
and transformed himself into water. When
he finally regained his natural form, his
mind was addled from his prolonged inter-
mingling with the ocean and he was
paranoically frightened of anyone with
superhuman power. A chance battle with
the Hulk cured him of his paranoia, however. Returning to America, he stalked the
mutant Dazzler to acquire her light-powers
to use against the Avengers. He was defeated, however, by the Dazzler and the Inhuman Black Bolt. He was abducted from
prison by the Beyonder to fight in the "Sec-

ret Wars" (see *Beyonder*). Following the wars, he was restored to Earth.

Height: 6′ 4″   **Eyes:** Blue
Weight: 365 lbs   **Hair:** Bald

Strength level: Variable. When he is not absorbing the properties of anything, the Absorbing Man possesses the normal human strength of a man of his age, height, and build who engages in regular exercise. Depending on what he absorbs and how long he can remain in contact with it, his strength can increase to the Class 100 range (able to routinely lift 100+ tons).

Known superhuman powers: The Absorbing Man possesses the ability to bodily duplicate at will the physical properties of anything he touches or that touches him. This power extends to both animate and inanimate objects and certain forms of energy. The matter of the Absorbing Man's body magically undergoes a material and physiological change so that his body becomes composed of the matter or energy with which he is making contact. While he is in this altered state, he still possesses his sentience despite the fact that his brain is now composed of the same material as the rest of him. Among the more ordinary materials he has been transformed into include steel, stone, wood, and glass. More unusual have been his transformations into water, fire, snow, helium, and silk. His most powerful transformations have been into energy-states such as cosmic, nuclear, thermal or light.

The Absorbing Man can also absorb specific properties relating to the form or mass of an object he touches. For example, he can assume the height of a skyscraper or the spikes of a mace. He can also assimilate mystical properties of objects or beings. He can mimic the properties of Thor's hammer as well as the strength of Thor himself.

If the Absorbing Man's body is broken or dispersed somehow when he is in non-human state, his sentience is capable of reassembling himself over a period of time and returning himself to human form. For example, he was able to return to normal after being shattered in glass form and dissipated in liquid form. During the first "Secret War" his arm was severed while he was in non-human form, but the Absorbing Man was able to reattach it to himself by holding the severed arm to its correct position on his body and then transforming it and himself back to human form.

Limitations: There are undefined limits to the amount of power that the Absorbing Man can absorb. He met his first defeat when he exploded upon attempting to absorb the power of the entire planet Earth.

Weapons: The Absorbing Man's prison ball and chain, which he was wearing at the time of his original transformation, magically possess the same properties of transformation as his body, providing he is in contact with them. ∎

BALL AND CHAIN

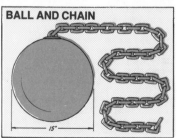

—15″—

ADAMANTIUM

Adamantium is a virtually indestructible man-made steel alloy which does not occur in nature and whose exact chemical composition is a United States government classified secret. Adamantium is not an element: its properties do not qualify it for any known space on the Periodic Table of Elements. Rather, Adamantium is a series of closely related compounds of iron created through a secret process discovered by the American metallurgist Dr. Myron MacLain.

MacLain began experimenting with the process that created Adamantium as a young scientist in the employ of the United States government in the early 1940s. Assigned to create a super-metal with which to build tanks, MacLain labored for months, experimenting with various iron alloys. One of his experiments utilized the rare meteoric ore now known as Wakandan Vibranium (see *Vibranium*). He tried to fuse the Vibranium to the iron alloy numerous times without success. Then one night when he dozed off, some as yet unknown factor entered the process, and permitted the fusion to occur. Upon discovering his success, MacLain poured the molten metal into a disc-shaped mold. The disc, once solidified, has proven to be the most impervious object ever created on Earth. MacLain turned the disc over to the government and it was given to Captain America to use as his shield (see *Captain America*). Neither MacLain nor anyone else has ever been able to discover what was the x-factor that entered the process, or has been able to fuse Vibranium with another metal. (The unknown iron-Vibranium alloy of which the shield is com-

posed resembles True Adamantium, although Adamantium itself contains no Vibranium.)

Over the following decades MacLain experimented, attempting to duplicate the process that created the shield. Finally, in recent years, he succeeded in developing the process by which the substance known as True Adamantium is created. True Adamantium is nearly as strong as Captain America's shield, and is, for all practical purposes, indestructible. The degree of impermeability varies directly with the thickness of the Adamantium. A direct blow from Thor's hammer, conveyed with the thunder god's full strength, will only slightly dent a solid cylinder of True Adamantium (see *Thor*). A sufficient mass of Adamantium could survive a direct hit from a nuclear weapon.

Adamantium is created through the mixing of certain chemical resins whose composition is a United States government secret. For eight minutes after the resins are mixed, the Adamantium can be molded into a particular shape as long as it is kept at a temperature of 1,500 degrees Fahrenheit. After this brief period the process of creating Adamantium is completed. The extremely stable molecular structure of the Adamantium prevents it from being molded further, even if the temperature remains high enough to keep it in liquefied form. Only a device called a Molecular Rearranger can alter the form of hardened Adamantium.

The United States government has shared the secret of Adamantium's composition with certain of its allies, and the secret

has also fallen into the hands of various criminals, such as the Constrictor, who has made special weaponry from Adamantium (see *Constrictor*). Wolverine possesses artificial claws made of True Adamantium and his bones have been fused with Adamantium in an unexplained manner so as to greatly increase their tensile strength (see *Wolverine*). The outer portion of the robotic body of Ultron is also composed entirely of True Adamantium, although Ultron's inner mechanisms are not (see *Ultron*).

Adamantium is extraordinarily expensive to produce. Therefore, certain parties who wish to use Adamantium on a large scale have resorted to utilizing a similar but somewhat weaker compound similar to True Adamantium called Secondary Adamantium. Although Secondary Adamantium is still far stronger than even titanium steel, it can be destroyed by sufficiently great amounts of force. Blastaar's energy discharges and the vibratory force created by the Overkill Horn have both proved able to destroy Secondary Adamantium (see *Blastaar, HYDRA*). The sentient computer known as F.A.U.S.T. had a casing made of Secondary Adamantium which Thor and Iron Man managed to destroy. The Red Skull and the original Hate-Monger had a dome of Secondary Adamantium constructed to protect their island fortress but the dome was destroyed by the vibratory force of the Overkill Horn and by powerful incendiary bombs.

First appearance: AVENGERS #66. ∎

DR. MYRON MacLAIN

WOLVERINE

ULTRON-7

AGUILA

Real Name: Alejandro Montoya
Occupation: Wealthy swashbuckler
Legal status: Citizen of Spain with no criminal record. Currently on extended visa in U.S. in his civilian identity.
Other current aliases: "The Eagle" ("El Águila" in English), "The Master"
Identity: Secret
Place of birth: Madrid, Spain
Marital status: Single
Known relatives: None
Group affiliation: None
Base of operations: New York City
First appearance: POWER MAN / IRON FIST #58

History: Little is as yet known about the life of Alejandro Montoya, the costumed swashbuckler called El Aguila. Born in Spain, Montoya is a mutant whose super-human power manifested itself while he was a teenager. It is not known when or where Montoya undertook the art of fencing or if he adopted the identity of El Águila before coming to America or after. Once in America, El Águila began to prey upon criminals, particularly drug dealers, slum-lords, and those whose criminal activities most affected the poor. It is probable that the money he confiscated from these criminals was redistributed to the poor. Since his activities have been outside the law, El Águila has been wanted by the police and has found himself in conflict with Power Man and Iron Fist on several occasions.

Height: 6′
Weight: 190 lbs
Eyes: Brown
Hair: Black
Strength level: El Águila possesses the normal human strength of a man of his age, height, and build who engages in intensive regular exercise.

Known superhuman powers: El Aguila possesses the ability to discharge electrostatic charges generated by his own body through a conductive medium. His body discharges a maximum of 100,000 volts at one time, sufficient to kill a man or to stun a rhinoceros at ten feet. He can mentally control the intensity of the blast, keeping it well within the non-lethal range. After fully depleting his store of bioelectricity, be it in one blast or successive blasts, it takes him one half hour to recharge back to full strength. When his power reaches its full charge, his body will naturally discharge any excess energy in minute, harmless quantities. His body generates and stores this bioelectricity in his central nervous system. The maximum range at which his blast can propagate through air at sea level is 30 feet.

Limitations: The major limitation of El Águila's bioelectric blast is that he must be in contact with a conductive metal in order to release it. Accordingly, he carries a sword through which he shoots his power. To protect the secret of his mutant nature, El Águila deliberately misleads the public to believe that his sword houses an electric blaster.

Abilities: El Águila is an expert swordsman.

Weapons: El Águila carries a double-edged steel sword, 36 inches long, weighing 2½ pounds. It has a hand guard that curves around the knuckles. ∎

AIM (ADVANCED IDEA MECHANICS)

AIM (Advanced Idea Mechanics) is an organization of brilliant scientists and their hirelings dedicated to the acquisition of power and the overthrow of all governments by technological means.

AIM began as a group of scientists organized during World War II by Baron Wolfgang von Strucker to develop advanced technological weaponry for his secret subversive organization HYDRA (see *Deceased: Baron Strucker, HYDRA*). Although HYDRA suffered a major defeat during the war, it continued to exist secretly over the following decades, growing and building its strength. The group of scientists grew in number over the years, and made great advances in various fields, including robotics, bioengineerings, bionics, and physics. Eventually the scientists publicly incorporated their organization under the name of Advanced Idea Mechanics (AIM). No one outside AIM or HYDRA knew of AIM's subversive goals and activities, nor of their scientific achievements, nor of the fact that AIM was actually the scientific research division of HYDRA. (Indeed, HYDRA's very existence remained unknown for most of this time.) Instead, AIM was believed by both the public and by intelligence organizations to be an international cartel dealing with the development and marketing of new technological products. AIM gained great influence with the U.S. government in its role as a supplier of hardware and weapons to governmental and quasi-governmental agencies.

After the initial defeat of HYDRA by SHIELD, AIM, whose connection with HYDRA had not been exposed, attempted to discredit SHIELD Director Nicholas Fury, and thereby force him out of his position (see *SHIELD*). This attempt, publicly led by Count Bornag Royale, failed, and instead Fury exposed AIM as a subversive organization. Although SHIELD believed it had put an end to AIM's operations, much of the organization escaped capture, and its links with the still secretly active HYDRA remained undiscovered. However, immediately upon the demise of Baron Strucker and the deaths of most of HYDRA's leading members in the destruction of HYDRA Island, AIM, now under the leadership of Modok, severed its ties with HYDRA, and has remained an independent organization ever since.

AIM has created a wide variety of advanced technological weaponry, and during the period when it was an arm of HYDRA, made great strides in creating androids, which the organization employed as assassins. (During this period AIM members sometimes referred to themselves as agents of THEM. THEM was the code name of the HYDRA core group which governed HYDRA and its subsidiary organizations, including AIM, during the period between HYDRA's first seeming destruction by SHIELD and its later re-emergence.) However, AIM has created three major instruments of deadly potential which stand out above the rest. The first is the Super-Adaptoid, an android capable of duplicating the form and superhuman powers of another being (see *Super-Adaptoid*). The second instrument was the Cosmic Cube, an unimaginably powerful object capable of restructuring reality. AIM manufactured the containing device — the cube — not the reality-transforming energy itself, whose nature and origin remain mysteries (see *Shaper of Worlds*).

The third major achievement of AIM is the creation of Modok (Mental Organization Designed Only for Killing), an artificially mutated human being with an enormous head and a stunted body who possesses superhuman intelligence and various psionic abilities (see *Modok*). Modok was originally an ordinary AIM member who was selected by AIM's leader, the so-called Scientist Supreme, to be the subject of vast bionic experiments that turned him into Modok. After being transformed, Modok slew the Scientist Supreme and seized control of AIM, severing its ties with the demolished HYDRA. For years AIM existed merely to serve Modok's ambitions for power. Under his leadership, AIM stagnated intellectually, created no truly impressive weapon, and launched no major attack on any nation.

However, two different splinter groups of AIM agents who had escaped being taken over by Modok emerged. One of the groups often clashed with Modok's AIM; another unsuccessfully attempted to create another active Cosmic Cube. Finally, dissension with Modok's rule grew within Modok's own organization and broke out in rebellion against him. Modok's AIM joined forces with the two splinter groups and drove Modok out of the organization. The three factions of AIM again combined, so that today AIM once more stands as a united organization. Modok has recently been captured by AIM and reprogrammed to obey the ruling council.

First appearance: STRANGE TALES #146.

■

ALPHA FLIGHT

Alpha Flight is a Canadian team of adventurers, most of whom have superhuman powers, which was organized under the auspices of the Canadian government's now defunct Department H. Roughly ten years ago James MacDonald Hudson, an engineer, resigned from the Am-Can Petro-Chemical Company in Canada when he learned that a special super-powered suit he had built for the company for use in geological exploration was going to be used by the United States military instead. Hudson secretly destroyed Am-Can's copies of the plans for the suit and made off with the psycho-cybernetic helmet that was necessary to make the suit work, and which he could claim as his own property with legal justification. Shocked by what had happened to Hudson at Am-Can, Heather McNeil, the executive secretary to Hudson's immediate superior there, Jerome Jaxon, also resigned from the company. McNeil arranged for herself and Hudson to meet with officials of the Canadian government, who heard their story and settled with Am-Can for any damages incurred when Hudson reclaimed his helmet. Hudson was then invited by the Canadian prime minister to participate in the creation of Department H, a top secret research and development agency within the Canadian Ministry of Defense. Soon afterwards Hudson married McNeil, and within the next few years Hudson had recruited the mutant called Wolverine as one of the Department's special agents (see *Wolverine*).

Reading a newspaper account of how Reed Richards and three of his friends became the Fantastic Four inspired James Hudson to create a team of superhumanly powerful agents to go on missions for the Canadian government. Wolverine aided Hudson in the initial phases of the creation of the team, which would be called Alpha Flight, and it was planned that Wolverine would lead the team. However, Wolverine eventually left Department H for his own reasons and joined the X-Men. Hudson continued to develop his super-powered suit, and it eventually became the costume that he himself wore as a member of Alpha Flight. As a costumed agent Hudson at first called himself Weapon Alpha, later changed his code name to Vindicator, and finally settled upon the name Guardian. Hudson reluctantly became the leader of Alpha Flight himself after Wolverine's resignation.

The standard procedure for recruits for Alpha Flight was that they would begin as members of a training team called Gamma Flight. Upon successfully completing their initial training, recruits would move into a transitional team, Beta Flight, to receive more advanced training. Those who proved to be successes in Beta Flight as well would finally join Alpha Flight, the team of agents who would participate in major missions.

Alpha Flight had six members when Department H was disbanded by the Canadian government for financial reason: Aurora, Guardian, Northstar, Sasquatch, Shaman, and Snowbird. However, the six members decided to continue acting as a team performing altruistic missions, and were joined by two trainees from Beta Flight, Marrina and Puck. In practice, however, the majority of the members undertook the same mission infrequently after the team became independent of the government, simply because the various members lived in different parts of Canada.

James Hudson died in the course of Alpha Flight's first major battle with a group called Omega Flight (see *Omega Flight*). Alpha Flight, however, continues as a team despite the loss of its founder, and the members have chosen Hudson's highly capable wife Heather, to act as their new leader. Heather adopted her husband's costume and his name of Vindicator. The Canadian government recently resumed funding Alpha Flight, and the team has established a headquarters on Tamarind Island off British Columbia. ■

GUARDIAN
(James MacDonald Hudson)
First appearance: X-MEN #109
Died in ALPHA FLIGHT #12

HEATHER HUDSON
First appearance: X-MEN #139

SHAMAN
(Michael Twoyoungmen)
Active as of X-MEN #120

SASQUATCH
(Walter Langkowski)
Active as of X-MEN #120
Died in ALPHA FLIGHT #23

AURORA
(Jeanne-Marie Beaubier)
Active as of X-MEN #120

NORTHSTAR
(Jean-Paul Beaubier)
Active as of X-MEN #120

SNOWBIRD
(Narya, Anne McKenzie)
Active as of X-MEN #120

MARINNA
(Marrina Smallwood)
Joined in ALPHA FLIGHT #1

PUCK
(Eugene Milton Judd)
Joined in ALPHA FLIGHT #1

TALISMAN
(Elizabeth Twoyoungmen)
Joined in ALPHA FLIGHT #20

BOX
(Roger Bochs, engineer)
Active as of ALPHA FLIGHT #24

VINDICATOR
(Heather Hudson)
Active as of ALPHA FLIGHT #31

ALPHA PRIMITIVES

The Alpha Primitives are a race of sub-human worker drones once employed by the Inhumans to perform manual labor and menial tasks (see *Inhumans*). They came into existence about four thousand years ago when the geneticist Avadar convinced the ruling Council of Genetics that a race of sub-human servants would free the Inhumans from the need to toil for subsistence, so all could devote themselves to the pursuits of knowledge. Avadar bio-engineered the prototype of the Alphas, and within a decade five hundred Alpha Primitives were bred to perform all of the support services for the entire city of Attilan: sanitation, food production, manufacturing and so forth (see *Attilan*).

The Alpha Primitives are basically docile creatures with simple thoughts and emotions. They are all the same neuter sex, preventing them from procreating naturally. Cloning is the sole means by which they may propagate. Each Alpha is exactly like every other. They are all five foot seven inches tall, have green eyes and hairless bodies. They are slightly superior in strength to the average human being, being able to lift (press) approximately 1000 pounds under optimal conditions. They work eighteen hours a day, and sleep the other six. They have no culture or need for recreation. They have been taught to speak and understand the basic vocabulary of a six year old human being. They have a life expectancy of forty-two years.

The Alpha Primitives have occasionally been the subjects of unlawful genetic experimentation. In recent years, Maximus, the brilliant but demented brother to the Inhumans' king Black Bolt, has performed experiments on them (see *Maximus*). In his first experiment, Maximus subjected three Alpha Primitives to a highly potent quantity of the mutagenic Terrigen Mist, causing them to become glowing globules of energy, collectively called the Trikon. The Trikon aided Maximus in his first attempt to seize the crown from his brother Black Bolt, and forced the Royal Family of the Inhumans into exile for a number of years. The Trikon was eventually vanquished from Attilan. Maximus's second experiment on the Alpha Primitives was less direct. Constructing a giant synthetic humanoid body as a receptable, Maximus built a device that could siphon the *psi* energy generated by the collective guilt that most modern Inhumans felt toward their slaves and transform it into physical energy. This energy empowered the giant humanoid, who became known as Omega, the ultimate Alpha. Omega was rendered inert when the Inhumans ceased their open warfare against their rebellious worker class.

Following the Omega incident, the Inhumans emancipated the Alpha Primitives from their labors and set them free to live as they please in the sub-city beneath Attilan. Having no culture and no knowledge of recreation, many of them have gone about their tasks as usual, despite their freedom. Since it is now illegal to clone replacement Alpha Primitives, their ranks are dwindling. Inhuman missionaries have been sent beneath the city to tutor the Alphas and administer to their welfare.

First appearance: FANTASTIC FOUR #47.

∎

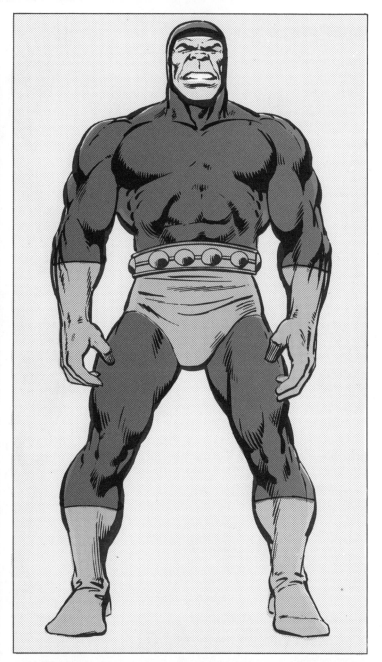

AMERICAN EAGLE

Real Name: Jason Strongbow
Occupation: Tribal leader
Legal status: United States citizen with no criminal record
Identity: Secret
Place of birth: Kaibito, Arizona
Marital status: Single
Known relatives: Ward (brother, deceased)
Group affiliation: None
Base of operations: Navaho Reservation, Arizona
First appearance and origin: MARVEL TWO-IN-ONE ANNUAL #6

History: Jason Strongbow, a representative of the Navaho tribe of Indians, attempted to stop a mining company from excavating a mountain sacred to the tribe by obtaining a court order. Failing in that, he led a peaceful protest group at the mining site. When the night watchman panicked and shot a protester, Strongbow followed him into the mine. There he discovered that the mining company was in league with Klaw, the master of sound, who sought uranium to fortify his sonic powers (see *Klaw*). He also found his brother Ward, who did not share his ideas of preserving the tribal grounds and soon allowed their argument to erupt into violence. During their fight, Klaw appeared and blasted the brothers with his sonic blaster. The bombardment of sonic energy and the exposure to an unknown isotope of uranium found in the mine combined to mutagenically enhance the strength and senses of the Strongbow brothers. Klaw, who had contracted the mining company to acquire uranium with which he hoped to fortify his powers, fled with his hirelings to the Savage Land in Antarctica, where Klaw hoped to acquire Vibranium (see *Vibranium, Appendix: Savage Land*).

Strongbow emerged from the mine and was hailed as a champion of his tribe. Taking the flight of a nearby eagle as an omen, Strongbow fashioned for himself the costumed identity of the American Eagle. Learning that his brother had gone to the Savage Land with the mining company, he set out in pursuit. In the Savage Land, the American Eagle was met by Ka-Zar, the Thing, and Wyatt Wingfoot. The four of them opposed and defeated Klaw and his hirelings. In the course of the battle, Strongbow's brother Ward, who had allied himself with Klaw, was killed by one of the miner's bullets. American Eagle has since returned to his people to be their champion.

Height: 6′   **Eyes** Brown
Weight: 200 lbs   **Hair:** Black
Strength level: The American Eagle possesses superhuman strength, enabling him to lift (press) approximately 15 tons under optimal conditions.

Known superhuman powers: The American Eagle possesses superhuman strength, speed, agility, and endurance. He can run at a maximum speed of 65 miles per hour. He has several times the endurance of an average human being.

The American Eagle's sensory organs have also been fortified. Like his namesake, the eagle, he has keen eyesight and is able to see 800 feet what the average human being sees at 20 feet. His senses of smell, taste, and hearing are approximately three times as acute as those of a normal human being.

Weapons: American Eagle carries a crossbow which fires specially designed bolts. He has a bolt to which a line of braided fiberglass is connected, enabling him to swing from overhead objects or to climb its length. He also has specially blunted bolts in order to stun an opponent at a distance. ∎

ANACONDA

Real Name: Blanche "Blondie" Sitznski
Occupation: Ex-steelworker, now free-lance criminal
Legal status: United States citizen with no criminal record as yet
Former aliases: None known
Place of birth: Pittsburgh, Pennsylvania
Marital status: Single
Known relatives: None
Group affiliation: Serpent Squad II, Serpent Society
Base of operations: Mobile
First appearance: MARVEL TWO-IN-ONE #64

History: Blanche Sitznski was selected by executives in the Roxxon Oil Company to be a special agent in covert operations (see *Roxxon Oil*). At the Mutagenics Laboratory of Roxxon's now-defunct subsidiary, the Brand Corporation, Sitznksi was bioengineered to have various permanent serpentine adaptations. Her first mission, as part of the new Serpent Squad, was to retrieve the ancient power object called the Serpent Crown for Roxxon president Hugh Jones. Following this mission, Anaconda and two of her fellow Serpent Squad cohorts left Roxxon to become mercenaries for hire. Recently, Anaconda was invited to join the Serpent Society by her former associate Sidewinder. After some persuasion, she accepted and has been an active member ever since (see *Serpent Society*).

Height: 6' 2"
Weight: 220 lbs
Eyes: Green
Hair: Blonde
Unusual features: Anaconda has scales on her face, neck, and chest, and small fins on her cheeks.
Strength level: Anaconda possesses superhuman strength enabling her to lift (press) approximately 2 tons on land under optimal conditions. Using her strength to constrict rather than lift, Anaconda has a grip that cannot be broken by those whose strength exceeds her own by factors up to 30 (see Known superhuman powers).
Known superhuman powers: Anaconda possesses the ability to elongate her limbs, entwine them around persons or objects, and constrict. The entire skeletal structure of her arms and legs has been replaced by artificial Adamantium alloy-based bones in the basic configuration of a snake's bodily skeleton. Her arms, normally 24 inches from armpit to wrist, and her legs, normally 35 inches from hipbone to ankle, are able to elongate to about one and a half times their normal length. When she extends her limbs in this fashion, the muscle tissue gorges with blood, swelling the limbs so that each looks like a massive, powerful snake. These four constricting limbs are capable of exerting enough pressure to radically deform a one inch-thick steel tube, two feet in diameter. Once Anaconda has fully entwined her serpentine limbs around a human-sized foe, there are few human beings able to get sufficient leverage and possessing sufficient strength to break her grip.

Anaconda has been surgically given artificial gills to enable her to extract oxygen from water in order to breath. She can now breathe while underwater indefinitely, as well as breathe on land. As a by-product of the extensive bio-engineering done to her body, Anaconda possesses superhuman recuperative abilities. Her body can heal from any non-fatal wound many times faster than a normal human being. ∎

ANDROMEDA

Real Name: Andromeda (a corruption of her name in the Atlantean language

Occupation: Warrior, adventurer

Identity: Unknown to the American general public

Legal status: Unknown. She claims to be a citizen of Atlantis.

Former aliases: Andrea McPhee

Place of birth: Unknown, presumably Atlantis

Marital status: Single

Known relatives: None known

Group affiliation: Ally of the Defenders

Base of operations: Currently mobile

First appearance: DEFENDERS #143, (in costume) DEFENDERS #146

History: Very little is definitely known about Andromeda. She claims to be a major in the Atlantean armed forces. Since Atlantean society, including the military, is so male-dominated, she says that she believed she could advance no further within it. Therefore, she asserts, she came to the surface world, inspired by the stories of the adventures that the Sub-Mariner, Atlantis's former ruler, had there, and sought out the team of adventurers to which he once belonged, the Defenders. At first Andromeda posed as a surface woman, aided by a serum that enabled her to breathe air and that changed her skin color, and called herself Andrea McPhee. She has recently revealed to the Defenders that she is a member of the Atlantean race.

Height: 5' 8"

Weight: 180 lbs.

Eyes: Green

Hair: Auburn

Skin: Blue

Strength level: The limits on Andromeda's strength have yet to be determined, but it is known that she is considerably stronger than the average Atlantean male. The average Atlantean male can lift (press) about 4 tons in air; at the very least, Andromeda can lift (press) 14 tons in air.

Known superhuman powers: Andromeda possesses the conventional attributes of the *Homo mermanus* species (see *Atlanteans, Atlantis*): gills to enable her to extract oxygen from water, superhumanly strong physiology to enable her to withstand the great water pressure changes that occur beneath the sea, blood circulation enabling her to withstand freezing temperatures, and specially-developed vision which is more sensitive to the green portion of the visible spectrum, enabling her to see in the murky ocean depths.

As noted, Andromeda possesses unusual strength for an Atlantean female. She can also swim (and move on the surface, as well) faster than the average Atlantean. The average Atlantean can swim at a maximum speed of about 26 knots (30 miles per hour) for several hours before tiring. Andromeda can maintain a greater swimming speed over that period, but its limits have yet to be determined.

Like all *Homo mermani* except for the Sub-Mariner and Namorita, Andromeda cannot breathe out of water unaided. She is capable of lasting approximately 10 minutes on the surface without artificial means for intaking oxygen before she begins to suffocate. However, in order to survive in the surface world, Andromeda used a serum employed on past occasions by the Atlanteans Krang and Dorma. When imbibed by a *Homo mermanus*, it allows him or her to absorb oxygen and expel carbon dioxide directly through the skin for a period of approximately 12 hours. The serum also alters his or her skin pigmentation to that of an average Caucasian human for the same amount of time.

Other abilities: Andromeda is highly proficient in all Atlantean methods of armed and unarmed combat.

Weaponry: Andromeda is highly skilled in the use of all standard Atlantean weaponry, but she most often uses a trident, which she can hurl with great force. Andromeda also possesses a warship of Atlantean manufacture, which can be used both for flight and for undersea travel, and which is armed with various Atlantean weaponry. ∎

ANGAR THE SCREAMER

Real Name: David Alan Angar
Occupation: Former activist, now criminal for hire
Legal status: United States citizen with a criminal record
Identity: Publicly known
Place of birth: San Francisco, California
Marital status: Single
Known relatives: None
Group affiliation: None
Base of operations: San Francisco
First appearance: DAREDEVIL #100
Origin: DAREDEVIL #101
History: David Angar, a radical social activist, volunteered to undergo an experiment to confer upon him superhuman powers. Subjected to technology brought to Earth from Titan by the priestess Moondragon, Angar acquired unusual vocal powers (see *Moondragon*). While Moondragon hoped to create more allies against the mad Titan Thanos, her erstwhile partner, Kerwin J. Broderick, employed Angar as a special operative for his own criminal enterprises. Angar's first assignment was to destroy Daredevil and the Black Widow, but Daredevil talked him out of becoming a murderer. Since then, Angar has used his power for personal gain, and his schemes have brought him in conflict with Iron Fist and the original Spider-Woman, among others.
Height: 5' 10"
Weight: 155 lbs
Eyes: Brown
Hair: Brown
Strength level: Angar possesses the normal human strength of a man of his age, height, and build who engages in moderate regular exercise.
Known superhuman powers: Angar possesses the ability to vocally emit piercing screams that create convincing, seemingly tangible hallucinations in anyone who hears his voice. His screams sonically stimulate the chemicals of the brain, creating natural toxins that induce hallucinations. Angar cannot control the specific content of his victim's hallucinations. Instead they are products of the victim's own subconscious. His power does tend to induce psychotic and nightmarish fantasies, however.

Angar's scream will affect anyone within the sound of his voice to some degree. The closer one is to the source, the longer one will hallucinate. Recovery time for the average human being standing 50 feet from his scream is approximately one hour. Recovery time for the average human being at three feet from him is approximately twelve hours. Angar is able to scream at an amplitude of 180 deciBels (in the gigacycle range). The audible portion of his scream, which is only a harmonic of the full range of sound produced, is around 138 dB. He can cause permanent hearing damage to those standing too close to him.

Angar is immune to the toxic effects of his own power. His vocal cords have more stamina than those of normal humans, enabling him to scream at maximum power for over an hour, pausing only for breath.

A side effect of his power is that very few people can remember that he was nearby when their hallucinations began. How this selective amnesia effect works is not yet known. ∎

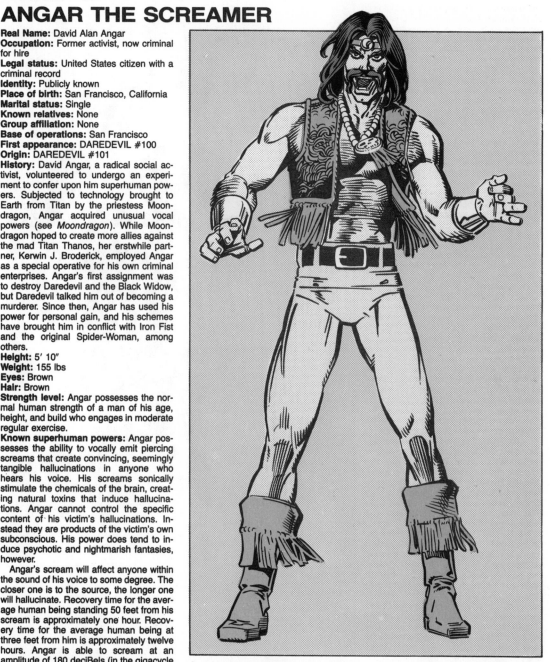

ANGEL

Real Name: Warren Kenneth Worthington III
Occupation: Chairman of the board and principal stockholder of Worthington Industries, adventurer
Identity: Publicly known. However, Warren Worthington is not publicly known to be an agent of X-Factor, although he is publicly known to be its financial backer.
Legal status: Citizen of the United States with no criminal record
Former aliases: The Avenging Angel
Place of birth: Centerport, Long Island, New York
Marital status: Single
Known relatives; Warren K. (grandfather, deceased), Warren K., Jr. (father, deceased), Kathryn (mother, deceased), Burt (alias the Dazzler, paternal uncle)
Group affiliation: Former member of the X-Men, the Champions of Los Angeles, and the Defenders, founding member of X-Factor
Base of operations: X-Factor headquarters, New York City. Worthington maintains residences in several cities and is co-owner of a mansion in the New Mexico Rocky Mountains.
First appearance: X-MEN #1
Origin: X-MEN #54–56
History: Warren Worthington III was attending a private school in his adolescence when wings began to grow from his shoulder blades. The wings reached their full adult size within months, but Worthington kept them a secret by strapping them tightly to his back and concealing them under his clothes. At first he thought himself a freak. However, Worthington learned that he could use his wings to fly, and came to enjoy his new ability. Then, one night there was a fire in his dormitory, and he resolved to use his flying power to rescue the people inside. To conceal his identity, Worthington wore a long blond wig and a long nightshirt, so that he looked like an angel. The rescue was successful, and his identity remained a secret. Shortly thereafter Worthington became a costumed crimefighter in New York City under the name of the Avenging Angel. He was then contacted by the X-Men and agreed to join them (see X-Men).

Shortly after Professor Charles Xavier, the founder of the X-Men, recruited several new members for the group, the Angel decided to leave the X-Men (see Professor X). After his parents' deaths, Worthington inherited their vast fortune, and he used part of it to found a Los Angeles-based organization of super-human adventurers called the Champions (see Appendix: Champions of Los Angeles). Worthington also publicly revealed that he was the Angel, although he and Xavier managed to keep secret Worthington's connection with Xavier's school, the cover and home base for the X-Men. When the Champions failed as an organization, Worthington decided to devote his time from then on to his business duties and to his renewed romance with his longtime girlfriend Candace "Candy" Southern. Worthington also briefly returned to the X-Men.

Recently the Angel joined the Defenders and remained with them after the Beast reorganized the group (see Beast, Appendix: Defenders). The Defenders used the mansion and estate that Worthington and associate Candace Southern jointly own in the New Mexico Rocky Mountains as their base of operations. When the Defenders disbanded, the Angel helped found X-Factor (see X-Factor).

Recently, the Angel's wings were severely injured in a battle with the Marauders during their massacre of most of the Morlocks (see *Morlocks, Appendix: Marauders*). He has been told that his wings have been permanently crippled, leaving him unable to fly, and that they must be amputated. Whether the Angel will live the rest of his life without wings remains to be seen.

Height: 6'
Weight: 150 lbs.
Eyes: Blue
Hair: Blond

Strength level: The Angel possesses the normal human strength of a man of his age, height, and build, who engages in intensive regular exercise. His wings can create enough lift to enable his to carry aloft at least 200 pounds in addition to his own weight.

Known superhuman powers: The Angel is a mutant who can fly by means of his natural wings which span sixteen feet from wingtip to wingtip. Fully feathered like a bird's, the wings have a very flexible skeletal structure, enabling him to press them to the back of his torso and legs with only the slightest bulge visible under his clothing.

The Angel's entire anatomy is naturally adapted to flying. His bones are hollow like a bird's, making him weigh far less than is usual for a man of his weight and build. His body is virtually devoid of fat, and possesses greater proportionate muscle mass than an ordinary human does. His eyes are specially adapted to be able to withstand high speed winds which would hurt the average human eye. He possesses a special membrane in his respiratory system enabling him to extract oxygen from the air at high velocities or high altitudes.

The Angel flies by flapping his wings, as a bird does. His normal cruising speed averages around 70 miles per hour, though he is capable of diving swoops that reach up to 180 miles per hour. He can fly at 150 miles per hour without the help of a tail wind for up to half an hour at a time before tiring to an appreciable degree.

Though he generally flies beneath the height of the clouds (6,500 feet), he can reach a height of 10,000 feet with little effort. With severe strain he can attain the highest recorded altitude of a bird in flight (African geese at 29,000 feet above sea level), but he can only remain that high for several minutes.

The Angel can fly non-stop under his own power for a maximum of approximately twelve hours. Contrary to some reports, he cannot make a transatlantic flight solely on his own power. During his one attempt to do so, he hitched a ride on an airplane for part of the way. ◼

ANNIHILUS

Real Name: Annihilus
Occupation: Conqueror, destroyer of life
Identity: Annihilus's existence is not known to the general public of Earth.
Legal status: Citizen of Arthros, planet in Sector 17 A of the Negative Zone (as charted by Reed Richards)
Place of birth: Planet of Arthros, Negative Zone
Marital status: Single, perhaps inapplicable
Known relatives: None
Group affiliation: Sometime partner of Blastaar
Base of operation: Sector 17 A of the Negative Zone
First appearance: FANTASTIC FOUR ANNUAL #6
Origin: FANTASTIC FOUR #140
History: Untold years ago, voyagers from the world Tyanna in the Negative Zone, an extradimensional universe made of anti-matter, set forth to seed the barren worlds of the Zone with living organisms that they had bioengineered in the form of spores (see *Appendix: Other Dimensions*). One of the Tyannan ships crashed upon the barren volcanic planet Arthros, and the dying voyagers released all of their life spores as their final act.

One of the spores grew into an insectoid being who possessed great intelligence through mutation. This being, who would become known as Annihilus, discovered the Tyannan starship and found within it a knowledge transference helmet. Annihilus used the helmet to learn the history and the accumulated knowledge of the Tyannans. Using that knowledge, Annihilus increased his strength and intelligence and created the Cosmic Control Rod from the cannisters that held the life spores and the technology of the starship. The Cosmic Control Rod not only enabled Annihilus to wield great power, but also extended his life span indefinitely as long as he possessed it. Annihilus used his newly acquired power to become the master of the other life forms that had arisen on Arthros from the spores, and soon he set forth to conquer the neighboring worlds in the Negative Zone.

Annihilus was driven by an insane obsession with averting his own death at any cost. In order to prevent his death, Annihilus obsessively guarded his Cosmic Control Rod and sought to destroy any other living being whom he imagined, justifiably or irrationally, of being a possible threat to his existence. In recent years Annihilus formed a partnership with Blastaar (see *Blastaar*), another powerful being of the Negative Zone, who stole his Cosmic Control Rod. As a result, Annihilus's body, which had been prevented from aging for untold years by the Rod, rapidly began to deteriorate. Driven to further insanity by the realization of his fast approaching death, Annihilus made an attack upon Earth, home of his longtime adversaries, the Fantastic Four, which ended in Annihilus's own apparent destruction. Whether or not Annihilus was truly destroyed, however, remains to be seen.

Height: 5′ 11″
Weight: 200 lbs.
Eyes: Green
Hair: None
Skin: Green
Strength level: Annihilus possesses superhuman strength, and can lift (press) approximately 50 tons, Earth gravity, under optimal conditions.

Known superhuman powers: Possessing a highly evolved exoskeleton, Annihilus can withstand external pressures of up to 1,500 pounds per square inch, or pressure equal to that 3,250 feet below the ocean surface. He can breathe at a low activity level for up to a year in the void of interplanetary space by storage and efficient conversion of oxygen molecules. He possesses slightly greater than human intelligence. Annihilus possesses wings that enable him to fly at a speed of up to 150 miles per hour in an Earth-like atmosphere. He was capable of even greater speeds in the airless void of space, but there his source of propulsion was the Cosmic Control Rod.

Weapons: Annihilus's major weapon was his Cosmic Control Rod, a six inch long, two inch diameter cylinder that contains the essence of the Tyannan starship's stardrive. Harnessing the power of the Cosmic Control Rod by cybernetic micro-circuitry, Annihilus was able to wield vast amounts of cosmic energy. This energy can be made through the Rod to alter the atomic structures of matter into new configurations, or to shoot in destructive beams with the maximum power of ten megatons of TNT. Exposure to the energies manipulated by the Rod also greatly retarded (and possibly stopped altogether) the process of aging in Annihilus's body.

Annihilus has access to the highly advanced technology of the Tyannans, and possesses other secondary weapons and vehicles which he created by cannibalizing the Tyannan starship. These include energy pistols and flying tank-like gun ships.

Note: One account appears to portray Annihilus as a colony of small insect-like beings inhabiting the Annihilus costume. This colony was not the true Annihilus, but was placed in the costume by the real Annihilus in order to mislead and attack an adversary on a particular occasion. ■

ANT-MAN

Real Name: Scott Edward Lang
Occupation: Former burglar, now electronics technician
Legal status: Citizen of the United States with criminal record
Identity: Secret
Place of birth: Coral Gables, Florida
Marital status: Divorced
Known relatives: Peggy Rae (wife), Cassandra Eleanor (daughter), Ruth (sister), Carl (brother-in-law)
Group affiliation: None
Base of operations: New York City
First appearance: (as Lang) AVENGERS #187, (as Ant-Man) MARVEL PREMIERE #47

History: Scott Lang was an electronics expert who could not support his family doing repair work so he turned his talents to burglary. Apprehended, he served his prison sentence and was paroled in three years for good behavior. Lang had furthered his studies of electronics while in prison and was soon hired by Stark International to work in its design department. When his daughter was diagnosed as having a serious congenital heart condition, Lang sought the aid of surgeon Dr. Erica Sondheim, whom he believed to have been held prisoner at Cross Technological Enterprises. Desperate to help his daughter, Lang decided to resort to burglary. Breaking into the New Jersey home of Dr. Henry Pym, Lang stole his Ant-Man uniform and shrinking gas canisters. Unknown to him, Pym observed the theft and in his then-current guise as Yellowjacket, followed Lang, curious to see to what use he would put the paraphernalia (see *Pym, Henry*). Garbed as Ant-Man, Lang broke into Cross, and discovered Dr. Sondheim was indeed being held prisoner by Darren Cross, president of Cross Technological Enterprises, who needed her expertise to correct his own heart condition. Rescuing her and defeating Cross, Lang was relieved when Sondheim was able to save the life of his daughter. Lang intended to return the Ant-Man costume to its owner and turn himself in, but Henry Pym, aware of the use to which Lang put the stolen goods, offered to let him keep them, providing he put them to a lawful use.

Since that time, Lang has donned the Ant-Man costume on various occasions to assist Iron Man, the Avengers, or the law, although he still considers himself a part-time costumed crimefighter. When Stark International became Stane International, Scott Lang resigned out of respect to Anthony Stark, its former head. Lang currently operates his own electronics store.
Height: 6'
Weight: 190 lbs
Eyes: Blue
Hair: Blond
Strength level: Ant-Man possesses the normal human strength of a man of his age, height, and weight who engages in moderate regular exercise. When he shrinks to ant-size, he retains his full-size human strength.
Known superhuman powers: Ant-Man possesses the power to reduce himself to the size of an ant, approximately one-half inch in height, by means of a rare group of subatomic particles called the Pym Particles after the man who discovered them, Henry Pym. The nature, the source, and the mechanics of the Pym Particles remain a mystery, but their properties and behavior

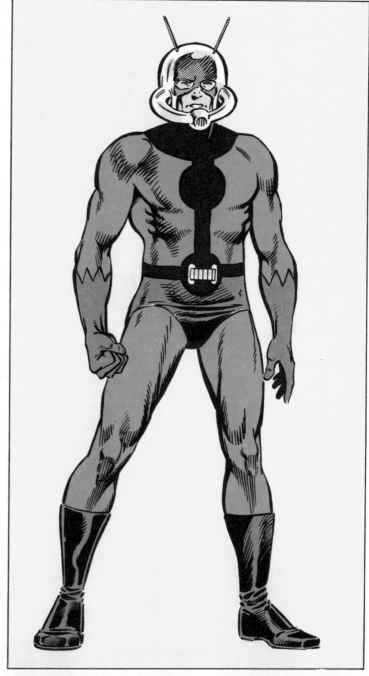

can be determined. The Pym Particles are suspended within an unknown gas which is confined and stored in special magnetic-field generating cylinders (see Paraphernalia).

When Ant-Man releases a certain quantity of the gas containing the Pym Particles in his immediate vicinity, the particles penetrate his skin, touch the nearest nerve endings in the skin, and are transmitted by the nervous system to the brain. Interacting with the electrical impulses of the brain, the particles create an organism-wide "reducing field," which is energized by mental command. Thus activated, the field reduces Ant-Man's entire body at a uniform rate to the size he has determined, which is usually ant-size (½ inch), although he can adopt sizes between his normal size and that of an ant, if he so desires.. Ant-Man's mass is not compressed into the reduced stature. Instead it is somehow extended into an extraphysical dimension that is opened by the activating of the Pym Particles, from which the mass can later be reclaimed. It takes about two seconds from the time the Pym Particles reach his brain for Ant-Man to reduce to ant-size.

It is not known how many Pym Particles constitute a sufficient quantity to enable the generation of a "reducing field." The quantity of particles, however, does not determine how small an organism can shrink. (That is determined by the mental command of the user.) It is also not known what effect, if any, the exposure to an overabundance of Pym Particles at a single time will have. It is known, however, that continuous exposure to Pym Particles over a prolonged period of time enables certain brains (such as Henry Pym's) to generate "reducing fields" spontaneously, without contact with a new quantity of particles. (Scott Lang has not been exposed to the particles long enough to determine if he will be similarly affected.) Whether this ability to spontaneously generate "reducing fields" is permanent or if it fades in time is unknown. Also unknown is the time limit, if any, of the potency of the particles. So far Ant-Man has been able to remain ant-size for as long as he has wished, a matter of hours. If Ant-Man is rendered unconscious while in his reduced state, he remains at that size and does not spontaneously revert to normal size.

To return to normal size, Ant-Man releases a certain quantity of the gas containing another type of Pym Particles in his immediate vicinity. Like the particles that produced the "reducing field," these particles also penetrate the skin, touch the nerve endings, and are transmitted by the nervous system to the brain. Also interacting with the electrical impulses of the brain, the particles create an organism-wide "enlarging field," which is energized by mental command. Ant-Man's body grows at a uniform rate, until he has reclaimed all of the mass that was extended extradimensionally. At that point, since there is no more of his mass within the extraphysical dimension, the "enlarging field" is no longer energized, and the enlargement process stops. (The particles of this "enlarging gas" can be used by certain individuals to grow larger than their normal stature. In this case, extra pseudo-organic mass is acquired from the same extraphysical dimension where excess organic mass is extended in the reducing process, and the "reducing gas" is used to regain normal stature. See *Goliath*.)

How Ant-Man mentally determines when

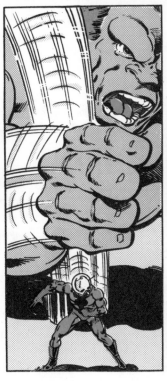

he has reduced himself to precisely the size he wishes (ant-size) is not fully understood. Certainly there are visual indicators in his surrounding environment, but the process occurs so quickly that it would be remarkable to be able to see these scale indicators. Presumably, knowing the precise rate at which the shrinking process occurs, he could time the process so that he deactivates the "reducing field" when he reaches the desired stature. Again, this would involve split-second timing. However he manages to do it, Ant-Man has been able to calibrate his shrinking process so that he attains within 1/32 of an inch of his usual half inch size. (He could use successive dosages of the "shrinking gas" or "enlarging gas" to make fine adjustments on his height.)

The smallest size the Pym Particles can enable an organism to attain is not known. Both Henry Pym and Scott Lang have used multiple dosages of the "shrinking gas" to shrink to sub-microscopic stature. (The successive dosages enabled them to mentally adjust to the experience with short "rest stops"; a single dosage would theoretically be enough to make the "journey" nonstop.) When 99.99+ per cent of an organism's mass is extradimensionally shunted, the organism is automatically sent into a "subatomic universe," one of countless alternate universes accessible to Earth only by the mass-shunting process. (For more information on these "microverses," see *Appendix: Other Dimensions*.)

Ant-Man can use the Pym Particles to reduce other objects and organisms at the same time he reduces himself. Touching the object or organism he wishes to shrink, he generates the "reducing field" in the usual manner, and then mentally extends that field to encompass his "baggage" or "passenger." How far he can extend this field is unknown. So far all he has "carried" with him has been one other person or ant. Ant-Man's uniform and paraphernalia shrink with him by this process.

Paraphernalia: Ant-Man stores the "reducing gas" and "enlarging gas" in separate cylindrical canisters on his belt. These canisters generate a magnetic field which keeps the Pym Particles from escaping. A button at the center of the canister activates the nozzle-release at the top of the canister. The nozzle releases a measured quantity of "gas" no matter how long or hard the button is depressed.

Ant-Man wears a cybernetic helmet permitting him rudimentary telepathic communication with ants. He can broadcast to a range of one mile, depending on environmental conditions. Directed by cybernetic-telepathic command, ants are able to perform certain simple tasks. There does not appear to be a limit to the number of ants he can command at once. Frequently Ant-Man employs an entire army of worker ants. The helmet also contains sound amplification equipment which shifts the frequency of his voice as well as augmenting the volume, so that he can be heard by normal-sized human beings despite his diminutive size. ∎

ANT-MAN'S GAS CANISTERS

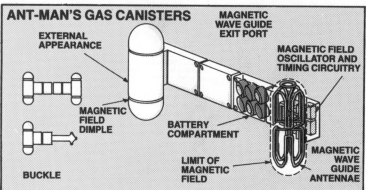

EXTERNAL APPEARANCE

MAGNETIC WAVE GUIDE EXIT PORT

MAGNETIC FIELD OSCILLATOR AND TIMING CIRCUITRY

MAGNETIC FIELD DIMPLE

BATTERY COMPARTMENT

BUCKLE

LIMIT OF MAGNETIC FIELD

MAGNETIC WAVE GUIDE ANTENNAE

ANT-MAN'S HELMET

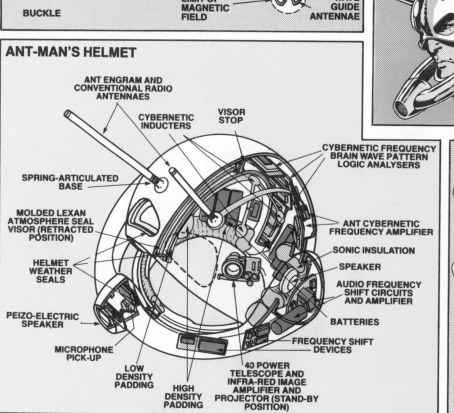

ANT ENGRAM AND CONVENTIONAL RADIO ANTENNAES

CYBERNETIC INDUCTERS

VISOR STOP

SPRING-ARTICULATED BASE

MOLDED LEXAN ATMOSPHERE SEAL VISOR (RETRACTED POSITION)

HELMET WEATHER SEALS

PEIZO-ELECTRIC SPEAKER

MICROPHONE PICK-UP

LOW DENSITY PADDING

HIGH DENSITY PADDING

40 POWER TELESCOPE AND INFRA-RED IMAGE AMPLIFIER AND PROJECTOR (STAND-BY POSITION)

CYBERNETIC FREQUENCY BRAIN WAVE PATTERN LOGIC ANALYSERS

ANT CYBERNETIC FREQUENCY AMPLIFIER

SONIC INSULATION

SPEAKER

AUDIO FREQUENCY SHIFT CIRCUITS AND AMPLIFIER

BATTERIES

FREQUENCY SHIFT DEVICES

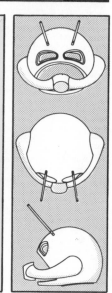

AQUARIAN

Real Name: Wundarr
Occupation: Prophet
Legal status: Citizen of Dakkam, illegal alien on Earth.
Identity: The fact that he is an alien is not widely known.
Other current aliases: Herald of the New Age
Place of birth: Dakkam, second planet in the R Aquarii system (Earth designation)
Marital status: Single
Known relatives: Hektu (father, deceased), Soja (mother, deceased)
Group affiliation: None
Base of operations: Mobile
First appearance: (as Wundarr) FEAR #17, (as the Aquarian) MARVEL TWO-IN-ONE #58
Origin: FEAR #17
History: Wundarr was born on the planet Dakkam to the extremely humanoid-looking alien race native to the world. As an infant, Wundarr was placed inside a rocket and sent into space when his father incorrectly predicted planetwide destruction. Spending the interstellar voyage in suspended animation, Wundarr eventually came within the gravitational influence of Earth and was bombarded by cosmic rays in Earth's outer atmosphere. This radiation endowed him with certain superhuman physical powers. Crashlanding on Earth, Wundarr grew to maturity within the ship, having been released from suspended animation by the crash. Eventually he was set free by the Man-Thing (see *Man-Thing*). Due to his lack of experience and education, Wundarr acted mentally and emotionally retarded. For a brief time he was placed in the custody of the Thing, but Namorita "adopted" him shortly thereafter (see *Namorita, Thing*). Government agents learned of his super human abilities and illegal alien status and brought him to the government energy research facility, Project: Pegasus, for study (see *Project: Pegasus*).

Wundarr's mild energy-dampening powers were used to probe the power object called the Cosmic Cube (see *Shaper of Worlds*). In an accidental power overload, Wundarr's mind and body were overwhelmed by the Cube's energies. Consequently, Wundarr's energy-dampening abilities were greatly heightened but his mind was shut down, as it was not yet able to cope with the influx of new power. In communion with the sentience of the Cosmic Cube, Wundarr gained great knowledge and a sense of purpose. Emerging from his coma, he renamed himself the Aquarian and set forth to use his new powers to bring peace and enlightenment to the world. He has since helped the sentient lifeform in the Cosmic Cube metamorphose into its next state of being.
Height: 5′ 10″
Weight: 165 lbs
Eyes: Brown
Hair: Brown
Strength level: The Aquarian possesses superhuman strength enabling him to lift (press) approximately 1 ton under optimal conditions. Before his powers changed due to exposure to the Cosmic Cube, he could absorb energy to increase his physical strength to about 15 times its normal level, thus enabling him to lift (press) 15 tons.
Known superhuman powers: The Aquarian possesses certain superhuman physi-

cal and energy-manipulating powers due to mutagenic changes wrought in his cellular structure by cosmic radiation.

Prior to his exposure to the Cosmic Cube, the Aquarian's body absorbed various energies from the environment and transformed them into kinetic energy with which to augment his body's strength and endurance. The Aquarian could not only use his augmented strength to lift things, but also to propel himself through the air by jumping. The Aquarian could cover several miles in a single bound. The energy absorption process continued involuntarily and if the Aquarian had not expended it in some physical activity before it reached the threshold of his body's capacity to retain energy, the energy would explosively discharge in a sphere of concussive force. (Reed Richards designed him a containment suit which enabled his body to expel small, non-concussive amounts of energy so it would not build up.)

After the Cosmic Cube experiment, the Aquarian's former energy-dampening ability was transformed into something different and more powerful. The Aquarian's body is now surrounded by a field of entropy ("null-force") which, at equilibrium, radiates to a distance of five feet from any point on his body. With concentration, the Aquarian can contract the null-field to about five inches in thickness, or expand it to a maximum distance of approximately 500 feet. He can never shut the field down completely.

The null-field neutralizes most energies within the electromagnetic spectrum over a certain as yet unmeasured intensity. This includes light, electricity, magnetism, high-frequency energies, sound, and even gravity.

The Aquarian's entropic field also neutralizes kinetic energy. His body's null-field is of opposite polarity to that of the fields of normal atomic matter. Hence his field nullifies kinetic energy in direct ratio to the inertia (resistance of object in motion to changes of motion) of the moving object. Only objects with kinetic energy below a certain as yet unmea-

sured value are permitted through his field without any cancellation of inertia. The net effect of any object of greater inertia entering his null-field is that it loses its kinetic energy. Hence, a speeding bullet, a thrown knife, or a hurled punch are unable to strike him.

Because this kinetic energy-cancelling property affects him as well as other objects in his field, the Aquarian cannot move faster than his null-field will allow. Therefore, his ability to leap is useless. However, since he can negate gravity's influence on him, he can walk on air.

The kinetic and electromagnetic energies possessed by most other superhumanly powered beings is also canceled within his field. Hence, those who possess superhuman physical strength would be unable to exercise it within his field, and those with energy-manipulating powers would also be unable to use them. The field does not take these innate capacities away; it simply prevents their use in his presence. ∎

ARABIAN KNIGHT

Real Name: Abdul Qamar
Occupation: Bedouin chieftain
Identity: Secret
Legal status: Citizen of Saudi Arabia, with no criminal record.
Other known aliases: None
Place of birth: Aqabah, Saudi Arabia
Known relatives: Maya, Rana, Almira (wives), Faisal, Hassim (sons)
Group affiliation: None
Base of operations: Mobile; region of Saudi Arabia and Ahmet, Egypt.
First appearance and origin: INCREDIBLE HULK #257
History: Seeking shelter in an underground tomb in the eastern desert of Egypt, Abdul Qamar discovered a magic scimitar and flying carpet that had belonged to a Thirteenth Century ancestor who had been a champion of his people. Qamar decided to carry on his ancestor's tradition by battling evil as the Arabian Knight.

Height: 5' 10"	**Eyes:** Brown
Weight: 170 lbs	**Hair:** Black

Strength level: The Arabian Knight possesses the normal human strength of a man of his age, height, and build, who engages in moderate regular exercise.

Known superhuman powers: None. The Arabian Knight's power derives from his three magical weapons.

Weapons: The Arabian Knight wields a "magic carpet" that responds solely to his mental commands. The carpet can levitate off the ground and propel itself through the air at any speed that the Knight commands. The Arabian Knight seldom has it fly beyond the speed at which he can breathe, approximately 90 miles per hour. The carpet can levitate to any height the Knight commands it, although he has not yet attempted to fly higher than 20,000 feet, the point at which the atmosphere becomes too thin to breathe. Besides its use as transportation, the carpet can be commanded to perform such feats as wrapping around an object or person, or rolling itself into a cylinder and striking like a whip or battering ram. The carpet, empowered by unknown magical forces, is virtually impervious to harm.

The Arabian Knight also wields a golden scimitar which is capable of emitting beams of concussive magical force. The maximum amount of concussive force the sword can emit at one time is not known, nor is how long (if at all) it takes the sword to "recharge" in between discharges. The Arabian Knight can mentally control the amount of force the sword emits. The sword possesses an enchantment that causes it to discharge magical energy against anyone other than the Knight who touches it. The Knight can also use the scimitar for slashing and stabbing. It can cut through steel, stone and other hard materials.

The belt-sash at the Arabian Knight's waist can also be animated by mental command, to serve as bonds, lariat, whip or climbing rope. It is made of the same substance as the flying carpet and is similarly indestructible. It can magically extend in length to almost ten times its ordinary length of four feet. ∎

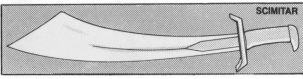

SCIMITAR

ARAGORN

Aragorn is a winged horse ridden by Brunnhilda the Valkyrie and previously owned and ridden by Dr. Dane Whitman, the Black Knight (see *Black Knight, Valkyrie*). Whitman was the nephew of Professor Nathan Garrett, who had adopted the guise of the earlier, criminal Black Knight (see *Appendix: Black Knight II*). In this role, Garrett had ridden a horse whom he had mutated using genetic engineering techniques that he had developed. The artificial mutations gave the horse large feathered wings and other special adaptations which enabled him to fly. After Garrett's final defeat by the original Iron Man, this winged horse escaped and eventually was further mutated and fell into the possession of the Dreadknight (see *Dreadknight*). Garrett, dying from the fall he had suffered in the battle, persuaded Whitman to vow to use the scientific discoveries he had used as the criminal Black Knight for good. Whitman decided to do so by becoming a new, heroic Black Knight. In pursuit of this goal, Whitman used Garrett's genetic techniques to mutate another horse, whom he named Aragorn, into a flying steed. When the new Black Knight left his own time for a temporary stay in the Twelfth Century A.D., he entrusted Aragorn to the care of Brunnhilda the Valkyrie, who remains his owner to this day. The Black Knight, having returned to his own time, now rides a mechanical flying steed.

Aragorn can fly by means of various adaptations given him through artificial mutation. The most prominent of these are his wings, which span eighteen and a half feet from wingtip to wingtip. The wings are fully feathered, like a bird's.

Aragorn's entire anatomy has been adapted to flying. His bones are hollower than a normal horse's, making him weigh less than a normal horse of his size would. His body is virtually devoid of fat, possessing greater proportionate muscle mass than human. His eyes are specially adapted to be able to withstand high speed winds which would hurt the average equine eye. He possesses a special membrane in his respiratory system enabling him to extract oxygen from the air at high velocity or at high altitudes.

Aragorn flies by flapping his wings, creating enough lift to hold aloft at least 2000 pounds; in other words, he can support aloft his own weight, that of the Valkyrie (who, as an Asgardian goddess, weighs more than an ordinary human of her size and build: 475 pounds), and other passengers as well. Aragorn can fly at speeds ranging up to 125 miles per hour. He can fly at his top speed for about one hour before needing to rest. Though he generally flies beneath the height of the clouds (6500 feet), Aragorn can reach a height of 10,000 feet with little effort.

Aragorn is highly intelligent, and will respond to a wide range of verbal commands given by the Valkyrie.

First appearance: AVENGERS #48 ∎

ARCADE

Real Name: Unknown
Occupation: Playboy, assassin
Legal status: United States citizen with no criminal record as yet
Identity: Secret
Former aliases: None known
Place of birth: Said to be Beverly Hills, California
Marital status: Single
Known relatives: None
Group affiliation: None
Base of operations: Various "Murderworlds" in undisclosed locations
First appearance: MARVEL TEAM-UP #65
Origin (possible): X-MEN #124
History: Arcade has given differing accounts of his past life, and as yet there is no evidence to substantiate any of these accounts. Apparently Arcade will tell falsehoods about his past to mislead and confuse his opponents for his own amusement.

One of Arcade's accounts states that he was the spoiled son of a millionaire living in Beverly Hills, California. When Arcade turned 21, his father cut off his allowance, claiming that Arcade did not deserve it. The next day Arcade killed his father in an explosion, and as a result, he inherited his father's vast wealth. In killing his father, Arcade discovered that he had a talent and liking for murder. He therefore became a "hit man" (an assassin for hire), and within a year became in his own view the best in the United States. However, Arcade became bored with killing by ordinary means, and so he used his great wealth to construct his first "Murderworld," a hidden complex of high-tech death traps designed in the manner of an amusement park.

Whatever the truth may be about his life to this point, the story of his life after he began using Murderworld is clear. Arcade now kills victims for money by trapping them within a Murderworld complex. He designs and constructs special traps within Murderworlds for individual victims after studying those victims' specific weaknesses. Arcade's customary fee is one million dollars per victim, which is a token fee, as his expenses incurred are often higher. To Arcade the game itself is more important than the expense or even the winning. Arcade employs two assistants, known only as Miss Locke and Mr. Chambers. Recently, seeking new challenges, he has attempted to kill various superhuman beings in his Murderworlds, including the X-Men, Spider-Man, and Captain Britain, but so far without success.

Height: 5' 6"
Weight: 140 lbs
Eyes: Blue
Hair: Red
Strength level: Arcade possesses the normal human strength of a man of his age, height, and build who engages in moderate regular exercise.
Known superhuman powers: None
Abilities: Arcade has a genius level I.Q. and a natural aptitude for mechanics, architecture, and applied technology. A brilliant and innovative self-taught designer, Arcade applies his talents to the construction of the amusement park-like complexes of death traps which he calls Murderworlds. ∎

ARES

Real Name: Ares
Occupation: God of War
Legal status: Citizen of Olympus
Identity: Ares' existence is not known to the general public of Earth, who believe him to be a fictional character of ancient myth.
Former aliases: Mars (his Roman name), Mister Talon
Place of birth: Olympus
Marital status: Married
Known relatives: Zeus (father), Hera (mother), Enyo (wife), Deimos, Phobos (sons), Neptune (Poseidon), Pluto (uncles), Demeter, Hestia (aunts), Hephaestus (brother), Apollo, Dionysius, Hercules, Hermes (half-brothers), Artemis, Athena, Venus (Aphrodite) (half-sisters)
Group affiliation: Gods of Olympus
Base of operations: Olympus
First modern appearance: THOR #129
History: Ares is the son of Zeus, monarch of the Olympian gods, and his wife Hera (see *Olympian Gods, Zeus*). Ares was worshipped as the god of war in ancient Greece and Rome. However, with the rise of Christianity in the Roman Empire, Zeus allowed the worship of the Olympians to die out, and Ares could no longer act as patron god of warriors. As a result, over the ensuing centuries Ares grew increasingly dissatisfied with Zeus's rule. He has three times attempted to conquer Olympus, twice in league with his uncle Pluto, god of the Olympian underworld; but each time he has been thwarted through the efforts of his half-brother Hercules and his Earthly allies (see *Hercules, Pluto*). Ares has hated Hercules since Hercules killed Ares' monstrous Stymphalian birds in the days of ancient Greece. Also, in recent years, Ares set two of Earth's nations at war with each other. The conflict threatened to spread over all of Earth, until Ares was forced to put an end to it by his half-sister Venus, whom he has long sought in marriage, and the Sub-Mariner (see *Sub-Mariner*). Venus and the Sub-Mariner extracted a pledge from Ares not to engage in further warmongering on Earth.

Height: 6′ 1″ **Eyes:** Brown
Weight: 500 lbs **Hair:** Brown
Strength level: Ares possesses greater strength than most Olympian gods, and can lift (press) approximately 70 tons under optimal conditions.

Known superhuman powers: As an immortal god, Ares possesses vast strength and endurance. His physical capabilities are superior to those of the majority of Olympian gods. He has virtually inexhaustible stamina, and does not tire appreciably after any exertion.

Like all Olympians, Ares is immortal, possessing a life essence that cannot be ended by any conventional means. He can be wounded in battle, but his godly life force gives him incredible recuperative abilities. He can fully recover from penetration wounds (such as by knife, sword, or bullet) in anywhere from minutes to hours, depending on their severity. Only an injury of such magnitude that it incinerates him or disperses a major portion of his bodily molecules could cause him physical death. Even then, his life essence may still be unharmed, and Zeus may be able to resurrect him.

Abilities: Ares possesses great skill in the use of all the implements of war used in the time of ancient Greece and Rome. ■

ARKON

Real Name: Arkon
Occupation: Imperion (ruler)
Legal status: Citizen of Polemachus.
Identity: Arkon has no dual identity. Although he appeared in public on Earth, his existence as an extradimensional being is not generally known.
Place of birth: Polemachus
Marital status: Single
Known relatives: None
Group affiliation: Former ally of the Enchantress
Base of operations: Polemachus
First appearance: AVENGERS #75

History: Arkon was born of noble lineage on the humanoid-inhabited extradimensional world Polemachus. The people of Polemachus developed a culture that glorifies warfare, and Arkon succeeded in becoming the greatest warrior of his people. Appointed imperion of the largest country on Polemachus, Arkon mounted military campaigns against neighboring countries in an effort to conquer the world. His dreams of conquest were forgotten when Polemachus was faced with a world-wide catastrophe: the light- and heat-providing planetary rings were disintegrating. Arkon's scientists determined that atomic explosions occurring on Earth somehow were extradimensionally translated to rekindle the energy rings for about a year. Although Polemachus had not developed nuclear weaponry, the scientist predicted that if they were to atomically annihilate the Earth, their world's energy-rings would be restored to power.

Towards this goal, Arkon manipulated the Scarlet Witch into reciting a magical spell found in a Polemachan book to enable him to transport himself to Earth. Attracted to the Witch, Arkon kidnapped her as well as a group of atomic scientists. The scientists were forced to yield information on nuclear weaponry, which Arkon's scientists used to construct an atomic device. Before Arkon could detonate it on Earth, however, Iron Man managed to build a machine that, when empowered by Thor's hammer, rekindled Polemachus's energy-rings (see *Thor*). Arkon then ceased hostilities with Earth.

The Avengers had cause to revisit Arkon's world when their comrade, the Black Knight, was taken captive by Arkon while searching for the Well at the Center of Time. Arkon ceased hostilities with the Earthmen when he learned that he was being duped by the Asgardian Enchantress (see *Enchantress*).

Although his world now possessed the capacity for atomic power, Arkon was dissatisfied with the length of time it took to build a nuclear arsenal. Thus he devised a plan to pit three extra-dimensional worlds, one of which was Earth, against one another, in hopes that energy from the resultant nuclear conflagration could be absorbed by his world. His elaborate machinations failed, due to the efforts of the Fantastic Four.

Arkon was forced to return to Earth yet again when the machine that Iron Man had once built failed due to Arkon's tinkering with it. Although Arkon's scientists managed to fix it, the machine needed to be re-energized before it could restore Polemachus's energy-rings. Arkon traveled to Earth to recruit Thor, but when he was unable to locate the thunder god, he settled for Storm of the X-Men, who also had the ability to summon lightning (see *Storm*). Apparently unaware of Arkon's two attempts to destroy Earth, Storm agreed to help, and with the assistance of her teammate Cyclops, rekindled Polemachus's rings (see *Cyclops*). Arkon returned the X-Men to Earth shortly thereafter. Still later, the X-Men and the Fantastic Four helped Arkon drive off an extra-dimensional invasion of Polemachus by the alien Badoon (see *Alien Races: Badoon*).

Height: 6'
Eyes: Brown
Weight: 400 lbs
Hair: Brown
Strength level: Arkon possesses superhuman strength, enabling him to lift (press) approximately 2 tons under optimal conditions.
Known superhuman powers: Arkon possesses superhuman strength, speed, agility, and stamina. His skin and muscle structure is denser than human, and his rate of recuperation is faster. Arkon is among the strongest beings of his race.
Weapons: Arkon wields three different kinds of energy weapons native to his world. Each of them are shaped like a stylized lightning bolt, and are solid until they hit their target. At that point, the bolts convert to pure energy. They are each thrown like a short javelin and are carried in a quiver. His golden bolts are designed to open temporary portals between dimensions, permitting him access to alternate worlds. The specific nature of the energy that creates these dimensional rifts is not yet known. His scarlet bolts are weapons of destruction, creating a force equivalent to 10 pounds of TNT, sufficient to blast Thor off his feet. His black bolts (sometimes called D-Bolts) are his most powerful energy weapons, capable of exerting a force equivalent to 20 tons of TNT, sufficient power to shatter a medium-sized mountain. ∎

ARMADILLO

Real name: Antonio Rodriguez
Occupation: Professional wrestler
Identity: Secret
Legal status: Citizen of the United States with a criminal record
Other known aliases: None
Place of birth: San Antonio, Texas
Marital status: Married
Known relatives: Maria (wife)
Group affiliation: Former henchman of Dr. Karl Malus
Base of operations: Mobile
First appearance and origin: CAPTAIN AMERICA #308

History: Little is known about the background of Antonio Rodriguez other than that he has a criminal record and a wife named Maria. His wife critically stricken with an undiagnosed disease, Rodriguez took her to every doctor who would see her but none were able to determine the nature of her illness, let alone help her. In desperation, he sought Dr. Karl Malus, a criminal scientist who specializes in the generation and bestowal of superhuman powers, whom he had heard about while in prison. Malus agreed to try to cure her in exchange for the man agreeing to become his test subject and employee for an indefinite period of time. Malus had long been interested in acquiring a superhuman henchman, particularly after his experiments on the Fly, the Hornet, the Werewolf, and Goliath failed to provide him one (see *Goliath, Werewolf*). Malus subjected the man to an experimental process that combined genetic material from an armadillo with the man's human genes. The process caused the man's strength to increase drastically, his skin to transform into a tough, organic armored plate, and his hands to grow thick tough claws. Malus dubbed him the Armadillo and assigned him to break into the West Coast Avengers Compound to steal the comatose body of Goliath, who was being held there. The Armadillo complied and soon found himself in combat with the visiting Captain America. Although physically superior to him, the Armadillo was defeated by the Captain's superior combat skills. Taking compassion on the Armadillo's plight because of his wife's condition, Captain America refused to turn the Armadillo over to the authorities. After Malus cured Maria, Armadillo joined the Unlimited Class Wrestling Federation.

Height: 7″ 6″ **Eyes:** Brown
Weight: 540 lbs. **Hair:** None

Strength level: The Armadillo possesses superhuman strength, enabling him to lift (press) approximately 25 tons under optimal conditions.

Known superhuman powers: The Armadillo possesses superhuman strength, a high degree of resistance to bodily harm, and sharp claws on his hands and feet. The armor plating and tough hide covering his entire body enables him to withstand the force of ballistic weaponry up to light anti-tank weapons without penetration. His skin can withstand brief exposure to flame, ice, and acid without damage. His bones and muscles have been augmented to such a degree that he can withstand the impact of being hit by a truck carrying ten tons of cargo traveling at 60 miles per hour without serious injury. The Armadillo possesses superhuman endurance as well, enabling him to exert himself at peak capacity for over an hour before fatigue begins to impair his performance. Despite his mass, he can move as quickly as a normal-sized athletically inclined man.

The Armadillo's claws are strong enough to rend gouges in cinderblock and medium-density steel with minimal wear on the nails. Coupled with his great strength, he can break through a standard 4 inch steel-reinforced cinderblock wall in a matter of seconds, or dig a hole in the earth deep enough to fit his entire body in less than a minute. ∎

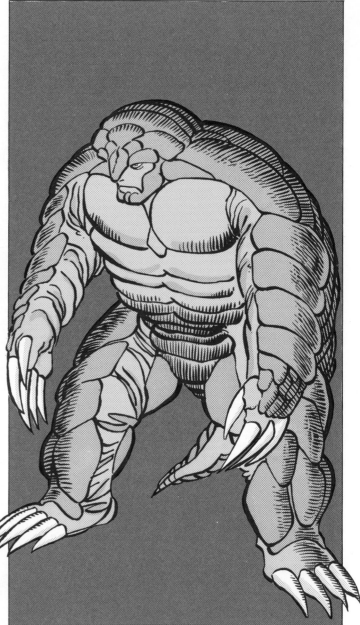

ASGARD

Asgard is a small otherdimensional planetary body (its surface area being about the same as that of the continental United States), whose nature and physics are different from those of planetary bodies in the Earthly dimension. Asgard is not a sphere like the Earth or Moon, but a relatively flat asteroid-like landmass suspended in space. Asgard does not rotate about its axis, nor does it revolve around a sun. Asgard has intervals of night and day (of undisclosed durations) even though it does not rotate. There is no evidence of changing seasons, however. It is not known if Asgard's source of light and heat is the Earth's sun, a sun in the Asgardian dimension whose gravity does not exert itself on Asgard, or a glowing ball of light dissimilar to a star in most of its properties. Unlike Earth, where the force of gravitation radiates from the center of the sphere, Asgard's gravity apparently radiates from some point or object beneath the suspended landmass. Consequently, there is a top side to Asgard, upon which beings can stand, and a bottom side where beings cannot stand and from which they will fall through space toward the source of gravitation. At the boundaries of Asgard's landmass, a being or object can step off into the void.

There is apparently some force that keeps the bottom and edges of Asgard's landmass from eroding away. Whatever this force is also prevents the bodies of water which are at certain of Asgard's boundaries from pouring off into the void, as well as preventing Asgard's atmosphere from escaping. Asgard has been described as floating on a "Sea of Space." This sea apparently has a surface, one that is navigable by certain Asgardian ships that resemble Viking longboats. The exact nature of space in the Asgardian dimension is unknown.

While the gravity of Asgard is roughly analogous to Earth's, common matter is considerably denser on an average. Consequently a chair made of Asgardian wood would be more massive (and heavier) than a chair made of analagous Earthly wood. Rocks, water, flesh, bone, steel — all matter is denser and thus more durable.

Besides all of the anomalies described above, Asgard is connected in some as yet unknown way with at least two other dimensional planes, one of which is that of the Earth (whom the Asgardians call *Midgard*, a word meaning "Middle Realm"). The Asgardians refer to all of the major known inhabited realms of their cosmology as the "Nine Worlds." Only four of the Nine Worlds are located on the main Asgardian landmass: *Asgard*, home of the Gods, *Vanaheim*, home of the Asgardians' sister race, the Vanir, *Nidavellir*, home of the Dwarves, and *Alfheim*, home of the Light Elves.

The remainder of the Nine Worlds are on separate landmasses isolated from one another by interdimensional space. (For the sake of creating a comprehensible diagram, the Nine Worlds of Asgard are placed in a multi-leveled configuration. These levels do not represent any real physical distances or relationships. Instead, they represent the interdimensional relationships between the realms.) *Midgard*, our Earth, does not appear to be physically affected by the motions of any of the other physical bodies in the Asgardian cosmology, although Earth's axis (the imaginary pole around which it rotates) is in alignment with

one of the roots of Yggdrasil, the cosmic ash tree that stands in Asgard. *Jotunheim*, the world of the giants, is a flat ring-shaped realm with high mountains along its inner edge. It is apparently on its own separate dimension plane, discrete from Asgard's and Earth's. *Svartalfheim*, home of the Dark Elves, is another asteroid-like landmass, smaller than Asgard. There are numerous nexus-portals between the mountains of Jotunheim and Svartalfheim and the mountains of Asgard permitting easy passage by denizens of each realm. These passageways make Jotunheim and Svartalfheim seem like "underworlds" of the Asgardian continent itself.

The eighth of the Nine Worlds is *Hel*, realm of the dead, and its sister realm, *Niffleheim*. In the Asgardian scheme of afterlife, the heroes and honored dead go to Valhalla, a special region of Asgard, the common dead go to Hel, and the dishonored dead (murderers and other evildoers) go to Niffleheim. Hel, Niffleheim, and Valhalla possess the necessary physical conditions to permit the astral forms of the deceased to exist there for indefinite periods of time. At one time, Hela, goddess of the dead, usurped the rule of Valhalla, despite the fact it was on a different dimensional plane than Hel (see *Hela*). Odin has since reclaimed the land. The ninth of the Nine Worlds is *Muspelheim*, land of the fiery demons. Until his recent disappearance, the primordial demon Surter ruled Muspelheim. Muspelheim is on its own dimensional plane, separate from all the other Nine Worlds. In the Asgardians' account of the origin of their cosmology, Muspelheim, the land of fire, and Nifleheim, the land of ice, were said to predate recorded time, separated from one another by Ginnungagap, the Yawning Void.

Asgard is honeycombed with nexus-portals to the various extradimensional realms of the Nine Worlds, making the worlds (with the exception of Earth) sometimes seem like they are on a contiguous plain. (Indeed, early cartographers of Asgard mapped it this way.) The only permanent portal to

Earth, *Bifrost*, the Rainbow Bridge, has recently been shattered, severing Asgard's connection with Earth and making passage between realms difficult. There is a special passageway from Asgard to the extra-dimensional realm of Olympus, home of the Greek gods (see *Olympus*). Since Olympus is not a part of the Asgardian cosmology, this nexus-portal is believed to be an artificial rather than natural phenomenon. Another unique feature of Asgard is the Cave of Time, an apparently natural phenomenon through which passage to other time eras is possible.

It is probable that somewhere in Asgard's outlying Sea of Space there are floating nexus-portals to Earth's space. Beings of the Earthly dimension have in certain instances been able to travel from Earthly to Asgardian space. There may indeed be an edge to Asgard's Sea of Space, perhaps at the perimeter of the "Dome of the Sky" extending from the outer edge of ringed Jotunheim. At the edge of the Sea there would exist "dimensional borderlands" which serve as transitional areas between discrete dimensions.

Asgard and its sister realms are populated by six distinct humanoid races, described under *Asgardians*. Besides these, there are several singular creatures who exist upon various of the Nine Worlds. The first is the Midgard Serpent Jormungand, an immense snake-like dragon whose body encircles the inner edge of the mountains of Jotunheim closest to Midgard. The Midgard Serpent lies at the very edge of the dimensional boundary between Jotunheim and Midgard, and prevents passage between dimensions. The second is the winged dragon Nidhogg, who lives in Niffleheim and gnaws at one of the roots of Yggdrasil. The third is the giant wolf-god Fenris, who is responsible for the war-god Tyr's loss of a hand. Fenris is imprisoned in the distant land of Varinheim. The fourth creature is the primordial ice giant Ymir (see *Ymir*).

First appearance: JOURNEY INTO MYSTERY #85.

ASGARD: THE NINE WORLDS

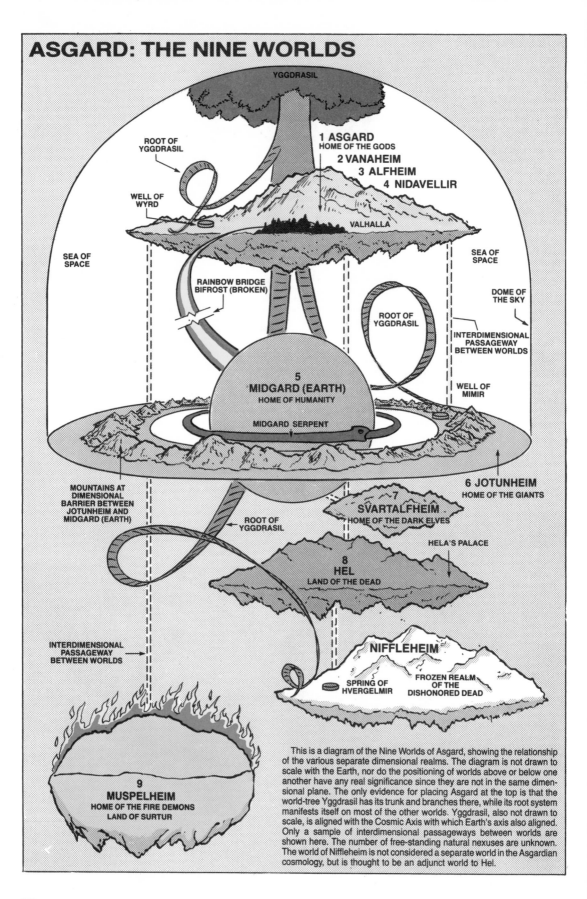

YGGDRASIL

ROOT OF YGGDRASIL

1 ASGARD
HOME OF THE GODS

2 VANAHEIM

3 ALFHEIM

4 NIDAVELLIR

WELL OF WYRD

VALHALLA

SEA OF SPACE

SEA OF SPACE

RAINBOW BRIDGE BIFROST (BROKEN)

DOME OF THE SKY

ROOT OF YGGDRASIL

INTERDIMENSIONAL PASSAGEWAY BETWEEN WORLDS

5 MIDGARD (EARTH)
HOME OF HUMANITY

MIDGARD SERPENT

WELL OF MIMIR

MOUNTAINS AT DIMENSIONAL BARRIER BETWEEN JOTUNHEIM AND MIDGARD (EARTH)

6 JOTUNHEIM
HOME OF THE GIANTS

ROOT OF YGGDRASIL

7 SVARTALFHEIM
HOME OF THE DARK ELVES

HELA'S PALACE

8 HEL
LAND OF THE DEAD

NIFFLEHEIM

INTERDIMENSIONAL PASSAGEWAY BETWEEN WORLDS

SPRING OF HVERGELMIR

FROZEN REALM OF THE DISHONORED DEAD

9 MUSPELHEIM
HOME OF THE FIRE DEMONS
LAND OF SURTUR

This is a diagram of the Nine Worlds of Asgard, showing the relationship of the various separate dimensional realms. The diagram is not drawn to scale with the Earth, nor do the positioning of worlds above or below one another have any real significance since they are not in the same dimensional plane. The only evidence for placing Asgard at the top is that the world-tree Yggdrasil has its trunk and branches there, while its root system manifests itself on most of the other worlds. Yggdrasil, also not drawn to scale, is aligned with the Cosmic Axis with which Earth's axis also aligned. Only a sample of interdimensional passageways between worlds are shown here. The number of free-standing natural nexuses are unknown. The world of Niffleheim is not considered a separate world in the Asgardian cosmology, but is thought to be an adjunct world to Hel.

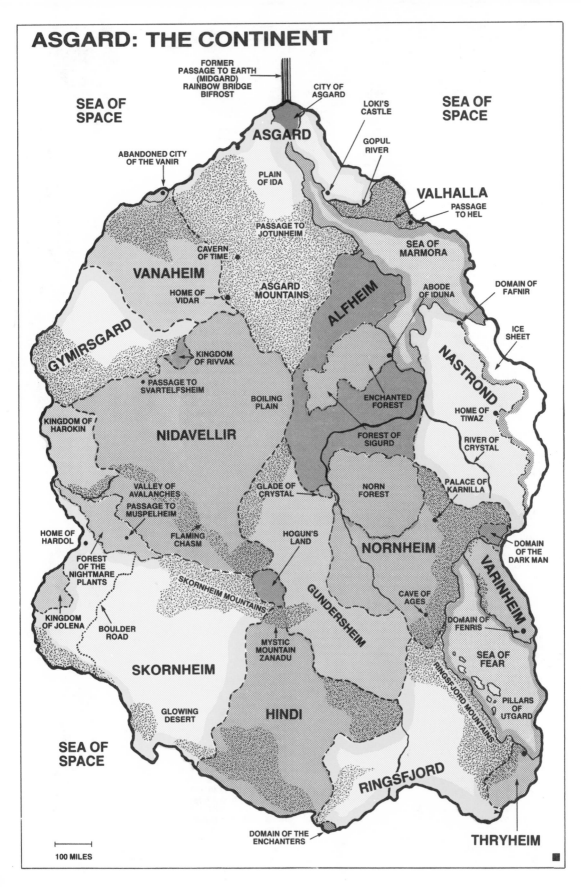

ASGARD: THE CONTINENT

SEA OF SPACE

FORMER PASSAGE TO EARTH (MIDGARD) RAINBOW BRIDGE BIFROST

CITY OF ASGARD

LOKI'S CASTLE

SEA OF SPACE

ASGARD

GOPUL RIVER

VALHALLA

PASSAGE TO HEL

ABANDONED CITY OF THE VANIR

PLAIN OF IDA

PASSAGE TO JOTUNHEIM

SEA OF MARMORA

DOMAIN OF FAFNIR

CAVERN OF TIME

ABODE OF IDUNA

VANAHEIM

ASGARD MOUNTAINS

ALFHEIM

ICE SHEET

HOME OF VIDAR

NASTROND

GYMIRSGARD

KINGDOM OF RIVVAK

ENCHANTED FOREST

HOME OF TIWAZ

PASSAGE TO SVARTELFSHEIM

BOILING PLAIN

RIVER OF CRYSTAL

KINGDOM OF HAROKIN

NIDAVELLIR

FOREST OF SIGURD

PALACE OF KARNILLA

GLADE OF CRYSTAL

NORN FOREST

VALLEY OF AVALANCHES

PASSAGE TO MUSPELHEIM

DOMAIN OF THE DARK MAN

HOME OF HARDOL

FLAMING CHASM

HOGUN'S LAND

NORNHEIM

VARINHEIM

FOREST OF THE NIGHTMARE PLANTS

SKORNHEIM MOUNTAINS

GUNDERSHEIM

CAVE OF AGES

DOMAIN OF FENRIS

KINGDOM OF JOLENA

BOULDER ROAD

MYSTIC MOUNTAIN ZANADU

SEA OF FEAR

SKORNHEIM

GLOWING DESERT

HINDI

RINGSFJORD MOUNTAINS

PILLARS OF UTGARD

SEA OF SPACE

RINGSFJORD

THRYHEIM

100 MILES

DOMAIN OF THE ENCHANTERS

ASGARDIANS

On the Nine Worlds of the Asgardian dimension system, there are six different races of intelligent humanoid beings. The gods are the most human-looking and powerful race of the six. The origin of the gods is shrouded in legend. It is believed that they are not native to the dimension of Asgard, but were born on Earth and relocated there at some point in the distant past. The gods of Asgard were worshipped about a millennium ago by the Norsemen of Scandinavia and various Germanic tribes (who called them by variant names; e.g. Wotan instead of Odin). The gods no longer have or actively seek worshippers on Earth. Certain gods, notably Thor and Odin, still take interest in the welfare of humanity. The gods possess certain superhuman physical attributes. They are extremely long-lived (though not immortal like the Olympian gods), aging at an extraordinarily slow rate upon reaching adulthood. Asgardian flesh and bone is about three times denser than similar human tissue, contributing to the gods' superhuman strength and weight. An average male god can lift (press) about 30 tons; an average female god can lift (press) about 25 tons. Gods are immune to all terrestrial diseases and resistant to conventional injury. The metabolism of the gods gives them superhuman endurance in all physical activities. Pictured here are many of the most prominent gods. Other important gods have their own entries.

The second race of Asgard is the *Giants*, whose dwelling place is Jotunheim. The Giants are basically humanoid in appearance and color, although they tend toward the neanderthalic in body and bone structure. Their most distinguishing feature is their height. The average Giant is twenty feet tall, although some reach up to thirty feet. On occasion, Giants will produce stunted offspring who look similar to the Gods. Loki and the Executioner are both children of Giants, despite their diminutive six or seven foot stature (see *Executioner, Loki*). Giants tend to lead a simple hunter / gatherer type of existence, but their great resentment of the Gods' superior attributes frequently incite them to wage war against the Gods. Giants are frequently sub-classified by their locale: Storm Giants live in the mountains, while Frost Giants live in the frozen tundra. The eldest Frost Giant is Ymir (see *Ymir*).

The third race of Asgard is the *Dwarves*. Dwarves are smaller in stature than the gods, and have squat, stocky bodies. Their average height is four feet. The Dwarves tend to be craftsmen and farmers who maintain friendly trade and peace relations with the Gods. Dwarves dwell in the land of Nidavellir, which is part of the landmass where Asgard and Vanaheim are situated. Dwarves have crafted such Asgardian weapons as the hammer Mjolnir and the spear Gungnir, although it was the magic of Odin that imbued these objects with their special enchantements.

The fourth race of Asgard is the *Elves*. There are two types of Elves, the Dark Elves and the Light Elves, and each dwell in their own separate world, Svartalfheim and Alfheim, respectively. Elves of both kinds vary greatly in size, from four to eight feet. They tend toward slender bodies with proportionately long limbs, although there are exceptions. The Light Elves tend to be lighter in color than the Dark Elves, and dwell on the surface while the Dark Elves dwell underground. Both types have a natural proclivity towards magic.

The fifth race of Asgard is the *Trolls*. The Trolls are the least human-looking of the denizens of the worlds of Asgard, possessing body characteristics that are almost simian. Trolls are stocky and massive, have thick body hair (almost fur), and tend toward a ruddy orange in color. They are on the average taller than the Gods but shorter than the Giants, around seven feet tall, although some Trolls are considerably taller. They live in scattered settlements throughout Asgard, Vanaheim, Jotunheim, and Svartalfheim, mostly underground. The Trolls toil as miners and metalworkers. As belligerent as the Giants, Trolls make up in craftiness what they lack in size. Trolls tend to be extremely strong, stronger than the average God, Dwarf, or Elf, and on a par with the Giants. Certain Trolls like Ulik rival the thunder god Thor in strength (see *Ulik*). The Trolls dislike the other races of Agard, particularly the Gods, and have as little to do with them as possible unless the opportunity for conquest presents itself. The Trolls of the Asgard Mountains are currently united under the leadership of Geirrodur, although revolutions are commonplace (see *Geirrodur*).

The sixth race of Asgard is the *Demons*. The Demons are beings of fire who dwell in Muspelheim, but sometimes venture to the other worlds in the name of war. A nomadic race, the Demons are the offspring of the great fire demon Surtur, whose existence is said to precede that of the Gods. The Demons tend to be about the same stature as the Gods. Other than Surtur, no other individual Asgardian Demon is known (see *Surtur*).

■

HEIMDALL

Real Name: Heimdall
Occupation: Sentry of Asgard, guardian of the Rainbow Bridge
Identity: The general public of Earth believes Heimdall to be a mythological character.
Marital status: Single
Known relatives: Sif (sister)
Base of operations: Asgard
History: Renowned for his heightened perceptions, Heimdall was appointed by Odin to be sentry of the Rainbow Bridge. For millennia, Heimdall remained at his post, venturing from it but once on a mission from Odin. Now that the Bridge has been destroyed, Heimdall stands at Asgard's gates.
First appearance: JOURNEY INTO MYSTERY #85
Height: 7' 2"
Weight: 575 lbs.
Eyes: Gray
Hair: Brown
Strength level: Heimdall can lift (press) about 35 tons.
Known superhuman powers: Heimdall has extraordinarily acute senses, bordering on the extrasensory. He can focus on certain sensory information or block it out from his consciousness as he chooses.

TYR

Real Name: Tyr
Occupation: God of war
Identity: The general public of Earth believes Tyr to be a mythological character.
Marital status: Single
Known relatives: None
Group affiliation: Gods of Asgard
Base of operations: Asgard
First appearance: JOURNEY INTO MYSTERY #85
History: Before Thor was born, Tyr had been a valiant defender of Asgard who lost his hand binding the wolf-god Fenris. Bitter about Thor's preeminence, Tyr has engaged in rebellion against Odin. He recently fought for Asgard against Surtur.
Height: 6' 7"   **Eyes:** Blue
Weight: 510 lbs.   **Hair:** Black
Strength level: Tyr can lift (press) about 35 tons.
Known superhuman powers: Tyr possesses the conventional superhuman physical attributes of an Asgardian god.
Abilities: As god of war, Tyr is a master of unarmed combat and of the use of all forms of Asgardian weaponry.

FRIGGA

Real Name: Frigga
Occupation: Queen of Asgard, goddess of marriage
Identity: The general public of Earth believes Frigga to be a mythological character.
Other current aliases: Fricka
Marital status: Married
Known relatives: Odin (husband), Loki, Thor (foster sons)
Group affiliation: Gods of Asgard
Base of operations: Asgard
First appearance: JOURNEY INTO MYSTERY #92
History: As Odin's wife, Frigga raised his son Thor, even though he was not her natural son. Frigga cast the spells to protect Balder from mortal harm. Frigga also supervised the efforts of the Asgardian goddesses to locate and train members of the Young Gods, the apprentices to the Celestials.
Height: 5′ 11″
Weight: 370 lbs.
Eyes: Blue
Hair: White, formerly black
Strength level: Frigga, a relatively old Asgardian goddess, can still lift (press) about 20 tons.
Known superhuman powers: Besides the conventional superhuman physical attributes of an Asgardian goddess, Frigga possesses certain abilities to wield magic which have not yet been defined.

IDUNN

Real Name: Idunn
Occupation: Goddess of immortality
Identity: The general public of Earth believes Idunn to be a mythological character.
Other current aliases: Freia, Freya
Marital status: Single
Known relatives: Frey (brother)
Base of operations: Asgard
First appearance: JOURNEY INTO MYSTERY #114
History: Odin appointed Idunn Keeper of the Golden Apples, whose mystical properties retard aging among the Asgardians.
Height: 5′ 9″
Weight: 370 lbs.
Eyes: Blue
Hair: Blonde
Strength level: Idunn can lift (press) about 25 tons.
Known superhuman powers: Idunn possesses the conventional superhuman physical attributes of an Asgardian goddess.

VOLLA

Real Name: Volla
Occupation: Prophetess
Identity: Unknown to the people of Earth
Place of birth: Asgard
Place of death: Asgard
Marital status: Single
Known relatives: None
Base of operations: Hel and Niffleheim
First appearance: THOR #127
History: Volla died after making known her prophecies of Ragnarok, but those who are brave and powerful enough to journey into the realm of the dead may still obtain prophecies from her.
Height: 5′ 7″
Weight: 225 lbs.
Eyes: Silver
Hair: White
Strength level: As a wraith, Volla's physical strength is negligible.
Known superhuman powers: Volla possesses precognitive powers, enabling her to envision alternate futures.

HERMOD

Real Name: Hermod
Occupation: God of speed
Identity: The general public of Earth believes Hermod to be a mythological character.
Marital status: Single
Known relatives: None
Base of operations: Asgard
First appearance: THOR #274
Height: 5′ 11″
Weight: 415 lbs.
Eyes: Blue
Hair: Brown
History: Very little is known of Hermod except that he is a relatively young Asgardian god. Noted for his fleetness, he is occasionally employed by Odin as a messenger. His most celebrated mission took him to Hela to learn how Balder might be revived.
Strength level: Hermod can lift (press) about 30 tons.
Known superhuman powers: Besides the conventional superhuman physical attributes of an Asgardian god, Hermod possesses the ability to move at speeds many times greater than an ordinary Asgardian can.

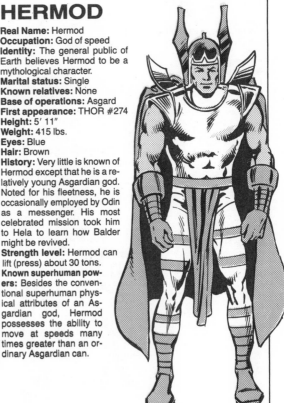

HODER

Real Name: Hoder
Occupation: God of winter
Identity: The general public of Earth believes Hoder to be a mythological character.
Marital status: Single
Known relatives: None
Base of operations: Asgard
First appearance: THOR #274
History: Hoder is an elderly god who nearly killed Balder when Loki tricked him into shooting Balder with an arrow tipped with mistletoe wood, to which Balder was vulnerable (see *Balder*).
Height: 5′ 10″
Weight: 390 lbs.
Eyes: None
Hair: White
Unusual physical characteristics: Hoder is totally blind.
Strength level: Hoder can lift (press) about 20 tons.
Known superhuman powers: Hoder possesses the conventional superhuman physical attributes of an Asgardian god. In addition, Hoder possesses psychic abilities which give him visions of events that are far distant or that lie in alternate futures.

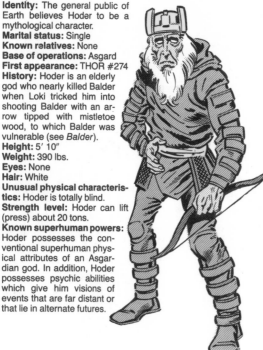

SIGYN

Real Name: Sigyn
Occupation: Goddess of fidelity
Identity: The general public of Earth believes Sigyn to be a mythological character.
Legal status: Princess of Asgard (through marriage to Loki)
Place of birth: Asgard
Marital status: Married
Known relatives: Loki (husband), Odin (father-in-law), Frigga (mother-in-law), Thor (brother-in-law)
Base of operations: Asgard
First appearance: THOR #275
History: The circumstances of Sigyn's marriage to Loki have yet to be revealed. They were estranged for several centuries, and only recently has Sigyn tried to revive their marriage. Sigyn steadfastly aided Loki while he was being punished by Odin, but after Loki regained his freedom, he abandoned her.
Height: 5′ 8″
Weight: 340 lbs.
Eyes: Blue
Hair: Black
Strength level: Sigyn (press) about 25 tons.
Known superhuman powers: Sigyn possesses the conventional superhuman physical attributes of an Asgardian goddess.

FREY

Real Name: Frey
Occupation: God of the harvest
Identity: The general public of Earth believes Frey to be a mythological character.
Marital status: Single
Known relatives: Idunn (sister)
Base of operations: Asgard
First appearance: THOR #294
History: Very little is known about Frey's life and exploits save for his role in the building of the palace of Valhalla.
Height: 6′
Weight: 425 lbs.
Eyes: Blue
Hair: Blond
Strength level: Frey can lift (press) about 30 tons.
Known superhuman powers: Frey possesses the conventional superhuman physical attributes of an Asgardian god.

VIDAR

Real Name: Vidar
Occupation: Huntsman, warrior
Identity: The general public of Earth believe Vidar to be a mythological character.
Legal status: Exiled citizen of Asgard
Marital status: Widower
Known relatives: Odin (father), Grid (mother), Solveig (wife, deceased), Thor, Loki (half-brothers)
Base of operations: A valley in the Asgard Mountains
First appearance: THOR ANNUAL #12
History: The product of Odin's dalliance with a giantess, Vidar lived outside the city of Asgard, his existence known to few. He ventured into the city but once to seek redress for the slaying of his wife.
Height: 10′
Weight: 690 lbs.
Eyes: Blue
Hair: Blond
Strength level: Vidar can lift (press) 50 tons.
Known superhuman powers: Vidar possesses the conventional superhuman physical attributes of an Asgardian god. His half-Giant heritage makes him stronger than the average Asgardian god.

ASP

Real name: Unknown
Occupation: Professional criminal
Identity: Secret
Legal status: Citizen of Egypt with no criminal record
Place of birth: Tanta, Egypt
Marital status: Unknown
Known relatives: None
Group affiliation: Member of the Serpent Society
Base of operations: Mobile
First appearance: CAPTAIN AMERICA #309
History: As yet, nothing is known about the Asp's life before she was invited to join Sidewinder's Serpent Society (see *Serpent Society*). The Asp accepted the invitation, and has been active in the group ever since. One of her first recorded missions undertaken with her fellow Serpents was the attempt to assassinate Modok (see *Modok*).
Height: 5′ 9″
Weight: 115 lbs.
Eyes: Brown
Hair: Black
Strength level: The Asp possesses the normal human strength of a woman of her age, height and build who engages in intensive regular exercise.
Known superhuman powers: The Asp possesses the ability to generate and project an unknown form of radiant energy which causes paralysis in those exposed to it. Her body constantly produces this energy, which upon exceeding her body's storage capacity, discharges itself in minute amounts through her skin. (Prolonged physical contact with the Asp is fatal to human beings.) By tapping her body's total store of energy, she can emit directed, visible lightning-like discharges she calls her "venom bolts." She generally projects them from her fingertips. At maximum strength, these venom-bolts can kill an average-size man standing six feet from her. The energy causes a rapid paralysis of its victim's nervous system. A non-fatal discharge will retain its potency for about four hours, depending upon the strength of the blast and the strength of the nervous system of the victim. The venom-bolt has no effect on anything other than living organisms.

After discharging her body's total store of energy, it takes the Asp about one half hour to regenerate her power to peak levels. She can recharge her body's store of energy faster by accelerating her metabolic rate through physical activity. She generally rebuilds her energy level by making swaying and undulating motions with her torso and arms. An accomplished dancer with superb muscular control, the Asp moves in a manner that is almost hypnotic in its provocativeness. Engaging in her "snake-dance," the Asp can regenerate her energy to peak capacity within ten minutes.
Abilities: As noted above, the Asp possesses the skill, grace, coordination and muscle control of an accomplished dancer. Deploring violence, she has never learned traditional methods of hand to hand combat. ∎

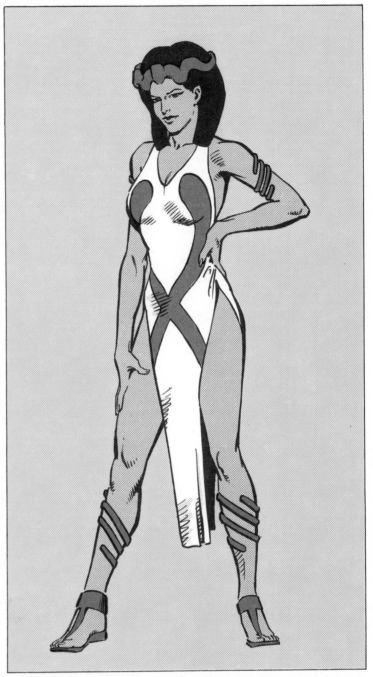

ATLANTEANS

The Atlanteans are a genetic offshoot of mainstream *Homo sapiens* called *Homo mermanus*, who by as yet unknown means acquired various bodily attributes enabling them to live indefinitely beneath the sea. The name "Atlantean" is derived from the ancient civilization of Atlantis that sank beneath the sea in prehistory, and whose ruins were settled by the *Homo mermani* (see *Atlantis*).

Atlanteans possess twin gills located on their necks near the clavicle bone, which enable them to extract oxygen from the water. They possess physiologies far stronger and more durable than their surface counterparts, which enable them to withstand the vast water pressure at the ocean's bottom as well as the pressure changes encountered traveling from one depth to another. Compared to the average air-breather, the average Atlantean is about ten times stronger. The average Atlantean can swim at a maximum speed of 30 miles per hour. Atlanteans are warm-blooded, and their blood circulation is superior to that of land-dwellers, enabling them to withstand the near-freezing temperatures of the ocean depths with minimal discomfort. Atlanteans have specially-adapted eyes possessing vision more sensitive to the green portion of the spectrum. This enables them to see more acutely in the dimly-lit ocean depths. Atlanteans need water in order to breathe, and will suffocate in open air in about five minutes. Atlantean skin tends to be light blue in color, although certain individuals are darker. Atlanteans possess residual body hair primarily on their heads, a holdover from their surface-dwelling ancestry.

Despite their various marine characteristics, Atlanteans are mammals: they bear their young live and care for them during infancy. Although rare, it is possible for an Atlantean and an air-breather to mate. The physical characteristics such an offspring will inherit is subject to genetic chance. In the two known cases of such matings, the offspring acquired the capacity to breathe in air and underwater (see *Namorita, Sub-Mariner*). The life expectancy of an Atlantean is about 150 years.

It is not known precisely how many Atlanteans there are in the world today. The number is believed to be under ten thousand, an extremely small figure when compared to the surface human population of approximately four billion. About two thousand live in the capital city of Atlantis and its immediate vicinity. Others live in small enclaves from pole to pole. Millennia ago, the Atlantean population divided and there was a sizable emigration to the Pacific Ocean by way of the southern tip of South America. These *Homo mermani* are popularly called Lemurians (after the sunken surface civilization of Lemuria), and possess the same physical characteristics as Atlanteans except their skin tends to be more greenish and scaled. It is not known how the population of the Lemurians compares in size with that of the Atlanteans (see *Lemurians*).

Most Atlanteans live in caves on the ocean floor or the submerged portions of coral reefs. The inhabitants of the capital city of Atlantis live in the ruins of the ancient city of surface Atlantis. Because there can be no fire under water, the Atlanteans have lacked the capacity to forge steel or burn fossil fuel for energy. Because of the aquatic medium in which they live, they were also unable to isolate or mix chemicals. Consequently, the Atlanteans never developed a native technology beyond that of flint tool-making. Swords and armaments used in warfare were largely salvaged from the ruins of surface Atlantis or sunken ships of human construction. It is only in the past century, through interaction with scientists of the non-human Deviant race, that any form of advanced technology was developed (see *Deviants*). Astronomy, chemistry, biology, and physics remain virtually unknown sciences. Medicine has remained primitive, with drugs unheard of and surgery impossible under water. No system of mass communication has ever been developed, nor any means of mass transit. With Deviant technology, Atlanteans built their first warships at the outbreak of World War II. Atlanteans communicate by means of a limited range of high-pitched vocal sounds and elaborate "signing" gestures. A more varied spoken language is not possible due to the inherent limitations of sound transmission through water.

Atlantean government has traditionally been tribal, although the citizens of the capital city of Atlantis have adopted the stylings of a monarchistic republic from their long-dead surface predecessors. Besides an ancestral monarch, Atlantis has a Council of Elders, who serve as the judiciary and legislative branch of government. Atlantis has a standing militia who perform police functions in times of peace. Although the monarchy of Atlantis claims all *Homo mermani* dwelling in the Atlantic Ocean as its subjects, in actuality the monarchy neither provides services nor protection nor demands tribute or recognition from those who live beyond one day's swim from the capital city. Most *Homo mermani* continue to live tribally. The largest grouping of Atlanteans in the Atlantic Ocean outside the capital city

NAMOR
Sub-Mariner, Exiled Prince of Atlantis
First modern appearance:
FANTASTIC FOUR #4

ATTUMA
Barbarian Usurper
First appeared in FANTASTIC FOUR #33

DORMA
Royal Consort (deceased)
First modern appearance:
FF ANNUAL #1

KRANG
Warlord
First appeared in FF ANNUAL #1

VASHTI
Grand Vizier
First appeared in TALES TO
ASTONISH #71

BYRRAH
Treacherous Cousin of Namor
First modern appearance: TALES TO
ASTONISH #90

SETH
Advisor to Namor (deceased)
First appeared in TALES TO
ASTONISH #98

IKTHON
Treacherous Scientist (deceased)
First appeared in SUB-MARINER #7

THAKOS
Warlord
First appeared in SUB-MARINER #16

KORMOK
High Priest
First appeared in SUB-MARINER #17

are ruled by the barbarian warlord Attuma.

Atlanteans subsist on raw fish and seaweed. They are largely a hunter / gatherer society, who have made successful attempts to farm seaweed. In most of the Atlantean tribes, males hunt for fish and females gather seaweed. In the monarchy of the Atlantean capital, society is stratified so that there is a special guild of hunters and gatherers who provide food for the entire population. This frees the rest of society for other pursuits, such as the advancement of culture. The culture of the tribal Atlanteans remains primitive, with ritualistic dance and storytelling at its core. The culture of monarchistic Atlantis is slightly more sophisticated, with its class or guild of entertainers. The religion of most tribal Atlanteans is pantheistic nature-worship. The state religion of monarchistic Atlantis reveres the Greek god of the sea Neptune, who once lived among the Atlanteans two millennia ago. The Atlantean Empire in many ways resembles the ancient Roman Empire at its zenith.

Also see *Andromeda, Atlantis, Krang, Namorita, Orka,* and *Sub-Mariner.* ∎

ORKA
Mutated renegade
First appeared in SUB-MARINER #23

THAKORR
Namor's Grandfather (deceased)
First modern appearance:
SUB-MARINER #38

FEN
Namor's mother (deceased)
First modern appearance:
SUB-MARINER #38

NAMORA
Cousin of Namor (deceased)
First modern appearance:
SUB-MARINER #51

NAMORITA
Second Cousin of Namor
First appeared in SUB-MARINER #51

LORVEX
Barbarian
First appeared in SUB-MARINER #54

CORAL
Citizen
First appeared in SUB-MARINER #56

ARKUS
Military Officer
First appeared in SUB-MARINER #63

VOLPAN
Technician
First appeared in SUB-MARINER #63

MADOXX
Elder Statesman
First appeared in SUB-MARINER #64

RAMAN
Gatekeeper
First appeared in SUB-MARINER #66

TYRAK
Krang's Lieutenant
First appeared in AVENGERS #156

MERANNO
U-Man, Nazi sympathizer
First appeared in INVADERS #3

DRAGONRIDER
Outlaw
First appeared in SUB-MARINER LS #1

DARA
Cousin of Namor
First appeared in SUB-MARINER LS #1

PROTEUS
Rebel shape-changer
First appeared in SUB-MARINER LS #2

ANDROMEDA
Warrior
First appeared in DEFENDERS #143

ATLANTIS

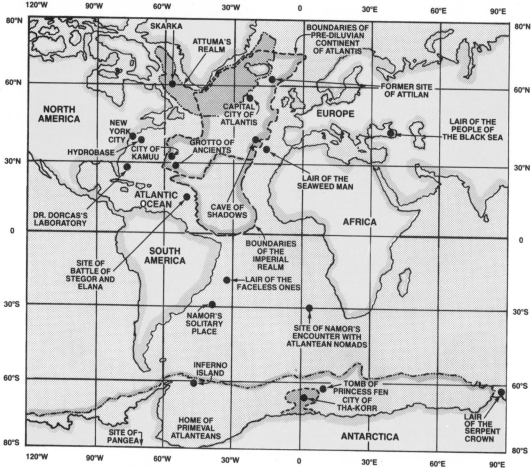

Ancient Atlantis was a small continent (about the size of present day Australia) located in the Atlantic Ocean between North America and Europe, which sank beneath the sea approximately twenty thousand years ago. The continent of Atlantis boasted one of the most highly advanced civilizations of its age. Founded about twenty-one thousand years ago (19,000 BC), the civilization of Atlantis predates that of any other known human civilization, and began a mere four thousand years after the retreat of the last Ice Age. Originally, Atlantis was a land of barbarians, one of whom, Kull, left and gained the throne of the nearby kingdom of Valusia. Over the 500 years between Kull's time and the sinking of Atlantis, Atlantis became the center of a small empire of sailors, craftsmen, traders, astrologers and alchemists. Atlantean sea vessels reached as far as the South Pole where they discovered the Antarctic jungle and game preserve they named Pangea (meaning "Paradise"). Atlantean alchemists created the Serpent Crown, a vessel empowered by the demonic Elder God Set (see *Demons*). The Serpent Crown is one of the few artifacts of ancient Atlantis to have survived until modern times. Few historical personages of the Atlantean Age are known today. One of the few is Kull, the barbarian-king who ruled Atlantis about 500 years before it sank. Kull was renowned as the slayer of the arch-wizard Thulsa Doom and as the enemy of the Serpent People, non-human but humanoid offspring of Set.

The last years of ancient Atlantis saw the erection of a giant glass-like dome over the capital city of the empire (also called Atlantis). Its last rulers were King Kamuu and his wife Queen Zartra, a native of the Lemurian Isles, which had been conquered by the non-human race of Deviants (see *Deviants, Lemuria*). The Atlantean empire had been in a state of decline after Kull's era. The empire was reeling with civil war in all of its provinces and the fighting kept encroaching closer and closer to the capital city. Finally barbarians from the Lemurian Isles attached Atlantis on behalf of the Deviant Empire, and to rout their forces King Kamuu opened the magma-pits which were the city's means of heating. The Lemu-

rian invaders were destroyed by the molten lava, but due to unprecedented volcanic pressures beneath the city, the magma release triggered a seismological cataclysm. First the capital city, and then the entire continent of Atlantis itself was wracked by earthquakes and volcanic eruptions. At the same time, the Deviants themseles launched an attack on the arriving Second Host of the alien Celestials (see *Celestials*). The Celestials retaliated by causing a nuclear cataclysm which sank Lemuria and created shock waves that shook the entire world. As a result of the local geological convulsions and the after effects of the Lemurian cataclysm, the entire continent of Atlantis fragmented and vanished beneath the Atlantic Ocean in about a week.

There were a few survivors of the Atlantean catastrophe. The largest concentration of survivors was in the southern city of Netheria, whose priests and intellectuals foresaw an attack by the Lemurians. They enclosed their small city in a dome of an unknown plastic-like substance and excavated and fortified their city's foundation. Consequently, when the continent of Atlantis fragmented, Netheria remained intact as it sank, coming to a rest in a huge sub-sea cavern. Finding a way to recycle their air supply, the Netherians renamed their realm the Netherworld. The Netherworld, now under the rule of Queen Kala, exists today (see *Appendix: Kala*).

Tiny bands of Atlanteans managed to find refuge on neighboring islands and the European continent, which were buffeted by the Atlantis catastrophe but not destroyed. The nearby island of Attilan, home of the genetically advanced but reclusive Inhumans, also survived the cataclysm virtually unscathed (see *Attilan, Inhumans*).

About ten thousand years ago, a new type of human being appeared in the Atlantic Ocean possessing gills to breathe underwater. The origins of *Homo mermanus* are lost. The capacity to breathe underwater, found prior to this time in certain individuals of both the Inhuman and Deviant races, may have been scientifically bestowed upon members of mainstream humanity by Inhuman or Deviant geneticists (see *Deviants*). The legends of the water-breathers themselves credit Neptune, god of the sea worshipped by the Greeks and Romans, with their transformation from air to water-breathers (see *Olympians*). The theory that *Homo mermanus* is a result of natural evolution is unsupportable.

For millenia, the tribe of *Homo mermani* were nomadic, wandering the Atlantic Ocean, preying upon small fish for food, using the shells of huge crustaceans for shelter, and developing but the most rudimentary tool-making culture. Finally, about 8,000 years ago, the undersea tribe discovered the ruins of the capital city of ancient Atlantis, which had lain undisturbed since Atlantis sank 12,000 years before. The prince of the sea people, named Kamuu after the legendary surface Atlantean ruler, happened upon the throne of his ancient namesake. Upon recovering the original Kamuu's sword, he was visited by the spirit of the last king of ancient Atlantis. The spirit of King Kamuu bade his water-breathing namesake to settle here on the site of old Atlantis and found a new Atlantis. The young Kamuu convinced his people to settle and they began to build a new city of Atlantis.

The undersea city of Atlantis fell victim to natural disasters and sieges by barbarian tribes over the next few millenia, but each time Atlantis was rebuilt in greater splendor. About 500 years after the founding of undersea Atlantis, a group of *Homo mermanus* left the city and made their way to the Pacific Ocean. This group founded the city of Lemuria on the opposite end of the now-submerged continent of Lemuria from that settled by the Deviants. Due to the acquisition and worship of the Serpent Crown, the magical artifact from pre-Cataclysmic Atlantis, the Lemurians' complexions and features have taken a more serpentine cast than their Atlantean forebears.

Little is known about Atlantean history between the time of the founding of Lemuria and the modern era. The Atlanteans' historical records, graven in stone until the relatively recent invention of a paper-like substance made from seaweed, have been all but lost in the dark ages of Atlantean history. The god Neptune is believed to have dwelled among the Atlanteans in mortal form during this period, promoting his worship, a practice that continues today. The Atlanteans also encountered Deviant refugees at some time in the past 200 years, and it was from them that they learned the rudiments of technology. The Atlanteans had very limited contact with their surface-dwelling parent race until recent times. This was largely due to the fact that neither water-breathers nor air-breathers could survive outside of their native environment for more than minutes without drowning. With the recent invention of a potion to enable a water-breather to breathe air for up to five hours, greater interaction between the races became possible.

About a century and a half ago, Atlantis was attacked by

hordes of undersea barbarians hailing from the nearby province of Skarka. Although the Atlanteans managed to repel the invaders, the city of Atlantis sustained heavy damages. Emperor Thakorr, who ascended the throne after former King Immanu died in battle with the barbarians, resolved to move the capital city of the empire from its traditional site. He led the Atlantean populace south, where they founded a new Atlantis not far from the continent of Antarctica. The Atlanteans lived in peace there until the 1920s, when an American ship was sent to Antarctica to clear a path through the icebergs. The detonation of explosive depth charges rocked the undersea city, killing a tenth of its inhabitants. Thakorr bade his daughter Fen to assign a scouting party to investigate the attack. The adventurous Fen decided to go herself. Fen learned that the bombardment was not an act of war, and became romantically attracted to the ship's captain, Leonard McKenzie. The American and Atlantean were soon wed and Fen later gave birth to Namor, a mutant hybrid of the two races (see *Sub-Mariner*). Most of McKenzie's crew were slain by the Atlanteans who believed they held Fen captive.

Namor possesses the ability to breathe in air and underwater and became the Atlantean's first emissary to the surface world. At first hostile to his father's people, he joined with American heroes to form the Invaders in order to battle Nazi aggression. After World War Two, Namor encountered Paul Destine, an American who unearthed the Serpent Crown from the Antarctic hiding place where a band of Lemurians had buried it. Destine used the crown to amplify his natural psionic powers and as an exercise of power, destroyed the nearby city of Atlantis with a mental blast. Namor's grandfather Thakorr and mother Fen were among the many casualties of Atlantis's destruction. Namor was rendered amnesiac by a blast of Destine's power, and wandered the surface world for decades before the Human Torch helped restore his memory. Namor returned to his native sea, but the Atlanteans who survived Destine's attack were not easily found.

Eventually, Namor was reunited with his people, and was crowned prince of Atlantis. Namor decided to rebuild Atlantis on its orginal site in the North Atlantic rather than his grandfather's chosen site near Antarctic. With the surface world learning of the existence of *Homo mermanus*, Atlantis was subjected to ever more tumultuous fortunes. Three times did Atlantis declare war on the surface world and bring troops onto Manhattan Island, only to withdraw them before casualties were sustained. Namor even petitioned the United Nations to accept Atlantis into its organization and was rejected on more than one occasion. Following the death of his betrothed, Lady Dorma, Namor abdicated the throne of Atlantis for a time. In his absence, Atlantis was besieged by barbarians and plunderers. Before long, the Atlanteans begged Namor to return to the throne and he agreed. The Atlanteans were then the victims of accidental nerve gas poisoning, leaving the thousands of *Homo mermani* who dwelled in the capital city in a death-like coma. When Namor had exhausted other possible sources of aid, he turned to his one-time ally, the power-hungry Doctor Doom (see *Doctor Doom*). Namor agreed to serve Doom for a time if Doom would use his scientific expertise to revive the Atlanteans. Both parties upheld their end of the bargain, and the Atlanteans were revived. For a time, the Atlanteans revered Namor for his role in their resuscitation with such fervor that it rankled him. Some time later, however, the ruling council of the Atlanteans assessed Namor's leadership, evaluated the impact of his continual leaves of absence from the kingdom, and voted that Namor give up his rule. Namor reluctantly agreed. The city of Atlantis and its small empire of colonies is currently ruled by Lord Vashti.

First modern appearance of the Atlanteans: FANTASTIC FOUR ANNUAL #1. ∎

ATTILAN

Attilan is the ancestral home of the Inhumans, a highly advanced offshoot of the human race (see *Inhumans*). About seven thousand years ago, the Inhumans grew tired of centuries of persecution by their more primitive parent race, and decided to create a place of refuge for themselves. Under the leadership of King Myran, the Inhumans chose as a site for their city a small island in the Northern Atlantic Ocean, located about two hundred miles southwest of Iceland. The city, which took several decades to complete, was named Attilan, a name derived from Atlantis, the former pinnacle of civilization on Earth that had vanished beneath the sea about three millennia before (see *Atlantis*). Attilan has been the sole center of the Inhuman population ever since.

For millennia, the Inhumans dwelled in Attilan, isolated from contact with mainstream humanity except for an occasional encounter with a lost Greek or Viking sailing vessel. Finally, in the mid-Twentieth Century, with the advent of steamships and airplanes, the Inhumans began to fear discovery by the human race. When one of his subjects was captured by human beings, young king Black Bolt determined that the Inhumans must move their civilization to some place more secure. Employing anti-gravity generators, the Inhumans moved their entire city and its foundation in one piece. The new site of Attilan, a hidden valley in the Himalayan Mountain range in China, was excavated by the Eternals, another variant offshoot of humanity (see *Eternals*). The Himalayan site of Attilan became known as "the Great Refuge." The Himalayas did not prove to be remote enough to enable the Inhumans to retain their secrecy, however, and soon the Inhumans' existence became known to several of the governments of the outside world, although not to the general public. While in the Himalayas, all of Attilan's ancient architecture was accidentally destroyed by Black Bolt and the city has been extensively redesigned and rebuilt.

In recent years, Attilan was relocated once again, this time to escape the effects of Earthly pollution and disease. Attilan is currently located in the "Blue Area of the Moon," nestled in the ruins of an ancient city built by the alien Kree (see *Kree*) whose technology gives the "Blue Area" its own artificially-created atmosphere.

First appearance: FANTASTIC FOUR #47. ∎

ATTILAN, CIRCA 10,000 BC

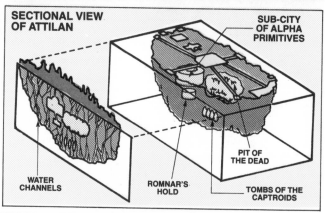

SECTIONAL VIEW OF ATTILAN

SUB-CITY OF ALPHA PRIMITIVES

WATER CHANNELS

ROMNAR'S HOLD

PIT OF THE DEAD

TOMBS OF THE CAPTROIDS

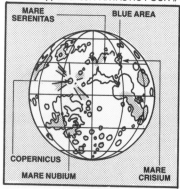

MARE SERENITAS

BLUE AREA

COPERNICUS

MARE NUBIUM

MARE CRISIUM

THE MOON

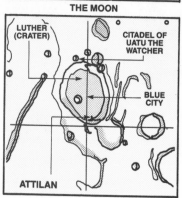

LUTHER (CRATER)

CITADEL OF UATU THE WATCHER

BLUE CITY

ATTILAN

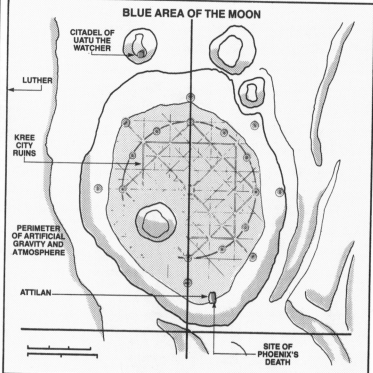

BLUE AREA OF THE MOON

CITADEL OF UATU THE WATCHER

LUTHER

KREE CITY RUINS

PERIMETER OF ARTIFICIAL GRAVITY AND ATMOSPHERE

ATTILAN

SITE OF PHOENIX'S DEATH

ATTILAN TODAY

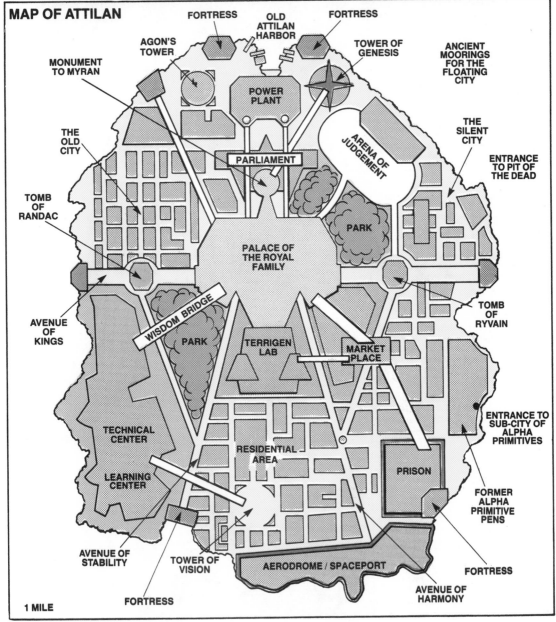

MAP OF ATTILAN

- FORTRESS
- OLD ATTILAN HARBOR
- FORTRESS
- TOWER OF GENESIS
- ANCIENT MOORINGS FOR THE FLOATING CITY
- AGON'S TOWER
- MONUMENT TO MYRAN
- POWER PLANT
- THE SILENT CITY
- THE OLD CITY
- PARLIAMENT
- ARENA OF JUDGEMENT
- ENTRANCE TO PIT OF THE DEAD
- TOMB OF RANDAC
- PARK
- PALACE OF THE ROYAL FAMILY
- AVENUE OF KINGS
- WISDOM BRIDGE
- PARK
- TERRIGEN LAB
- MARKET PLACE
- TOMB OF RYVAIN
- TECHNICAL CENTER
- RESIDENTIAL AREA
- ENTRANCE TO SUB-CITY OF ALPHA PRIMITIVES
- LEARNING CENTER
- PRISON
- AVENUE OF STABILITY
- TOWER OF VISION
- AERODROME / SPACEPORT
- FORMER ALPHA PRIMITIVE PENS
- FORTRESS
- FORTRESS
- AVENUE OF HARMONY

1 MILE

47

ATTUMA

Real Name: Attuma
Occupation: Barbarian chieftain
Legal status: Citizen of Skarka
Identity: Attuma does not use a dual identity. His existence is not known to the general public of the surface world.
Place of birth: Northern Atlantic Ocean
Marital status: Unknown
Known relatives: None known
Group affiliation: Former ally of Byrrah, Krang, Ikthon, Dr. Dorcas, Tiger Shark, Tyrak, and the Red Ghost
Base of operations: Atlantic Ocean
First appearance: FANTASTIC FOUR #33
History: Attuma was born into the tribe of *Homo mermanus* who eschewed civilization to live as nomadic barbarians. For some unrecorded reason, Attuma was endowed with strength far surpassing that of his people. Nearing adulthood, Attuma learned of a prophesy, in the lost Atlantean Chronicles, of a conqueror who would take the empire of Atlantis by force. Believing he is that conqueror, Attuma has launched numerous attacks on the city of Atlantis and its regent Prince Namor (see *Sub-Mariner*).

Unable to best Namor in personal combat, Attuma has frequently taken allies to further his ambitions. These alliances have also met with defeat. The first time Attuma attacked Atlantis, the Fantastic Four aided Namor in repulsing his attack. In recent years, Attuma has battled the Avengers as well. Not renowned for his intelligence, Attuma has frequently employed renegade Atlantean and human scientists. One of them created the Octo-Meks, octopus-shaped fighting machines. Another proposed that he mate with human mutants in order to produce a sire stronger than Namor himself. Toward this end he abducted the mutant Phoenix (see *Deceased: Phoenix I*), but she thwarted his plans. Although Attuma has never been able to claim a lasting victory over Namor, he was a party to the death of Namor's bride, Lady Dorma. Attuma is still at large in the Atlantic Ocean, having never been imprisoned for any of his deeds.

Height: 6′ 8″ **Hair:** Black
Weight: 410 lbs **Skin:** Blue
Eyes: Brown

Strength level: Attuma possesses superhuman strength enabling him to lift (press) approximately 40 tons on land, and somewhat more than that in his native element, the sea. Attuma is significantly stronger than the average member of *Homo mermanus*.

Known superhuman powers: Attuma possesses the typical attributes of *Homo mermanus*: gills to enable him to extract oxygen from the water, superhuman physiology to enable him to withstand the extreme water pressure changes beneath the sea, blood circulation enabling him to withstand freezing temperatures, and specially-developed vision which is more sensitive to the green portion of the spectrum enabling him to see in the murky depths.

Attuma is far stronger than the typical Atlantean. Whereas most Atlanteans can swim at a speed of 30 miles per hour, Attuma can swim at 60 miles per hour (see *Atlanteans*). Like all Atlanteans, Attuma cannot breathe air out of water. He is capable of lasting approximately ten minutes out of water before he begins to suffocate.

Weapons: Attuma customarily carries a three-pronged iron sword weighing approximately 50 pounds. ∎

AURORA

Real Name: Jeanne-Marie Beaubier
Occupation: Former teacher of history / geography, adventurer
Identity: Secret, known to certain Canadian government officials
Legal status: Canadian citizen with no criminal record
Former aliases: None
Place of birth: Montreal, Quebec, Canada
Marital status: Single
Known relatives: Jean-Paul Beaubier (Northstar), brother
Group affiliation: Alpha Flight
Base of operations: LaVelle, Quebec, Canada
First appearance: X-MEN #120

History: Jeanne-Marie Beaubier and her twin brother Jean-Paul were separated in infancy after their parents were killed under circumstances yet to be revealed. Jean-Paul was adopted by Mr. and Mrs. Louis Martin, who were cousins of his mother. The Martins could not afford to adopt Jeanne-Marie as well, however, and so they arranged for her to be raised at Madame DuPont's School for Girls in LaVelle, Quebec, a reactionary religious school. Soon afterward the Martins moved to Northern Quebec. Mr. and Mrs. Martin were killed in an accident several years later, and Jean-Paul was placed in a foster home, unaware that he had a sister (see *Northstar*).

Extremely nervous and introverted, Jeanne-Marie Beaubier was miserable at Madame DuPont's School, and, at the age of thirteen, she attempted suicide by throwing heself from the roof of one of the school's buildings. Instead of falling to her death, however, Beaubier discovered that she could fly at great speed. Unaware that she was a superhumanly powerful mutant, the deeply religous Beaubier believed that her flight was the result of a divine miracle. The next morning she explained to the school's headmistress, Soeur Anne, what she believed had happened. Believing the young girl to be guilty of blasphemy, Soeur Anne had Beaubier severely disciplined through means including corporal punishment. This incident triggered schizophrenia in the young woman. A second personality, extroverted and far more uninhibited, emerged. Under the influence of this second personality, Beaubier secretly left the school that same night. On returning three days later, she had no memory of where she had been or what she had done, and she was again physically punished. The resulting trauma was so great that Beaubier repressed her second personality for the next five years.

At the end of that time, Beaubier's application to become a teacher at the school was accepted. By this time Beaubier had adjusted to life at the school, and her everyday personality was that of a prim, proper, repressed woman. But the same night that her application was accepted, her second personality re-emerged, and she left to enjoy herself in Montreal. Confronted by muggers, she knocked one unconscious by moving at superhuman speeds. This was the first time that she had used her superhuman powers in five years. The second mugger was halted by Wolverine, who had witnessed the attempted assault (see *Wolverine*). Recognizing that Beaubier had superhuman powers, Wolverine invited her to go to Ottawa to meet James MacDonald Hudson, who was organizing a

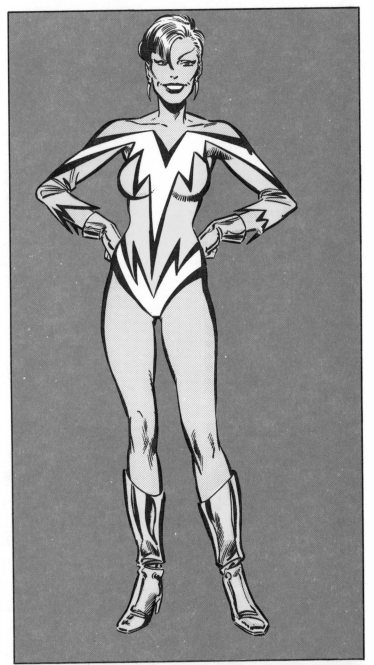

team of superhumanly powerful agents for the Canadian government's Department H. Hudson accepted her as a recruit and reunited her with her brother. After a period of training, both Beaubier siblings joined the team that Hudson created, Alpha Flight, under the code names Aurora and Northstar (see *Alpha Flight*).

Jeanne-Marie Beaubier, however, continues to have a split personality. She may unexpectedly shift from one of her personalities to the other. Each personality thinks of the other as if it belonged to an entirely different person. As Jeanne-Marie the teacher, Beaubier has little memory of her activities as Aurora. Each personality strongly dislikes the other. Fear or despair will sometimes cause Aurora to shift back into her Jeanne-Marie / teacher persona.

Recently, Beaubier underwent still further personality changes. For a time her "Aurora" and "Jeanne-Marie" personae have each manifested traits of the other, while nevertheless remaining distinctly separate personalities. Most of the time now, she manifests a third personality, which is basically Aurora's, but with more of a sense of responsiblity than before. Whether or not Beaubier's split personality will continue to evolve remains to be seen. Also in recent months, Dr. Walter Langkowski, the physicist who as Sasquatch was a member of Alpha Flight, performed an experiment in molecular rearrangement upon Beaubier which altered her superhuman abilities. It brought about three specific changes. First, it enabled her to create a bright light without being in physical contact with her brother Northstar. Second, it greatly reduced the potential limits of her superhuman speed. Third, according to Langkowski, it made it impossible for present day technology to detect that she is a mutant.

Height: 5' 11"
Weight: 125 lbs
Eyes: Blue
Hair: Black
Strength level: Aurora possesses the normal human strength of a woman of her age, height, and build who engages in regular intensive exericse.

Known superhuman powers: Aurora is a mutant who possesses the ability to propel her body at superhuman speed, becoming a living projectile. Through an act of concentration, Aurora can channel a portion of the kinetic energy of the atomic motion in her body's molecules in a single direction. This can accelerate her body in a velocity in direct proportion to the amount of kinetic energy she has tapped. It was once theoretically possible for her to reach 99% of the speed of light (286,272 miles per second in a vacuum), although she never traveled at anywhere near that speed since if she did, she would wreak great damage upon herself and her environment. Dr. Langkowski's actions in molecularly restructuring Aurora's body greatly reduced the potential limits of her speed. She now can move at speeds roughly up to the speed of sound (about 770 miles per hour at sea level). This reduction has made little difference in the use of her powers over short distances, since she can still move faster than the human eye can follow.

Aurora can generate from her body a bright white light equivalent at maximum intensity to a half million foot candles. Originally she could only generate light when in physical contact with her brother Northstar. However, Dr. Walter Langkowski's molecular restructuring of her body has enabled her to generate light on her own. She does so by varying the rate of acceleration of the molecules of her body out of phase with one another, thereby generating a cascade of photonic discharges. Should she link hands with Northstar, they could together generate a light equivalent to a lighthouse beacon (one million foot candles) by each sibling's varying the rate of acceleration of his or her own molecules out of phase with those of the other's. Aurora can project the light she generates in any direction for a number of offensive effects.

As a side effect of partially robbing her molecules of their atomic motion, the binding forces within and between the molecules increase. This enhances the sheer toughness of Aurora's entire body. This effect gives her skin enough durability to withstand the ravages of wind, friction and air turbulence. Aurora's costume is made of special materials to enable it to withstand these conditions as well.

Aurora can also move a portion of her body at superhuman speed at a time. Hence, she can overpower an opponent by hitting him repeatedly at superhuman speed with her fist. To hover in mid-air Aurora applies thrust downward in a carefully controlled manner.

When carrying another, unprotected human being aloft, Aurora does not move faster than 60 miles per hour in order that her "passenger" may be able to breathe easily (Aurora herself can breathe at somewhat higher rates due to training) and so that the "passenger" will not suffer harm from wind, friction, or air turbulence.

Note: Although she does not wear a mask, Beaubier is able to keep her identity as Aurora secret by not allowing herself to be photographed while in costume if she can help it, and by moving so swiftly in public that she cannot be positively identified. ■

AVALANCHE

Real Name: Dominic Petros
Occupation: Professional criminal
Identity: Publicly known
Legal status: Naturalized American citizen with a criminal record, former Greek citizen
Former aliases: None known
Place of birth: Unknown location in Crete
Marital status: Married
Known relatives: Helen (wife)
Group affiliation: Brotherhood of Evil Mutants II, now known as Freedom Force
Base of operations: A secret location within the Pentagon, Virginia
First appearance: X-MEN #141
History: Avalanche's past before Mystique recruited him for the second Brotherhood of Evil Mutants (see *Appendix: Brotherhood of Evil Mutants, Mystique*) is almost entirely unknown, except for the fact that he is an immigrant from Greece. He first publicly appeared with the Brotherhood when they unsuccessfully attempted to assassinate Senator Robert Kelly during his hearings on the menace that mutants allegedly pose to humanity in general. Avalanche briefly left the Brotherhood to attempt to blackmail the state of California into paying him an enormous sum to prevent him from using his power to trigger a major earthquake there. Avalanche fought the Hulk (see *Hulk*) on this occasion, and suffered serious injury (see Limitations). He has since returned to the Brotherhood. Recently, Mystique offered the Brotherhood's services to the United States government. Their first mission under their new name of Freedom Force was to capture the mutant Magneto (see *Freedom Force, Magneto*).

Height: 5′ 7″   **Eyes:** Brown
Weight: 195 lbs.   **Hair:** Brown
Strength level: Avalanche possesses the normal human strength of a man of his age, height, and build who engages in moderate regular exercise.
Known superhuman powers: Avalanche is a mutant with the superhuman ability to generate powerful waves of vibrations from his hands, creating highly destructive effects. The vibrations can cause an inorganic object to shatter or crumble into dust. When directed against large objects like buildings or upon the earth itself, the vibrations can produce effects similar to those of an earthquake or avalanches within limited areas. Avalanche need not touch an object to affect it: he can direct the vibrations against it from some distance away from it.

Avalanche is himself invulnerable to the effects of generating these intense vibratory waves. However, if the vibrations were to be reflected back upon him, he would be severely injured.
Limitations: For unknown reasons, Avalanche's power has little or no effect on organic tissue. When he once used his power against the Hulk, the Hulk was uninjured, but the resulting feedback shattered the bones of Avalanche's arms (which have since completely healed). Hence, although Avalanche's vibrations have little or no effect on organic tissue, the reflected vibrations ("feedback") can injure him.

As yet there is no known limit to the amount of area upon which Avalanche can use his powers at one time. However, there is no evidence that he could create an earthquake capable of destroying an entire city. ■

AVENGERS

The Avengers is one of Earth's foremost organizations of costumed superhuman adventurers dedicated to safeguarding the world from any threat beyond the power of conventional peacekeeping forces to handle. Founded several months after the incorporation of the Fantastic Four (see *Fantastic Four*), the Avengers became the first superhuman team to be granted official government sanctions by the National Security Council of the United States, the General Assembly of the United Nations, and later by the international intelligence agency, SHIELD. Unlike the Fantastic Four, whose ranks have been restricted to Reed Richards and his experimental rocket crew (except for an occasional substitute), membership in the Avengers has been open and in constant fluctuation. Only weeks after the Avengers' inception, one of its founding members, the Hulk, left the team, setting the precedent for future roster changes. Roughly a year into the organization's existence, all of the rest of the founding members took a leave of absence, leaving the Avengers' first recruit, Captain America, to fill the vacancies in the ranks. Eventually, all of the founding members returned for stints as active members with the exception of the Hulk.

The five founding members of the Avengers first banded together when Loki, the Asgardian god of mischief (see *Loki*), attempted to discredit the Hulk in order to draw the thunder god Thor into battle. The Hulk's teenage ally Rick Jones, believing the Hulk was innocent of the deed he was accused of, dispatched a radio call to the Fantastic Four for help. Loki intercepted the message, however, and relayed it to Thor. Inadvertently the message was also received by Iron Man, Ant-Man, and the Wasp. The four adventurers rendezvoused for the first time, tracked down the Hulk, learned that Loki was the true culprit, and apprehended him. Before they parted, Ant-Man suggested that they form a regular team. The five readily agreed, and the Wasp suggested the name "Avengers." The newly-formed team assembled a short time later at the midtown Manhattan mansion of industrialist Anthony Stark, who, unknown to them at the time, was their fellow member Iron Man. Stark soon donated the mansion to the Avengers for their exclusive use (see *Avengers Mansion*), and set up a foundation to cover all the operational expenses of the nonprofit team of adventurers. This foundation was set up under Stark's mother's name (The Maria Stark Foundation) so that his own business fortunes could not immediately affect the financial situation of the Avengers. The Stark family's trusted butler Edwin Jarvis was kept on as the principal regular domestic employee at Avengers Mansion.

Captain America became the first full-time resident of Avengers Mansion as well as the team's first recruit. When the founding members took a leave of absence, their replacements, Hawkeye, Quicksilver, and the Scarlet Witch, also made the Mansion their domicile, as did various subsequent members. Captain America became the first permanent chairman of the team, a post he held for a number of years. Chairmanship of the Avengers has been determined by election, and a number of individuals have held the positions over the years, including Iron Man, the Wasp, and the Vision. The ranks of active Avengers has varied in number from a mere three up to fifteen. In addition, certain individuals have enjoyed informal status with the group well before becoming official members. (In three cases, this informal status never culminated in official membership.)

As the official ties between the Avengers and the United States government grew to the extent that the Avengers computer system had direct access to certain U.S. governmental and military information networks, the National Security Council began to take a more active interest in the Avengers' internal affairs. In recent years, N.S.C. agent Henry Peter Gyrich was appointed to be the government's liaison with the Avengers. Gyrich instituted certain policies in the name of security which restricted active membership in the group and tightened admission requirements. Prior to this point, the Avengers screened candidates for membership themselves, and were flexible enough in their membership requirements to allow non-citizens, gods, mutants, and even synthetic humans to join. Gyrich initiated a strict screening procedure for new members and even dictated Avengers membership according to government standards of equal-opportunity employment. Happily for the Avengers, Gyrich was eventually reassigned to Project: Wideawake (see *Sentinels*), and was replaced by the more moderate Raymond Sikorsky, another N.S.C. agent. Captain America instituted a six-member ceiling on membership during his latest stint as chairman, and this ceiling has remained in effect since.

THOR
(Sigurd Jarlsen)
Founding Member

IRON MAN
(Anthony Stark)
Founding Member

ANT-MAN
(Henry Pym)
Founding Member

WASP
(Janet Van Dyne)
Founding Member

HULK
(Bruce Banner)
Founding Member

GIANT-MAN
(formerly Ant-Man)
Active AVENGERS #2

CAPTAIN AMERICA
(Steve Rogers)
Joined AVENGERS #4

HAWKEYE
(Clint Barton)
Joined AVENGERS #16

QUICKSILVER
(Pietro Maximoff)
Joined AVENGERS #16

SCARLET WITCH
(Wanda Maximoff)
Joined AVENGERS #16

In recent months, then-current chairman the Vision petitioned the U.S. government to approve the establishment of a second team of active Avengers to be based on the West Coast. Getting official clearance, the Vision appointed Hawkeye to be the new team's chairman and sent him to Los Angeles, California, to set up a base of operations (see *Avengers Compound*). With two independently operated but fully coordinated branches of Avengers, the organization now has slots for twelve active members, six on each coast. When it was learned that the Vision planned to take benevolent control of the world government (see *Vision*), certain punitive measures were taken by the United States, despite the fact that the Vision aborted his plan before it truly endangered anyone. The government has since limited the Avengers' access to security-related information, and has revoked various special sanctions, including the privilege of launching their supersonic Quinjets from their headquarters in Manhattan. The Avengers have joined with the Fantastic Four, whose Manhattan launch privileges were also rescinded, to establish a joint airbase in the Atlantic Ocean just outside U.S. territorial limits. The operations of the West Coast Avengers have been curtailed in regard to government sanctions but not airspace rights.

The East Coast and West Coast Avengers operate autonomously of one another, with no central authority. The informal dividing line for their United States operations is the Mississippi River. The two groups routinely share all information, and occasionally join forces to meet a single threat. Together, the two teams make up Earth's largest and most powerful organization of superhuman champions.

First appearance: AVENGERS #1, (West Coast Avengers) WEST COAST AVENGERS (Limited Series) #1.

MEMBERSHIP RECORD

THOR
Founding member. Thor has taken numerous leaves of absence of varying duration. He is currently a reserve member of the East Coast team, participating in Avengers business under special circumstances.

IRON MAN
Founding member. Iron Man has taken several leaves of absence, once while being investigated on murder charges, and most recently when alcoholism incapacitated him. He served as chairman once, and is currently an active member of the West Coast Avengers.

ANT-MAN I / GIANT-MAN I / GOLIATH I / YELLOWJACKET
Founding member. Ant-Man assumed the identity of Giant-Man before his second adventure with the group. After a short leave of absence, he returned to the team under the name of Goliath. Later he changed his identity to Yellowjacket, and married his fellow member, the Wasp, in this guise. He took several leaves of absence after this, occasionally reassuming his Ant-Man identity. Following a lengthy leave, Yellowjacket returned to active status and was expelled for dishonorable conduct. He has now retired from active costumed adventuring, but serves the West Coast Avengers as resident scientist.

WASP
Founding member. Wasp has taken a few leaves of absence of varying duration, usually to accompany her partner and later husband, Yellowjacket. She has since divorced him. She is currently serving her second term as chairman of the East Coast Avengers.

HULK
Founding member. The Hulk quit the team following their second adventure. He has been an unofficial ally of the team on rare occasions since.

CAPTAIN AMERICA
First recruit of the original team. Captain America has served several lengthy stints as chairman. He has taken a few leaves of absence of short duration. He is currently an active member of the East Coast Avengers.

HAWKEYE / GOLIATH II / HAWKEYE
Second recruit, filling a vacancy in the ranks left by the departing founding members. Hawkeye has taken a few leaves of absence of varying duration. He assumed the identity of Goliath II for a short time, but resumed his Hawkeye identity thereafter. He is a founding member and chairman of the West Coast Avengers.

QUICKSILVER
Third recruit, filling a vacancy in the ranks left by the departing founding members. Quicksilver has served two major stints with the East Coast Avengers. He resigned from active membership to marry outside the group. Residing on the moon, Quicksilver is inactive in the Avengers.

SWORDSMAN
(real name classified)
Joined AVENGERS #19

GOLIATH
(formerly Giant-Man)
Active AVENGERS #28

HERCULES
(no alias used)
Joined AVENGERS #45

BLACK PANTHER
(T'Challa)
Joined AVENGERS #52

VISION
(no alias used)
Joined AVENGERS #58

YELLOWJACKET
(formerly Goliath)
Active AVENGERS #63

GOLIATH II
(formerly Hawkeye)
Active AVENGERS #63

BLACK KNIGHT
(Dane Whitman)
Joined AVENGERS #71

BLACK WIDOW
(Natasha Romanova)
Joined AVENGERS #111

MANTIS
(real name classified)
Joined AVENGERS #114

SCARLET WITCH

Fourth recruit, filling a vacancy in the ranks left by the departing founding members. The Scarlet Witch has taken several leaves of absence of varying duration, once after her wedding to fellow Avenger, the Vision. She and the Vision later left active duty to become reserve members, but subsequently returned to active duty. Following an official investigation of her husband's activities as Avengers chairman, she resigned her membership.

SWORDSMAN

Fifth recruit. The Swordsman served a several day stint as a member, betrayed the Avengers, and was expelled. He returned years later, having reformed, and had his membership reinstated. The Swordsman died in action.

HERCULES

Sixth recruit. Hercules served the Avengers in an unofficial capacity for a brief period before being granted official membership. He took a long leave of absence shortly thereafter, serving as an unofficial ally to the Avengers on only two occasions. He was briefly a member of the short-lived team, the Champions. He is currently an active member of the East Coast Avengers.

BLACK PANTHER

Seventh recruit, served as Captain America's replacement during his first major leave of absence. The Panther eventually returned to Wakanda, the African nation of which he is king. He has since become a reserve Avenger, serving on an irregular basis.

VISION

Eighth recruit. The Vision served as an active member of the Avengers for years before taking his first leave of absence, after his wedding to fellow member, the Scarlet Witch. The Vision and the Scarlet Witch quickly returned to active duty and continued to live at Avengers Mansion until they had saved enough to buy a house of their own. They then became reserve Avengers. The Vision later returned to active duty and assumed chairmanship of the group. At his instigation, the Avengers formed the West Coast branch. He has since stepped down as chairman and resigned from active membership.

BLACK KNIGHT

Ninth recruit. The Black Knight assisted the Avengers on several cases unofficially before being elected to membership. Rather than joining the active roster, the Black Knight applied for reserve status, and left for England where he owned an estate. He then undertook a time trip to the Tenth Century in order to fight in the Crusades, and has only recently returned. Having forfeited his British estate, he has returned to his native America and has rejoined the Avengers. He is currently an active member of the East Coast team.

BLACK WIDOW

Tenth recruit. A long-time ally of the Avengers due to her now-terminated romantic relationship with Hawkeye, the Black Widow finally accepted membership in the group for the duration of a single adventure. She then elected to stay with Daredevil in San Francisco. She was a member of the short-lived Champions, and has worked with the East Coast Avengers on several occasions since the disbanding of the Champions. Residing in New York, she is currently a reserve member of the East Coast Avengers.

MANTIS

Eleventh recruit. Mantis served as a provisional member for several months in tandem with the Swordsman, whom she helped reform. She was elected to full membership after learning she was the Celestial Madonna, but she immediately resigned from active duty to pursue her destiny in space.

BEAST

Twelfth recruit. A graduate of the X-Men, the Beast applied for Avengers membership and after a period of provisional membership was elected to active status. He served an uninterrupted stint until during a major membership reshuffling, he decided to go off active duty to pursue a life of his own. He soon joined the Defenders, however, and resigned his reserve status with the Avengers. With the demise of the Defenders, he joined the original X-Men in X-Factor.

MOONDRAGON

Applicant. Moondragon accepted a period of provisional membership after aiding the Avengers in two major adventures. When she was offered a full active membership, she declined, preferring to remain a reserve member. She later assisted the Avengers in one mission, and then encountered them twice in an adversarial role. The second time she was expelled from the Avengers for dishonorable conduct. She has since joined the Defenders and was expelled from their ranks just prior to their disbanding.

BEAST
(Henry McCoy)
Joined AVENGERS #137

MOONDRAGON
(Heather Douglas)
Joined AVENGERS #137

HELLCAT
(Patsy Walker)
Applied AVENGERS #144

JOCASTA
(no alias used)

MS. MARVEL
(Carol Danvers)
Joined AVENGERS #183

FALCON
(Sam Wilson)
Joined AVENGERS #184

WONDER MAN
(Simon Williams)
Joined AVENGERS #194

TIGRA
(Greer Nelson)
Joined AVENGERS #211

SHE-HULK
(Jennifer Walters)
Joined AVENGERS #221

CAPTAIN MARVEL
(Monica Rambeau)
Joined AVENGERS #231

HELLCAT

Applicant. Hellcat applied for membership in the Avengers and was granted provisional status for a number of months. Before she could be elected to membership, however, fellow provisional member Moondragon convinced Hellcat to accompany her for further training. Although she never served as an active member of the Avengers, Hellcat was a member of the now-defunct Defenders.

JOCASTA

Applicant. Jocasta was a provisional member living in Avengers Mansion since shortly after her creation as a robot. She was never granted official status. She has since been deactivated.

MS. MARVEL

Thirteenth recruit. After sharing a number of adventures with the Avengers on an unofficial basis, Ms. Marvel applied for full membership and was accepted. She served a brief stint, and resigned from the team after an unwanted pregnancy. She is now a member of the Starjammers under the name of Binary.

FALCON

Fourteenth recruit. The Falcon was drafted for Avengers membership by Henry Peter Gyrich's government edict. He served for a brief period and resigned.

WONDER MAN

Fifteenth recruit. After a long term as a provisional member, Wonder Man was elected to active membership. He served for an uninterrupted stint until, during a major membership reshuffling, he decided to leave the active roster in order to pursue a career on the West Coast. When the West Coast Avengers were organized, he was asked to rejoin. Wonder Man is currently an active member of the West Coast team.

TIGRA

Sixteenth recruit. Tigra applied for membership to the East Coast Avengers and was accepted into the active ranks. She served for a brief time and resigned for personal reasons. When the West Coast Avengers were organized, she was asked to rejoin. Tigra is currently an active member of the West Coast team.

SHE-HULK

Seventeenth recruit. She-Hulk applied for membership and was accepted into the active ranks. She served for a short term, and then requested reserve status so that she could fill a vacancy in the Fantastic Four left by the Thing. She-Hulk remains a reserve member of the East Coast Avengers.

CAPTAIN MARVEL

Eighteenth recruit. Captain Marvel was nominated to enter the Avengers' new training program by the Wasp, and accepted. After a brief period as a provisional member, she was elected to active membership. Captain Marvel is currently an active member of the East Coast Avengers.

STARFOX

Nineteenth recruit. Starfox applied for membership and was accepted into the training program. After a brief period as a provisional member, he was awarded active status. After a distinguished tour of duty, Starfox elected to leave the team for personal reasons. He is currently a reserve member of the East Coast Avengers.

MOCKINGBIRD

First recruit of the West Coast Avengers. After her husband Hawkeye was appointed chairman, Mockingbird accepted active membership in the newly organized second team. She currently resides at the Avengers Compound and is an active member of the West Coast team. Due to her SHIELD credentials, she was appointed the West Coast team's security liason with the government.

IRON MAN II

Second recruit of the West Coast Avengers. Iron Man II was invited to join the newly organized second team by the Vision, who believed him to be the original Iron Man and not his hand-picked replacement. Iron Man II accepted the offer of membership, served for a brief time, and became a reserve member when the original Iron Man became active again.

THING

Applicant to the West Coast Avengers. While on leave from the Fantastic Four, the Thing was invited to join the West Coast Avengers by Hawkeye. Although he has shared some adventures with them, he has not accepted official membership.

STARFOX
(Eros)
Joined AVENGERS #231

MOCKINGBIRD
(Barbara Morse Barton)
Joined WEST COAST
AVENGERS LS #1

IRON MAN II
(James Rhodes)
Joined WEST COAST
AVENGERS LS #1

THING
(Benjamin Grimm)
Active WEST COAST
AVENGERS #4

SUB-MARINER
(Namor McKenzie)
Joined AVENGERS #264

FIREBIRD
(Bonita Juarez)
Active WEST COAST
AVENGERS #4

RICK JONES
Honorary member
Active AVENGERS #1

HENRY PYM
Resident scientist
Active WEST COAST
AVENGERS #1

FIREBIRD

Applicant to the West Coast Avengers. A member of the loosely-organized Rangers, Firebird was invited to join the West Coast Avengers. She is currently a provisional member of the West Coast team.

SUB-MARINER

Twentieth recruit to the East Coast Avengers. A former member of the Invaders and Defenders, the Sub-Mariner was offered membership in the Avengers by Captain America and accepted. He is currently an active member of the East Coast team. ∎

AVENGERS COMPOUND

The Avengers Compound is a 15 acre estate located on the Pacific coastline south of Los Angeles at 1800 Palos Verdes Drive. It is the headquarters of the West Coast Avengers. Built in 1921 as a home for the silent movie star Sylvia Powell, the estate remained unoccupied since the actress's death in 1969 until it was purchased by the Avengers as a base for their second team. Based on designs created by Anthony Stark for the East Coast Avengers Mansion and for his former facilities at Stark International, the Compound's planning and construction was supervised by Dr. William Barrett Foster, an engineer formerly of Stark International's Los Angeles plant. A special freelance construction crew hand-picked by Foster was contracted to do the building renovations. The mountainside beneath the main building was excavated to facilitate the installation of two levels about fifty feet beneath the mansion's basement. It is on these levels where the high-security functions of the West Coast Avengers are conducted. A garage and hangar facility for the supersonic Quinjets was built on the site of a private four-hole golf course. The actual hangar facilities are underground, and are accessible through a camouflaged area of cliffside. The servants' bungalows of the original estate were re-modeled to become quarters for all members in residence. The estate includes about 250 feet of private beachfront. The Avengers Compound has a permanent staff of five, including a butler, maid, cook, groundskeeper, and mechanic. The financing and maintenance of the Compound is made possible through the Maria Stark Trust Fund and several private grants.

First appearance: AVENGERS #246.

FRONT VIEW

BACK VIEW

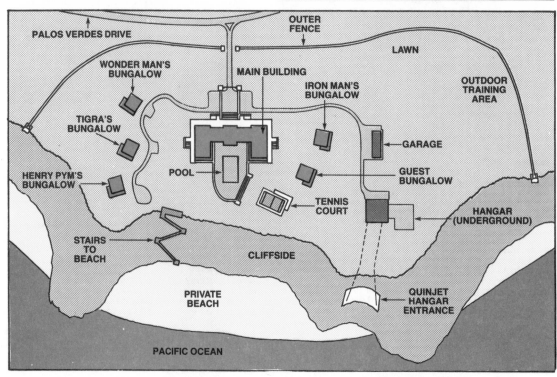

MAIN FLOOR

The Main Floor of the neo-Mediterranean styled villa retains most of its original functions and furnishings. Although there are numerous surveillance and detainment devices to intercept unauthorized personnel, this floor is relatively low security. Public functions of the Avengers, such as press conferences, are held in the east wing main ballroom, as is formal dining. Informal meetings are held in the west wing living room area. The library, which encompasses part of the second floor, has the capacity for 20,000 books. The kitchen and maid's and cook's quarters are also on this floor. On the same level as the Main Floor is the patio, sundeck, and Olympic size swimming pool.

SECOND FLOOR

The Second Floor of the main building contains the office / study where administrative affairs of the Avengers are conducted and non-classified organizational material is stored. This room is primarily used by the West Coast Avengers' chairman, Hawkeye. Also on this floor is the master bedroom shared by Hawkeye and his wife Mockingbird. In the west wing is the indoor recreation room and lounge where a billiards table, pinball machines, video arcades, and a wall-sized television screen are kept for the use of members and their guests. The second floor of the library contains fiction and recreational material, while the main floor of the library contains reference books. Second floor interior balconies overlook the front hall and both wings.

BASEMENT

The Basement of the main building contains the conventional support facilities for the above ground levels, including the heating system, the power generators, and the house computer. It is a low security area.

SUB-BASEMENT LEVEL ONE

The two Sub-Levels of the Avengers Compound are the high-security areas of the headquarters. On Level One is the private hospital and biological and chemical research facilities. As yet the Avengers employ no on-staff physician. Staff scientist Dr. Henry Pym makes use of the laboratory facilites.

SUB-BASEMENT LEVEL TWO

Level Two houses the high security Assembly Room where all operational and strategic meetings are held. The main computer is located here, containing the same crime forensic files, operational records, and world security data as its twin in the East Coast Avengers Mansion. The computers are constantly on line with one another, sharing all data. Like the East Coast Avengers, the West Coast Avengers have limited access to the national security data of the Pentagon and SHIELD. Both East and West Coast Avengers routinely trade information with the Fantastic Four, Inc. The power generators for the two Sub-Basement levels are located here.

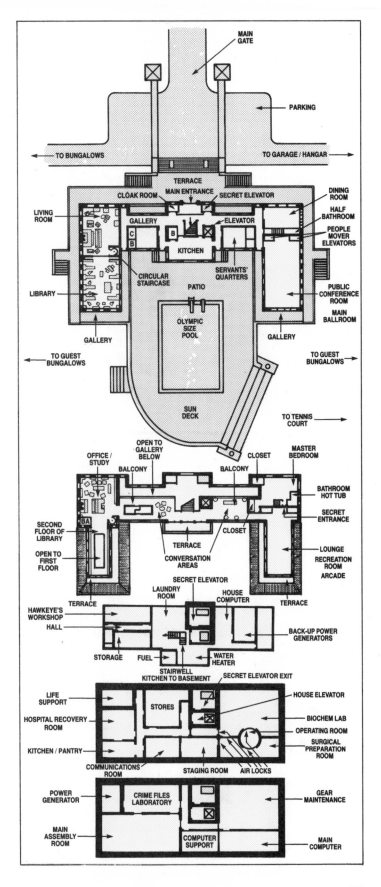

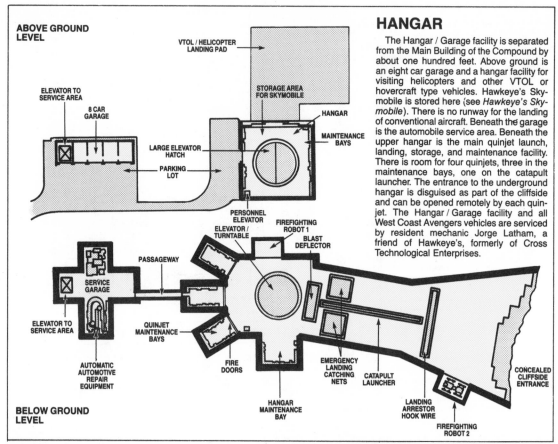

ABOVE GROUND LEVEL

VTOL / HELICOPTER LANDING PAD

ELEVATOR TO SERVICE AREA

8 CAR GARAGE

STORAGE AREA FOR SKYMOBILE

HANGAR

MAINTENANCE BAYS

LARGE ELEVATOR HATCH

PARKING LOT

PERSONNEL ELEVATOR

HANGAR

The Hangar / Garage facility is separated from the Main Building of the Compound by about one hundred feet. Above ground is an eight car garage and a hangar facility for visiting helicopters and other VTOL or hovercraft type vehicles. Hawkeye's Skymobile is stored here (see *Hawkeye's Skymobile*). There is no runway for the landing of conventional aircraft. Beneath the garage is the automobile service area. Beneath the upper hangar is the main quinjet launch, landing, storage, and maintenance facility. There is room for four quinjets, three in the maintenance bays, one on the catapult launcher. The entrance to the underground hangar is disguised as part of the cliffside and can be opened remotely by each quinjet. The Hangar / Garage facility and all West Coast Avengers vehicles are serviced by resident mechanic Jorge Latham, a friend of Hawkeye's, formerly of Cross Technological Enterprises.

ELEVATOR / TURNTABLE

FIREFIGHTING ROBOT 1

BLAST DEFLECTOR

PASSAGEWAY

SERVICE GARAGE

ELEVATOR TO SERVICE AREA

QUINJET MAINTENANCE BAYS

AUTOMATIC AUTOMOTIVE REPAIR EQUIPMENT

FIRE DOORS

EMERGENCY LANDING CATCHING NETS

CATAPULT LAUNCHER

CONCEALED CLIFFSIDE ENTRANCE

HANGAR MAINTENANCE BAY

LANDING ARRESTOR HOOK WIRE

FIREFIGHTING ROBOT 2

BELOW GROUND LEVEL

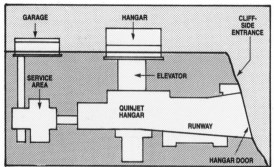

GARAGE

HANGAR

CLIFF-SIDE ENTRANCE

SERVICE AREA

ELEVATOR

QUINJET HANGAR

RUNWAY

HANGAR DOOR

HANGAR DOOR SWINGS OPEN

BUNGALOW

The Avengers Compound has five identical bungalows designed as living quarters for active members who request them.

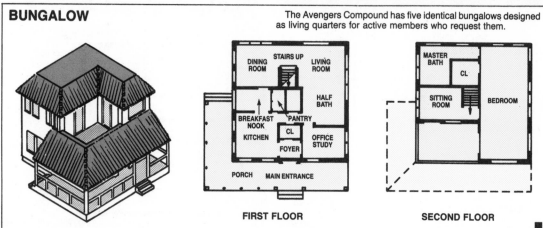

DINING ROOM

STAIRS UP

LIVING ROOM

HALF BATH

BREAKFAST NOOK

PANTRY

KITCHEN

CL

OFFICE STUDY

FOYER

PORCH

MAIN ENTRANCE

MASTER BATH

CL

SITTING ROOM

BEDROOM

FIRST FLOOR

SECOND FLOOR

AVENGERS MANSION

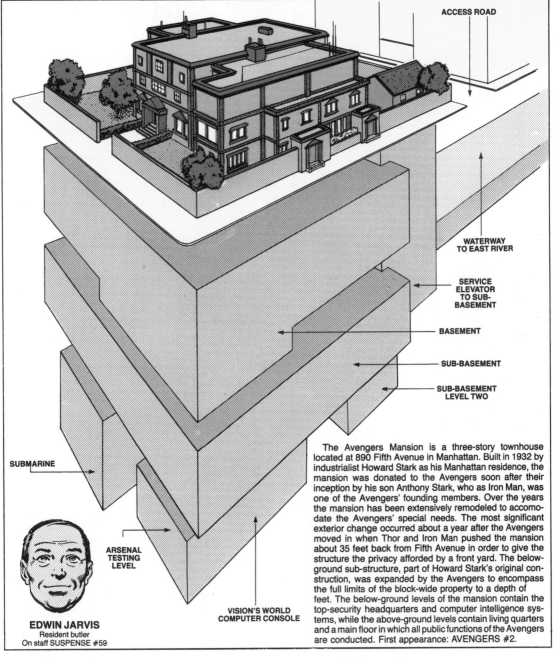

ACCESS ROAD

WATERWAY TO EAST RIVER

SERVICE ELEVATOR TO SUB-BASEMENT

BASEMENT

SUB-BASEMENT

SUB-BASEMENT LEVEL TWO

SUBMARINE

ARSENAL TESTING LEVEL

VISION'S WORLD COMPUTER CONSOLE

EDWIN JARVIS
Resident butler
On staff SUSPENSE #59

The Avengers Mansion is a three-story townhouse located at 890 Fifth Avenue in Manhattan. Built in 1932 by industrialist Howard Stark as his Manhattan residence, the mansion was donated to the Avengers soon after their inception by his son Anthony Stark, who as Iron Man, was one of the Avengers' founding members. Over the years the mansion has been extensively remodeled to accomodate the Avengers' special needs. The most significant exterior change occurred about a year after the Avengers moved in when Thor and Iron Man pushed the mansion about 35 feet back from Fifth Avenue in order to give the structure the privacy afforded by a front yard. The below-ground sub-structure, part of Howard Stark's original construction, was expanded by the Avengers to encompass the full limits of the block-wide property to a depth of feet. The below-ground levels of the mansion contain the top-security headquarters and computer intelligence systems, while the above-ground levels contain living quarters and a main floor in which all public functions of the Avengers are conducted. First appearance: AVENGERS #2.

THIRD FLOOR

The top floor of Avengers Mansion had long been the hangar and landing runway for the Avengers' supersonic Quinjets (see *Avengers Quinjet*). Employing the principles of a naval aircraft carrier landing deck, the third floor uses a wire (which catches the arresting hook of a quinjet) and a series of pistol-coupled pulleys which gradually decelerate the craft over a 30-foot distance. The third floor also contained computerized navigation aids, radar, and communications. The hangar had storage room for four Quinjets, three on storage dollies, and one in launch position. With the recent rescinding of launch privileges within city limits, the third floor hangar has been in disuse. All of the Quinjets have been moved to Hydrobase (see *Hydrobase*). Various members have suggested converting the facilities to other uses, but as yet what to do with the vacant hangar has not been decided.

SECOND FLOOR

Private quarters for any Avenger who requests them comprise the entire second floor of the mansion. Unlike the third floor which was completely gutted to make room for the hangar facility, the second floor closely resembled the original floorplan and architecture designed and constructed by Howard Stark. While many members of the Avengers maintain residences outside the mansion, many members over the years have lived at the mansion full-time during their term of active membership. When space was available, a member such as the Wasp, who had a residence elsewhere, could use one of the bedrooms as a Manhattan apartment. At only one time in Avengers history were all eight bedrooms occupied. Usually at least half of the rooms remain vacant. Since the Avengers' inception, there has always been at least one Avenger living full time at the mansion. The following Avengers are the only ones never to have resided at Avengers Mansion: Thor, Iron Man, Hulk, Black Widow, Moondragon, Hellcat, Ms. Marvel, Falcon, and Captain Marvel. Anthony Stark's quarters, used infrequently by the Avengers' benefactor and never as his alter ego Iron Man, are still reserved for Stark's exclusive use.

GROUNDS AND MAIN FLOOR

Avengers Mansion is surrounded on three sides by a twelve-foot high concrete and reinforced steel wall, with a steel fence along Fifth Avenue. The yard, doors, and windows all have numerous surveillance systems to ascertain the identities of all visitors and detainment devices to intercept unauthorized personnel. Visitors seeking entrance to the mansion are screened at the front gate. The garden and patio in the backyard have sufficient foliage to afford Avengers a fair degree of outdoor privacy. The main floor of the mansion contains no materials vital to the Avengers' security or functions and thus is occasionally opened to the public for press conferences and social functions. The Avengers' only dining facilities are on the main floor, as is the private library. The Avengers' butler Edwin Jarvis is the only person quartered on this floor.

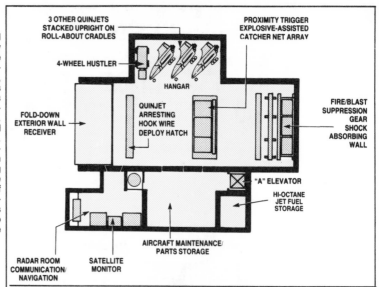

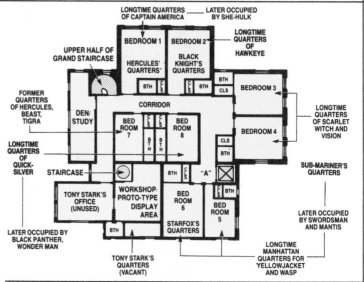

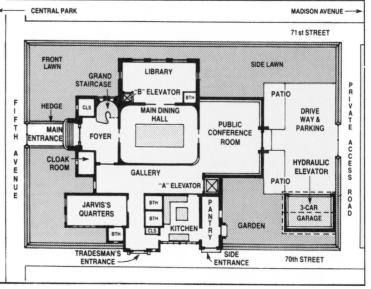

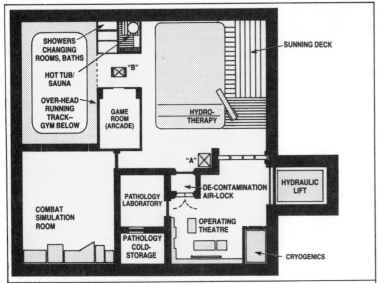

BASEMENT

Recreational, training, and medical facilities comprise the first sub-surface level of Avengers Mansion. A fully equipped gymnasium, an Olympic-size pool, sauna and steambath are available to the membership, as is a game room featuring a billiards table, pinball machines, and video arcade games. The Combat Simulation Room is a heavily-reinforced area in which various robotic devices simulating humanoid and mechanical attacks can be engaged for training purposes. The Combat Room is monitored and programmed by the mansion's main computer system. Also on this level are emergency medical facilities, once used by Dr. Donald Blake and Dr. Henry Pym. There is also a cryogenic storage area in which certain individuals (members or adversaries) suffering from degenerative ailments can be placed in suspended animation.

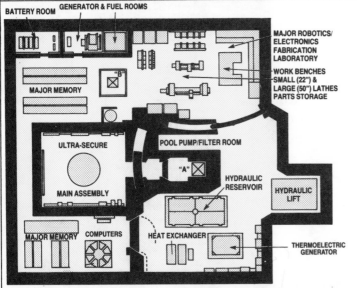

SUB-BASEMENT LEVEL ONE

Sub-Basement Level One contains the Avengers' high security Assembly Room where all operational meetings are held. The Assembly Room is the most secure place in the entire headquarters complex due to its massive reinforcements and vault-like entrance passageway. The first sub-basement houses the Avengers' computer system which contains all of their crime / forensic files, operational records, and world security data.

Until recently when the Avengers' governmental security clearances were revoked, the Avengers' computers had limited access to the national security data of the Pentagon's computer system, as well as a direct common database with SHIELD. Now the only outside agency with which the Avengers routinely trade information is the Fantastic Four, Inc. The mansion's power supply, a thermoelectric generator, along with its attendant back-up systems, are also housed on this floor, as is the Robotics / Electronics Fabrication Area once used by Dr. Henry Pym and Anthony Stark. This area is currently used by Dane Whitman (the Black Knight).

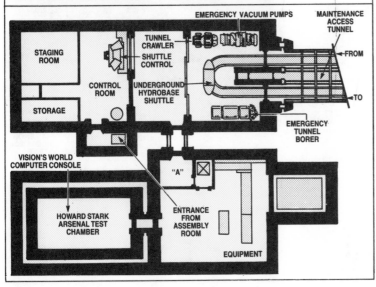

SUB-BASEMENT LEVEL TWO

Until recently, Sub-Basement Level Two had been primarily used for storage. Howard Stark built it for private weapons testing and storage, and constructed the robot named Arsenal there that would later menace the Avengers. The Avengers have a submarine pen with its own waterway to the East River, but with the adoption of the Quinjets as the major means of transit, the submarine system fell into disuse. In recent months, the submarine pen and waterway has been refurbished to create the UGABS (Underground Airbase Shuttle) system, a secret means of rapid transit to the Hydrobase nine miles off the coast of New York. The shuttle is easily accessible from the Assembly Room above, as well as other parts of the Mansion. ∎

AVENGERS QUINJET

STARK INTERNATIONAL QUINJET A-1 (UNITED STATES)
WAKANDA DESIGN GROUP, T'CHALLA, CHIEFTAIN

Data: Avengers Quinjet A-1
Power Plant: 2 × 2 symmetrically mounted modified Pratt & Whitney J48-P-8A Turbojet engines (each 8,5000 pounds static thrust). 1 modified Pratt & Whitney TF33-P-7 Turbofan engine (21,000 lb. S.T.) without afterburning).
Wing span: 23′ 9″
Length overall, inc. nose probe: 34′ 8″
Cabin: Max width: 10′ 4″
  Max. Height: 6′ 8″
Normal take-off weight: 29,000 lbs.
Max. level speed at Sea Level: Mach 2.1
Max. rate of climb at S / L: 7,900 feet per min.
Service ceiling: 130,000 feet, with afterburner: 220,000 feet
Range with max. fuel, 5% fuel reserve, 4,000 lbs. (max.) payload: 9,500 miles
Range with max. fuel, 5% fuel reserve: 11,000 miles
Accomodation: Flight crew of 2 on bi-directional, zero-height Weber escape harnesses, optional seating for 5 passengers.
Operational equipment: True Vertical Take-Off and Landing capability by routing 4 smaller engine's exhaust through vertical thrust deflectors.

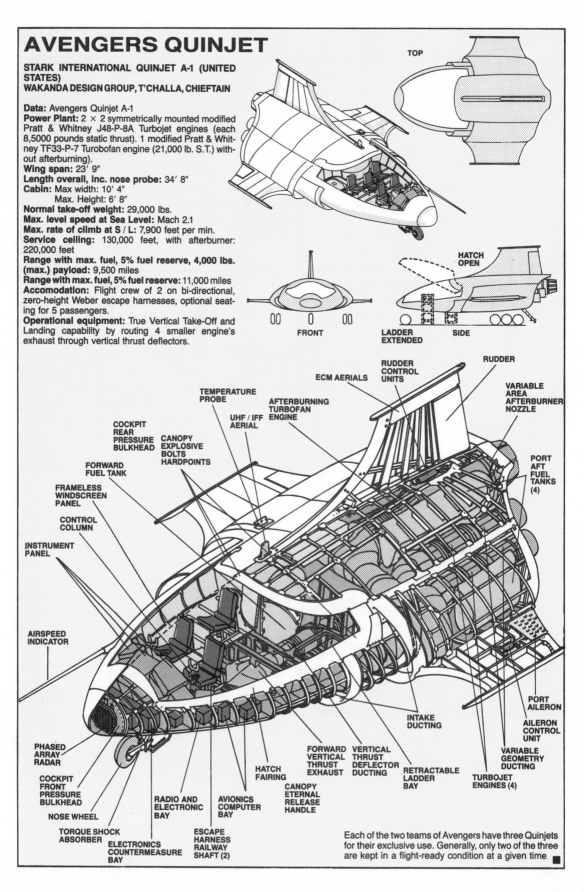

TOP

HATCH OPEN

FRONT

LADDER EXTENDED   SIDE

RUDDER CONTROL UNITS

ECM AERIALS

RUDDER

VARIABLE AREA AFTERBURNER NOZZLE

TEMPERATURE PROBE

AFTERBURNING TURBOFAN ENGINE

UHF / IFF AERIAL

COCKPIT REAR PRESSURE BULKHEAD

CANOPY EXPLOSIVE BOLTS HARDPOINTS

PORT AFT FUEL TANKS (4)

FORWARD FUEL TANK

FRAMELESS WINDSCREEN PANEL

CONTROL COLUMN

INSTRUMENT PANEL

AIRSPEED INDICATOR

PORT AILERON

AILERON CONTROL UNIT

PHASED ARRAY RADAR

COCKPIT FRONT PRESSURE BULKHEAD

NOSE WHEEL

HATCH FAIRING

INTAKE DUCTING

FORWARD VERTICAL THRUST EXHAUST

VERTICAL THRUST DEFLECTOR DUCTING

RETRACTABLE LADDER BAY

VARIABLE GEOMETRY DUCTING

TURBOJET ENGINES (4)

RADIO AND ELECTRONIC BAY

AVIONICS COMPUTER BAY

CANOPY ETERNAL RELEASE HANDLE

TORQUE SHOCK ABSORBER

ELECTRONICS COUNTERMEASURE BAY

ESCAPE HARNESS RAILWAY SHAFT (2)

Each of the two teams of Avengers have three Quinjets for their exclusive use. Generally, only two of the three are kept in a flight-ready condition at a given time. ■

BALDER

Real Name: Balder
Occupation: Warrior-god, Asgardian god of light
Identity: Publicly known on Earth, although the general public of Earth does not believe him to be the god of Norse mythology.
Legal status: Citizen of Asgard
Other current aliases: Balder the Brave

Place of birth: Asgard
Marital status: Single
Known relatives: None
Group affiliation: Gods of Asgard, frequent personal ally of Thor and the Warriors Three
Base of operations: Asgard
First appearance: JOURNEY INTO MYSTERY #85

History: Due to his many heroic deeds over the ages, Balder has long been regarded as Asgard's noblest god and its greatest warrior next to the thunder god Thor, who has long been Balder's closest friend (see *Asgard*). Balder has been unsuccessfully sought as a lover by the sorceress Karnilla the Norn Queen (see *Karnilla*).

63

Because of prophecies that Balder's death would help trigger the coming of Ragnarok, the destruction of Asgard and its inhabitants, Odin, ruler of Asgard, commanded his wife Frigga to make Balder invulnerable to harm. Frigga cast spells that would protect Balder from harm by any living or inanimate thing while he was in the Asgardian dimension. (The legends describe her as extracting promises from all of these things not to harm Balder, as if they were all sentient and capable of speech.) The sole exception was mistletoe. This omission is probably not due to forgetfulness on Frigga's part, since she has not made him invulnerable to harm from mistletoe since his vulnerability to it became known. It is more likely that his vulnerability to mistletoe is a necessary side effect of the spells making him invulnerable to harm from other things.

Loki, the god of mischief, learned of the prophecies tying Balder's death to the coming of Ragnarok, and also learned of Balder's vulnerability to mistletoe (see *Loki*). Seeking to bring about Ragnarok, Loki tricked the blind god Hoder into firing an arrow tipped with mistletoe wood at Balder. Balder was fatally wounded, but Odin's power prevented him from actually dying and instead kept him in a state resembling suspended animation (see *Odin*). Nevertheless, Balder's spirit journeyed to Hel, one of the Asgardian realms of the dead. There Balder was appalled at seeing the horrors endured by the spirits of so many of those whom he had slain in battle.

Odin finally restored Balder fully to life, but Balder's hair turned white as a result of his experiences in Hel. His beloved, Nanna, sacrificed her life to save him from entrapment in marriage by Karnilla, and Balder was so distraught that he has resolved never to speak of this incident or of her again. Anguished by Nanna's death and by what he had seen in the land of the dead, Balder forswore the life of a warrior, attempted unsuccessfully to forget his misery through eating, gaining considerable weight in the process, and finally rode out into the desert, hoping to die there. Instead, Balder encountered the Norns, the three goddesses who oversee the workings of destiny. The Norns gave Balder a vision that restored his faith in the value of life and in the need for him to continue living. Balder rode back to Asgard and was sent by Odin to Karnilla to seek her aid in the Asgardians' battle against Surtur and the legions of Muspelheim (see *Surtur*). Balder was successful in this mission, and his relationship appears to have changed in the process. Balder has also returned to his normal weight through vigorous exercise.

Height: 6' 4"
Weight: 320 lbs.
Eyes: Blue
Hair: White, formerly brown
Strength level: Balder is somewhat stronger than the average Asgardian male, and can lift (press) about 35 tons. (The average Asgardian male can lift about 30 tons.)
Known superhuman powers: Balder possesses the conventional superhuman physical attributes of an Asgardian. Like all Asgardians, Balder is extremely long-lived (though not immortal like the Olympians), superhumanly strong, and immune to all diseases. (Asgardian flesh and bone is about three times denser than similar human tissue, contributing to the Asgardians' superhuman strength and weight.)

His Asgardian metabolism gives him superhuman endurance in all physical activities.

Because of spells placed on him by Frigga, queen of Asgard, Balder cannot suffer injury by any living or non-living thing while he is in the Asgardian dimension. Any projectile hurled at Balder which is capable of killing or injuring an Asgardian will be magically deflected from its path before it can strike him. However, Balder can be injured or killed by weapons made of mistletoe wood. Presumably he can also be harmed by the power of Odin, and possibly by the spells and magical energies used by others. Balder could also die in the Asgardian dimension through means that do not involve weaponry: for example, he could starve to death or be asphyxiated. Moreover, Frigga's spells do not protect Balder when he is in the Earth dimension. It is not known whether Balder also becomes vulnerable when he is in dimensions other than those of Asgard and Earth.

Abilities: Balder is a brilliant warrior, greatly skilled in hand-to-hand combat, swordsmanship, and horsemanship. ■

BARON MORDO

Real Name: Karl Amadeus Mordo
Occupation: Sorcerer
Legal status: Transylvanian nobleman with no criminal record
Identity: The general public does not know that Baron Mordo is a sorcerer.
Place of birth: Varf Mandra, Transylvania
Marital status: Single
Known relatives: Viscount Crowler (grandfather)
Group affiliation: Former minion of Dormammu, former disciple of the Ancient One.
Base of operations: Castle Mordo, Varf Mandra, Transylvania
First appearance: STRANGE TALES #111
History: Karl Mordo acquired an interest in the occult from his maternal grandfather, Viscount Crowler, at an early age. When he became an adult, he sought out the mystic master known as the Ancient One in Tibet (see *Deceased: Ancient One*). The Ancient One recognized that Mordo had the innate ability to become a sorcerer of great power, but that Mordo was motivated solely by lust for power. The Ancient One decided to accept Mordo as a disciple in order to keep watch over him.

While still living at his mentor's palace, Mordo plotted to destroy the Ancient One. Mordo's scheming was overheard by the Ancient One's guest, Dr. Stephen Strange, a jaded physician. Witnessing Mordo's power and learning of his intent shocked Strange into a recognition of the meaning of evil. Strange sought to warn the Ancient One, but Mordo placed mystical restraints upon Strange that prevented him from telling the Ancient One of his plans. Strange, however, seeking a way to get around Mordo's spell, sincerely asked the Ancient One if he too could become his disciple. The Ancient One, who was aware of Mordo's schemes, freed Strange of Mordo's spell and accepted Strange as his disciple.

Eventually Mordo left the Ancient One, and Strange, over the years, gained mastery of the mystic arts. Strange and Mordo were thus rivals, and have clashed repeatedly over the years. Mordo has served the extradimensional entity Dormammu in the past, but he also seeks to amass more power for himself (see *Dormammu*). Mordo is obsessed with destroying Doctor Strange, who is now the sorcerer supreme of Earth's dimension (see *Doctor Strange*).

Height: 6′   **Eyes:** Brown
Weight: 250 lbs   **Hair:** Grey
Strength level: Baron Mordo possesses the normal human strength of a man of his age, height, and build who engages in no regular exercise.

Known superhuman powers: Baron Mordo is a powerful sorcerer motivated by ambition and megalomania. Though he is among the ten most powerful Earth-born sorcerers alive today, his power pales beside that of Earth's sorcerer supreme; Doctor Strange. Mordo's magic, like that of most magicians, is derived from three major sources: personal powers of the soul/mind/body (mesmerism, astral projection, thought-casting, etc.), powers gained by tapping this universe's ambient magical energy and employing it for specific effects (teleportation, illusion-casting, energy projection), and finally, powers gained through the tapping of extra-dimensional energy by

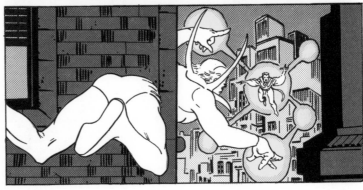

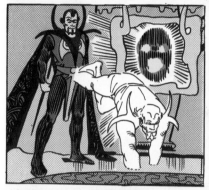

invoking entities or objects of power dwelling in mystical dimensions, tangential to our own. The latter means of power is usually gained by the recitation of spells, either ritualized ones found in various mystic texts or by original spells invoking extra-dimensional assistance.

To begin with his personal powers, Mordo has mastered the art of astral projection, the mental ability to separate his astral self — the sheath of the soul, or life-essence — from his physical self and travel through space unbounded by physical laws while retaining human consciousness. The astral form is invisible, intangible, and incapable of being harmed except by the most rigorous mystical means. Mordo is of such mastery that he can remain in his astral form for up to 24 hours before there is any corporeal deterioration of his physical form. The physical form is quite vulnerable to attack while the astral form is absent. If harm were to befall the physical body while he was in his astral form, he would be stranded in his wraith-like state.

Mordo has the ability to mesmerize people to do his bidding, both in person and at a distance. This mental domination is only possible over those minds less trained than his. His magical control over a person

persists until such time when the subject completes the finite task he or she was given, or Mordo wilfully releases him or her from control, or the spell is broken by a superior mage, or the spell fades from disuse. Mordo can also cast his thoughts over short or vast distances in a manner virtually identical with telepathy. The entire Earth is within reach of Mordo's mind, providing he knows where to contact the specific mind he may be seeking. Mordo can communicate with only one mind at a time.

Mordo is able to tap this universe's store of ambient magical energy and manipulate it for a variety of effects. He is able to form and hurl magical energy bolts with a high degree of potency and control. He is able to erect energy shields or screens with a high degree of imperviousness to both physical and magical damage. He is able to use the local magical energy for the conjuration of small physical objects like fetters or flowers, or for unusual luminescent effects.

Mordo is sometimes able to utilize local magical energy to teleport across the face of the Earth or into a mystic dimension (certain alternate realities where the physical laws are based on magic rather then science). Oddly enough, teleportation within a dimension is more taxing to a sorcerer

than teleportation between dimensions. Such expenditure of energy leaves all sorcerers (including Mordo) mystically debilitated for a varying length of time, making teleportation a dangerous and seldom-used ability. Physical teleportation across time rather than space is the most power-draining type of journey of all.

Mordo has a knowledge of a host of sorcerous spells and incantations invoking the names and aspects of various extra-dimensional objects and beings of power. Mordo (like his nemesis, Doctor Strange) is able to draw upon these extra-dimensional power sources for very specific effects without depleting his own capacity to draw upon local magical power and without taxing his own personal abilities. Some of these extra-dimensional phenomena called upon include the Vapors of Valtorr, the Crimson Bands of Cytorrak, and the Images of Ikonn. Some of the extra-dimensional beings of power invoked are Dormammu, Satannish and Tiboro. It is possible to accomplish a certain magical effect by a number of means. An adept sorcerer like Mordo will use the magic that least diminishes his overall ability to draw upon the many forms of magic. ∎

BARON ZEMO

Real Name: Helmut Zemo
Occupation: Scientist
Legal status: Citizen of Germany with no criminal record
Identity: Baron Zemo does not use a dual identity.
Former aliases: The Phoenix
Place of birth: Leipzig, Germany
Marital status: Single
Known relatives: Heinrich (father, deceased), Hilda (mother, deceased)
Group affiliation: Former partner of Primus, former ally of Mother Superior and the Red Skull
Base of operations: Castle Zemo, Sierra Madre Oriental Mountains, Mexico
First appearance and origin: (as Phoenix) CAPTAIN AMERICA #168, (as Zemo) CAPTAIN AMERICA #276
History: Helmut Zemo is the son of Baron Heinrich Zemo, the master Nazi scientist and enemy of Captain America (see *Captain America, Deceased: Baron Zemo I*). During World War Two, the elder Zemo made many scientific discoveries for the Third Reich, among which was Adhesive X, a powerful bonding agent. In battle with Captain America, Zemo was doused with Adhesive X, permanently affixing the mask Zemo wore to conceal his identity to his face. Zemo's only son, Helmut, believed this led to his father's insanity. When Captain America was revived from his decades-long suspended animation, the elder Zemo, estranged from his wife and son, came out of hiding in South America to battle him. The elder Zemo eventually died in battle with Captain America, when the former accidentally triggered a rockslide with his dis integrator gun and was buried by it.

Eventually learning the circumstances of his father's demise, young Helmut Zemo blamed Captain America and decided to follow in his father's footsteps and avenge him. Zemo recreated many of his father's devices and formulae, including Adhesive X. Calling himself the Phoenix, Zemo captured Captain America and his then-partner the Falcon and chained them above a boiling cauldron of Adhesive X. Escaping, Captain America grappled with the young Zemo and accidentally caused him to topple into the vat of liquid. Captain America left, believing Zemo dead.

Helmut Zemo had, in fact, escaped through a secret pipe at the bottom of the cauldron. The passage through the boiling liquid left its mark, however, and Zemo's face was severely scarred. Zemo kept out of sight for a period of time, building a retreat for himself in Mexico, recreating more of his father's inventions, and plotting revenge against Captain America. Allying himself with Primus, the shape-changing mutate created by geneticist Arnim Zola (see *Arnim Zola, Primus*), Zemo finally launched his first major campaign against Captain America, using Captain America's childhood friend Arnold Roth as his pawn. Captain America managed to escape, however.

Zemo's second attack on Captain America was launched under the auspices of the Nazi mastermind, the Red Skull, and his daughter, Mother Superior (see *Appendix: Mother Superior, Deceased: Red Skull*). After Zemo underwent tutelage at the side of Mother Superior, the Skull provided Zemo with the opportunity to defeat Captain America by making him relive his greatest tragedy, the death of his young ally Bucky (a death that occurred due to the machinations of Zemo's father). Captain America managed to survive the ordeal. Later, hostilities erupted between Zemo and Mother Superior over who would become the Red Skull's heir. Zemo lost the fight, falling prey to Mother Superior's mental blasts. Zemo's current whereabouts and mental condition are unknown.

Height: 5' 10"
Weight: 180 lbs
Eyes: Blue
Hair: Blond (what is left of it)
Unusual features: Zemo's face is severely disfigured, having the appearance of melted wax.
Strength level: Baron Zemo possesses the normal human strength of a man of his age, height, and build who engages in moderate exercise.
Known superhuman powers: None.
Abilities: Baron Zemo is highly intelligent, although not a scientific genius like his father. He is very capable of carrying out the experiments devised by his father, although it is unlikely he will make any significant scientific breakthroughs of his own. The depth of his hatred for Captain America, coupled with his great wealth, makes him a formidable enemy. ∎

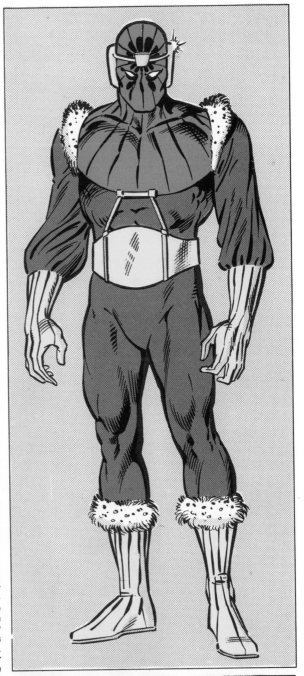

BATROC'S BRIGADE

Batroc's Brigade is the name of various bands of mercenaries, martial artists, and assassins organized by the French savate master, Georges Batroc. Although Batroc has worked alone, he often recruited fellow rogues and criminals when a job he has been hired for so requires it.

To locate the "seismo-bomb" for an undisclosed foreign power, Batroc organized his first Brigade, composed of the Swordsman and the Living Laser (now both deceased). Following the unsuccessful completion of the mission, the first Brigade disbanded. Shortly thereafter, Batroc was hired by the Red Skull to attack Captain America. To carry out this assignment, Batroc recruited the Porcupine and Whirlwind. Again, the team disbanded upon failure. Batroc abandoned superhuman criminals for his next two Brigades, and hired dozens of ordinary "muscle men" and martial artists.

Recently, Batroc was hired by criminal industrialist Obadiah Stane to steal Captain America's shield. For this assignment, he hired the British weapons master Zaran, and the South American revolutionary Machete. Zaran and Machete proved to be Batroc's most resouceful allies yet, having successfully completed the task they were hired for. Batroc has kept this Brigade intact for future missions.
First appearance: (original Brigade) CAPTAIN AMERICA #105, (new Brigade) CAPTAIN AMERICA #302. ∎

BATROC

Real name: Georges Batroc
Occupation: Mercenary
Legal status: French citizen with a criminal record
Other aliases: The Leaper
Place of birth: Marseilles, France
Marital status: Single
Known relatives: None
Base of operations: Mobile
First appearance: TALES OF SUSPENSE #75
History: Batroc trained himself in savate while in the French Foreign Legion, and later became a costumed mercenary.
Height: 6′
Weight: 225 lbs.
Eyes: Brown
Hair: Black
Strength level: Human athlete
Known superhuman powers: None
Abilities: Batroc is a master of *savate*, a French form of foot-boxing.

ZARAN

Real name: Maximillian Zaran
Occupation: Mercenary, assassin
Legal status: Citizen of Great Britain with criminal record
Identity: Secret
Other aliases: The Weapons Master
Place of birth:
Marital status: Single
Known relatives: None
Base of operations: Mobile
First appearance: MASTER OF KUNG FU #77
History: Zaran was an agent of the British Secret Service, MI-6, who defected to the employ of Fah Lo Suee, the daughter of Fu Manchu. Spurned by her, Zaran became a mercenary.
Height: 6′ 1″
Weight: 235 lbs.
Eyes: Blue
Hair: Red
Strength level: Human athlete
Known superhuman powers: None
Abilities: Mastery of ancient and modern weapons including knives, bows, staffs, maces, spears, nunchakus, shurikens, guns.
Weapons: Zaran wears gauntlets and a collarpiece studded with small *sais*.

MACHETE

Real name: Ferdinand Lopez
Occupation: Former revolutionary, now mercenary
Legal status: Citizen of San Diablo with no criminal record
Identity: Secret
Place of birth: San Diablo
Marital status: Unknown
Known relatives: None
Base of operations: Mobile
First appearance: CAPTAIN AMERICA #302
History: Machete was a revolutionary in the tiny South American republic of San Diablo who decided to become a mercenary to help finance the revolution.
Height: 6′ 2″
Weight: 200 lbs.
Eyes: Blue
Hair: Black
Strength level: Human athlete
Known superhuman powers: None
Abilities: High proficiency at the throwing of knives and blades
Weapons: Machete carries two 3-foot machetes and numerous tiny throwing knives.

BEAST

Real Name: Henry ("Hank") McCoy
Occupation: Biochemist, adventurer
Legal status: Citizen of the United States with no criminal record
Identity: Publicly known. However, Henry McCoy is not publicly known to be a member of X-Factor.
Place of birth: Dunfee, Illinois
Marital status: Single
Known relatives: Norton (father), Edna (mother), Robert (uncle)
Group affiliation: Former member of the X-Men, the Avengers, and the Defenders, founding member of X-Factor
Base of operations: X-Factor headquarters, New York City
First appearance: X-MEN #1, (in furry form) AMAZING ADVENTURES #11
Origin: X-MEN #15, 49-53
History: Henry McCoy is a mutant whose powers were in evidence since birth. The probable cause of his mutation was his father's exposure to massive amounts of radiation during a nuclear power plant "incident." As a youth, McCoy's superhuman agility and athletic prowess earned him recognition in school as a star football player. It was then that Professor Charles Xavier learned of him and invited him to join his School for Gifted Youngsters. As a member of Professor Xavier's original X-Men, McCoy was given the code name "Beast" (see *Professor X, X-Men*). Upon graduation, McCoy was hired as a genetic researcher at the Brand Corporation. There he isolated a chemical catalyst that triggered mutations and sampled the serum in hopes of changing his appearance enough so he could ferret out enemy agents at the facility. The serum caused fur to grow over his entire body, enlarged his canine teeth, and increased his already prodigious athletic ability. By remaining too long in this altered state, McCoy learned that he could not return to his former appearance. He later learned to accept his more beast-like appearance. Leaving Brand, he joined the Avengers and became a full-time adventurer. The Beast left the Avengers after a distinguished stint of service and joined the Defenders, which he decided to reorganize into a more formal and cohesive team. Still later, he and the other members of Xavier's first "class" of X-Men reunited to form the team known as X-Factor (see *X-Factor*).

Recently geneticist Dr. Carl Maddicks kidnapped the Beast and performed an experiment that reversed the effects of the serum that had produced the Beast's furry mutated form. As a result the Beast again has his original human appearance, although, as always, he still has unusually large hands and feet. His superhuman abilities are still the same as when he was in his furry form. Whether Maddicks' treatment will have further effects on the Beast remains to be seen.

Height: 5′ 11″
Weight: 350 lbs.
Eyes: Blue
Hair: (originally) Brown, (in furry form) Bluish black, (currently) Black
Strength level: The Beast possesses superhuman strength enabling him to lift (press) 1 ton under optimal conditions.
Known superhuman powers: In addition to his superhuman strength, the Beast possesses superhuman agility, endurance, speed, and dexterity. The Beast has the agility of a great ape and the acrobatic prowess of an accomplished circus aerialist and acrobat. He can walk a tightrope or a slackrope with minimal effort. He can walk on his hands for many hours, or perform a complicated sequence of gymnastic stunts such as flips, rolls and springs. Further, his manual and pedal dexterity are so great that he can write using both hands at once or tie knots in rope with his toes. He can crawl up brick walls by wedging his fingers and toes into the smallest cracks and applying a vise-like grip on them.

BEETLE

Real Name: Abner Jenkins
Occupation: Former mechanic, now professional criminal
Legal status: Citizen of the United States with a criminal record
Identity: Publicly known
Place of birth: Baltimore, Maryland
Marital status: Single
Known relatives: None
Group affiliation: Former employee of the Collector and Justin Hammer, former partner of the Gladiator, former member of Egghead's Masters of Evil
Base of operations: New York area
First appearance and origin: STRANGE TALES #123, (in current battle-suit) SPECTACULAR SPIDER-MAN #58
History: Abner Jenkins was a master mechanic at an aircraft parts factory who became dissatisfied with his boring, low-paying job. Using his considerable mechanical knowledge, Jenkins built an armor-plated, strength-augmenting suit, a pair of gravity-defying wings, and a pair of suction-fingered gloves, and a cybernetic control helmet. Calling himself the Beetle, Jenkins decided to use his battle-suit for fame, wealth, and adventure. The Beetle chose to lure the Human Torch and the Thing into battle, believing a victory over half the Fantastic Four would make him an overnight sensation. Unfortunately, the Thing and the Torch defeated him, and he was sent to prison. Paroled a short time later, he sought revenge on the Torch, but found himself in battle with Spider-Man instead. Once again he was defeated. Upon his release, he decided to forego petty revenge and concentrate on the acquisition of wealth. He battled Spider-Man and Daredevil separately on various occasions, and once was recruited by the Collector to serve as his unwilling agent (see *Collector*). Under the Collector's domination, the Beetle faced the Avengers.

Losing every battle against costumed crimefighters and failing to accumulate very much wealth, the Beetle offered his services to underworld financier Justin Hammer, who kept various superhuman criminals on retainer (see *Hammer, Justin*). His offer accepted, the Beetle was dispatched against the original Iron Man, as part of a battalion of costumed criminals. His Beetle armor was severely damaged by Iron Man during the fight.

Jenkins then invested all of the capital he could acquire into the modification and refinement of his Beetle armor. With the assistance of the Tinkerer, he produced a new battle-suit with far greater capacities than his old one. Before launching his comeback, the Beetle recruited the criminal Ringer to put Spider-Man through his paces. The Beetle wished to study Spider-Man's fighting style and program it into a computer system so he could anticipate his opponent's moves. Despite his preparations and new battle-suit, the Beetle was defeated by Spider-Man. He was later freed from prison by Egghead who recruited him for his Masters of Evil organization. The Beetle and the other Masters of Evil were defeated by the Avengers and arrested. Abner Jenkins is currently in jail, awaiting parole.

Height: 5' 11"
Weight: 175 lbs

Eyes: Brown
Hair: Brown

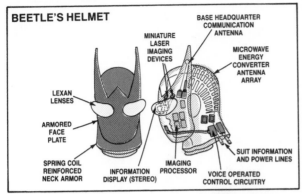

BEETLE'S HELMET

- BASE HEADQUARTER COMMUNICATION ANTENNA
- MINIATURE LASER IMAGING DEVICES
- MICROWAVE ENERGY CONVERTER ANTENNA ARRAY
- LEXAN LENSES
- ARMORED FACE PLATE
- SPRING COIL REINFORCED NECK ARMOR
- INFORMATION DISPLAY (STEREO)
- IMAGING PROCESSOR
- VOICE OPERATED CONTROL CIRCUITRY
- SUIT INFORMATION AND POWER LINES

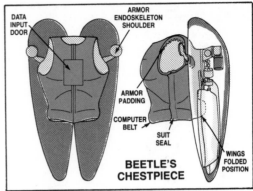

BEETLE'S CHESTPIECE

- DATA INPUT DOOR
- ARMOR ENDOSKELETON SHOULDER
- ARMOR PADDING
- COMPUTER BELT
- SUIT SEAL
- WINGS FOLDED POSITION

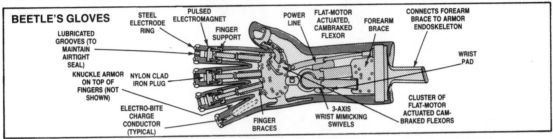

BEETLE'S GLOVES

- STEEL ELECTRODE RING
- PULSED ELECTROMAGNET
- FINGER SUPPORT
- POWER LINE
- FLAT-MOTOR ACTUATED, CAMBRAKED FLEXOR
- FOREARM BRACE
- CONNECTS FOREARM BRACE TO ARMOR ENDOSKELETON
- LUBRICATED GROOVES (TO MAINTAIN AIRTIGHT SEAL)
- KNUCKLE ARMOR ON TOP OF FINGERS (NOT SHOWN)
- NYLON CLAD IRON PLUG
- ELECTRO-BITE CHARGE CONDUCTOR (TYPICAL)
- FINGER BRACES
- 3-AXIS WRIST MIMICKING SWIVELS
- CLUSTER OF FLAT-MOTOR ACTUATED CAM-BRAKED FLEXORS
- WRIST PAD

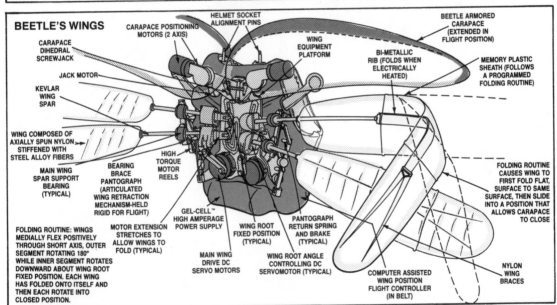

BEETLE'S WINGS

- HELMET SOCKET ALIGNMENT PINS
- CARAPACE POSITIONING MOTORS (2 AXIS)
- WING EQUIPMENT PLATFORM
- BEETLE ARMORED CARAPACE (EXTENDED IN FLIGHT POSITION)
- CARAPACE DIHEDRAL SCREWJACK
- JACK MOTOR
- KEVLAR WING SPAR
- BI-METALLIC RIB (FOLDS WHEN ELECTRICALLY HEATED)
- MEMORY PLASTIC SHEATH (FOLLOWS A PROGRAMMED FOLDING ROUTINE)
- WING COMPOSED OF AXIALLY SPUN NYLON STIFFENED WITH STEEL ALLOY FIBERS
- HIGH TORQUE MOTOR REELS
- MAIN WING SPAR SUPPORT BEARING (TYPICAL)
- BEARING BRACE PANTOGRAPH (ARTICULATED WING RETRACTION MECHANISM-HELD RIGID FOR FLIGHT)
- GEL-CELL™ HIGH AMPERAGE POWER SUPPLY
- PANTOGRAPH RETURN SPRING AND BRAKE (TYPICAL)
- FOLDING ROUTINE CAUSES WING TO FIRST FOLD FLAT, SURFACE TO SAME SURFACE, THEN SLIDE INTO A POSITION THAT ALLOWS CARAPACE TO CLOSE
- FOLDING ROUTINE: WINGS MEDIALLY FLEX POSITIVELY THROUGH SHORT AXIS, OUTER SEGMENT ROTATING 180° WHILE INNER SEGMENT ROTATES DOWNWARD ABOUT WING ROOT FIXED POSITION. EACH WING HAS FOLDED ONTO ITSELF AND THEN EACH ROTATE INTO CLOSED POSITION.
- MOTOR EXTENSION STRETCHES TO ALLOW WINGS TO FOLD (TYPICAL)
- WING ROOT FIXED POSITION (TYPICAL)
- MAIN WING DRIVE DC SERVO MOTORS
- WING ROOT ANGLE CONTROLLING DC SERVOMOTOR (TYPICAL)
- COMPUTER ASSISTED WING POSITION FLIGHT CONTROLLER (IN BELT)
- NYLON WING BRACES

Strength level: The Beetle possesses the normal human strength of a man of his age, height, and build who engages in moderate regular exercise. When his strength is augmented by his battle-suit, he can lift (press) about a ton, 1000 pounds per arm.

Known superhuman powers: None

Paraphernalia and weaponry: The Beetle wears a battle-suit constructed of a magnanium alloy, providing him with a high degree of protection against injury. The suit contains power-boosting circuitry which augments his strength to several times that of a normal human being (see Strength level). The suit's power source is a microwave processor built into his helmet. The helmet has a antenna path that allows reception and ultra-efficient conversion into energy of microwaves at many prevalent frequencies, giving his suit a constantly-re-plenishing power supply. This microwave processor sometimes jams nearby television reception. A mini-computer built into his chestpiece feeds data to his helmet on his opponents' probable movements, enabling him to anticipate their moves. In order for the computer to provide this tactical information, it must have sufficient data on that opponent.

The battle-suit contains a number of other special features. The gloves of each hand contain pneumatic suction-grippers, enabling the Beetle to cling to walls or lift things with his fingertips. Also, each glove contains circuitry that enables him to shoot an electrostatic blast he calls his "electro-bite." He discharges the electro-bite by touching the second and third finger sheath of each hand together and pointing with the first and fourth fingers. The electro-bite has sufficient power to blast a one foot diameter hole through a 3 foot thick brick wall at fifteen feet. (Such a blast would, however, necessitate his diverting all available power to his gloves, thus temporarily immobilizing his other weaponry.)

The final feature of the Beetle's armament are his ultra-tough mylar wings powered by super-efficient micro-motors which enable him to fly by mimicking the complex motion of an actual beetle's wings. Stored beneath dome-like armored sheaths on his back when not in use, the wings can be unsheathed by cybernetic command. The wings enable him to fly at a normal cruising speed of 60 miles per hour. By diverting all of his power into the wings, he can reach a top speed of 100 miles per hour for as long as his power holds out. ∎

BELASCO

Real Name: (allegedly) Belasco (rest of name unrevealed)

Occupation: Sorcerer serving the Elder Gods

Identity: His existence is unknown to the general population of Earth.

Legal status: Citizen of Italy believed to be dead

Former aliases: Unknown

Place of birth: (allegedly) Florence, Italy

Marital status: Unknown

Known relatives: None

Group affiliation: None

Base of operations: Formerly Florence, Italy, formerly Pangea, formerly Limbo, currently unknown

First appearance: KA-ZAR THE SAVAGE #11

History: The only recorded accounts of Belasco's origin are his own and the one in a book purported to be a ship's log kept by the poet Dante Alighieri, and there are reasons to doubt the veracity of both stories. According to these accounts, Belasco was a sorcerer in 13th Century Italy who used his knowledge of alchemy and the black arts to make contact with the so-called Elder Gods, extradimensional demonic beings bent on invading and ruling Earth. (It is not known whether the Elder Gods have any connection with the N'garai or the Undying Ones, two demonic races with similar goals, or whether they may be of the same race as the Elder Gods Chthon and Gaea. See *Chthon*, *Demons*, *Gaea*.) Belasco struck a bargain with these Elder Gods. He would enable them to cross the interdimensional boundaries between their cosmos and Earth's by means of a spell he would cast utilizing a pentagonal arrangement of five mystical "bloodstones." In exchange, the Elder Gods granted Belasco enormous mystical powers and immortality. They also designated him to become the father of a new race of Earth-born demons, and in order to make his role possible, made him partially demonic in form, giving him horns and a tail, among other features. This much of Belasco's account of his origin is probably true.

It is next asserted that Belasco kidnapped Bice "Beatrice" dei Portinari, the beloved of the poet Dante Alighieri, to serve as his mate in spawning this race of demons. Belasco fled with Beatrice aboard a ship, which was pursued by another vessel hired by Dante. Belasco sailed for Pangea, a land once settled by the pre-cataclysmic Atlanteans, who used climate-control machinery and other technology that had been left by its original inhabitants to turn the area into a recreation center with a tropical climate (see *Atlanteans*; *Appendix: Pangea*). The Elder Gods had indicated to Belasco that the spell to bring them to Earth could best be performed at Mt. Flavius, a volcano, there. Belasco had Beatrice wear a locket containing four of the bloodstones necessary to make the spell work, while he retained the last one. While on the voyage Belasco forced Beatrice to marry and mate with him, and she was in her ninth month of pregnancy when they finally arrived in Pangea.

Closely pursued by Dante, Belasco took Beatrice down into a network of underground passageways that the Atlanteans had allegedly designed for their own amusement to resemble hell. On arriving at the center of the exhibit, Beatrice died in

the process of giving birth to demonic creatures. Dante witnessed her death and, horrified and enraged, tried to kill Belasco. In the swordfight that ensued, Belasco accidentally cut an overhead pipe with his sword, causing an unknown freezing liquid to pour over him. Because of his immortality, Belasco did not die but was placed in suspended animation. Dante returned to Italy. The locket had somehow become lost while Belasco and Beatrice had made their way through the subterranean tunnels.

Belasco claims that he remained in suspended animation for centuries. Then, he asserts, in recent years the volcano became active again, causing an accident with the electrical wiring in the chamber where Belasco was, melting the frozen liquid around him and returning him to life. Belasco then studied the underground controls.

There are several reasons to doubt the entire veracity of these accounts. First, they are contradicted by the historical records of the lives of Dante and Beatrice. Second, it is impossible to believe that the pre-cataclysmic Atlantean scientists could have built a replica of hell that resembles in such close detail the visions of hell that were independently developed by the ancient Greek religion and by Christianity thousands of years later. It is far more likely that Belasco himself used Pangean technology to construct a mechanized replica of the underworld as it is depicted in Dante's poem, the *Inferno*. It may be that Dante's ship's log is a forgery by Belasco. Third, Belasco's own account of his origin conceals the fact that at some point he lost his right arm.

Only recently did Belasco regain the locket that would enable him to bring the Elder Gods to Earth. He placed Shanna O'Hara under his mental control, intending to make her the mother of his new demonic race (see *Shanna the She-Devil*). Placing the final bloodstone in the locket, Belasco began casting his spell, but just as the Elder Gods were about to emerge through an interdimensional rift, Shanna's lover Ka-Zar tore the locket from her neck and hurled it into the volcano's lava (see *Ka-Zar*). The rift closed, imprisoning the Elder Gods once again. In retribution, they apparently destroyed Belasco, but in fact trapped him within another dimension that he calls limbo.

Years may pass in Belasco's limbo while mere moments pass on Earth. Hence, it is impossible to determine how long Belasco remained there. He became the absolute master of this realm, and there battled and defeated the X-Men of a divergent Earth (see *X-Men*). He also brought the X-Men of our own Earth to limbo, including Illyana Rasputin, the seven-year-old sister of the X-Man Colossus (see *Colossus*). Belasco seized Illyana as the other X-Men escaped back to our Earth. He shaped a portion of her soul into a bloodstone, thereby infusing some of his own evil into her, enabling him to control her, and giving her great potential mystical power. Illyana became Belasco's apprentice, and he conjured two more bloodstones from her soul as years passed in limbo. Belasco intended to use her as his new means of bringing the Elder Gods to Earth once she reached adulthood. After turning fourteen, however, Illyana defeated Belasco in battle and drove him from limbo. She became its new master and returned to Earth at a point only seconds after the X-Men's escape back to it, and joined the New Mutants as Magik (see *Magik, New Mutants*).

In limbo, however, Belasco had already begun magically manipulating events in Pangea to bring about his release. When Ka-Zar placed a ring containing the only one of the original bloodstones to survive on the finger of Shanna, with whom Belasco had established a mystic link, Belasco was able to return to Pangea. This time he intended to turn Ka-Zar and Shanna into demons who would serve as parents to a new demonic race. He also planned to find Illyana and use her to bring the Elder Gods to Earth. However, Ka-Zar seized Belasco's sword, which the Elder Gods had forged, and impaled him with it just as Shanna recited a spell from a book of Belasco's that caused Belasco and the sword to vanish. Belasco's current whereabouts are unknown.

Height: 6′ 4″
Weight: 250 lbs.
Eyes: Black
Hair: Brown
Unusual physical characteristics: Belasco has various demonic features including red horns upon his forehead, a long, pointed tail, reddish skin, fangs, claws, and pointed ears. Belasco lost his right arm when it was severed, under circumstances yet to be revealed, by his own sword, which was forged by the Elder Gods.
Strength level: Unknown, but presumably that of a normal human in good physical condition.
Known superhuman powers: Belasco is one of the most powerful of all Earthborn sorcerers, and was granted most of his power by the Elder Gods he serves. Among other feats, he can hurl bolts of mystical force, mesmerize victims, transform people into animals, and raise the dead under certain circumstances. His long studies of the black arts have given him an encyclopedic knowledge of spells that he can use.

The Elder Gods also granted Belasco immortality and apparently invulnerability as well. Possibly the only means of killing him is his own sword, which was forged by the

Elder Gods and was used to sever his right arm.

Belasco's powers are somehow linked to those of Magik. When they fought their climactic battle in limbo, Magik took on a demonic form while simultaneously Belasco reverted to human form, losing most of his power and his invulnerability in the process. It is not known whether Belasco would lose his demonic form and powers whenever Magik takes on her demonic form.

Other abilities: Belasco has considerable knowledge of much of the technology that the pre-cataclysmic Atlanteans found in Pangea.
Weapons: Belasco carries a sword forged by the Elder Gods which is capable of harming Belasco himself.
Base of operations: Belasco was formerly master of a dimension he called limbo. The word "limbo" is frequently used to describe interdimensional voids. The one once ruled by Belasco is probably a small pocket dimension that is tenuously connected to True Limbo, where time does not pass in a physical sense and, as a result no one can age or die. Time does pass in a physical sense in Belasco's limbo, and Magik aged seven years while she was there. However, one might spend years in Belasco's limbo while no more than moments pass on Earth, due to the unknown temporal laws of the former place. The matter within Belasco's limbo can be shaped and transformed by the thoughts and emotions of the sorcerer who is its master.

Belasco's limbo is populated by demons who serve its master. The principal demon is known as S'ym (see *Appendix: S'ym*). ∎

BETA RAY BILL

Real Name: Beta Ray Bill (English equivalent of his name in his own language)
Occupation: Warrior
Identity: His existence is not known to the general public of Earth. His identity is known to the population of Asgard.
Legal status: Citizen of an unidentified planet, honorary citizen of Asgard.
Other current aliases: Beta Ray Thor
Place of birth: An unidentified planet in the "Burning Galaxy"
Marital status: Single

Known relatives: None
Group affiliation: Protector of an unidentified alien race, ally of Asgard
Base of operations: Beta Ray Bill usually accompanies his race's space fleet.
First appearance: THOR #337
Origin: THOR #338
History: Beta Ray Bill is a member of an extraterrestrial race of semi-humanoid beings which lived in a peaceful interplanetary empire in a distant galaxy now known as the "Burning Galaxy." Recently, the ancient

demon known as Surtur (see *Surtur*) caused the core of that galaxy to explode in order to release the tremendous amount of energy he needed to reforge his "Sword of Doom." This galactic cataclysm destroyed most of the empire, and the survivors made ready to flee in a fleet of ten thousand starships in order to find new homes in another galaxy.

The imperial leaders decided to choose a guardian for the space fleet who would be granted great powers. Athletic games

74

which proved to be grueling tests of strength and endurance were held to select physically acceptable candidates. These candidates were then subjected to psychological tests which left most of them dead or insane. Beta Ray Bill was among the small group of survivors.

The empire's scientists took specimens of the most ferocious carnivorous beast in the empire, and, using bioengineering techniques, restructured their bodies as to greatly increase their strength, speed, and agility. Then, in an excruitiatingly painful process, the life forces and consciousness of the candidates for guardian were transferred into these bioengineered cyborg bodies. Beta Ray Bill was the only one of the candidates to survive this process, and so it was that he became the guardian.

Beta Ray Bill was given a sentient warship, named Skuttlebutt. Because there was not enough food for everyone who was to ride in the space fleet for what might prove to be a very long journey, even with travel through hyperspace, all of them were put into a state of suspended animation called coldsleep. Only Beta Ray Bill, whose life span had been artificially lengthened through bioengineering, remained awake to serve as guardian. Almost immediately after the fleet had left the devastated empire, Beta Ray Bill discovered that it was being followed by a horde of demons coming from the exploded galactic core. These demons were in the employ of Surtur. Beta Ray Bill and Skuttlebutt fought the demons and held them off until the fleet had gotten a safe distance away. Beta Ray Bill then traveled ahead of the fleet, searching in vain for a world where his people could take refuge. Meanwhile, the demons continued to follow, even over intergalactic distance, drawing ever closer to the fleet.

After the space fleet had entered the Milky Way Galaxy, it was detected by a SHIELD hyperspatial probe, and then-SHIELD Director Nicholas Fury asked Thor to investigate. At this time Beta Ray Bill was in suspended animation aboard the Skuttlebutt, whose computers would awake him if they detected danger. They awakened him when Thor breached the hull of the ship, and the alien guardian and the thunder god began battling one another, not realizing each other's noble motives. As they fought, Thor was separated from his enchanted hammer Mjolnir, and the starship entered Earth's solar system. When it did so, Odin's spell, which caused Thor to revert to his mortal form of Dr. Donald Blake if he was out of contact with the hammer for sixty seconds or more, was activated (see *Thor*). Thor turned into Blake and the hammer, again according to Odin's spell, turned into a wooden cane. Beta Ray Bill seized the cane and, without realizing what would happen, struck it against a wall. He then found himself in possession of the powers of Thor, holding Mjolnir, and even garbed in a variation of Thor's costume. This was because the enchantments on the hammer were designed so as to bestow the power and form of Thor upon any bearer worthy of them. Odin had believed that only Thor himself was so worthy, but Beta Ray Bill, a great hero in his own right, was equally worthy.

Beta Ray Bill's ship landed on Earth, whereupon Odin cast a spell to transport Thor to Asgard. The spell took Beta Ray Bill there instead, leaving Blake on Earth. On learning his mistake, Odin transported Blake to Asgard as well, and endowed him

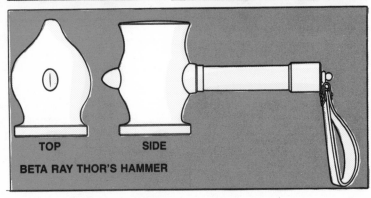

TOP   **SIDE**

BETA RAY THOR'S HAMMER

with the form of Thor again. Beta Ray Bill had assumed that Thor and the other Asgardians were in league with his demonic adversaries, but was convinced of his error. Nevertheless, he insisted on keeping Mjolnir, saying that he had won it fairly in combat, and that he needed it as a weapon to defend his race from the demons. Odin decreed that the matter be settled by a combat to the death between Thor and Beta Ray Bill, neither having the use of Mjolnir, and transported them to the land of Skartheim for the battle. Beta Ray Bill proved to be the victor in the ensuing battle, but he refused to kill Thor, whom he regarded as a noble adversary. Odin's motives in decreeing this combat are unclear, but he was apparently satisfied with the result, in that Beta Ray Bill proved his own nobility by sparing Thor's life, and Thor learned a lesson in humility in recognizing that he could be defeated in combat with an equal.

Beta Ray Bill had won the right to Thor's hammer, but he was torn between his need for such a powerful weapon to defend his people and his guilt over depriving Thor of the weapon he was meant to bear. Odin solved the problem by commissioning the creation of a new uru hammer from Eitri, the dwarf who had created Thor's hammer, and the other dwarves who worked at the forges of Nidavellir. Odin placed enchantments similar to those on Thor's hammer upon this new one, which he named Storm Breaker, and bestowed upon Beta Ray Bill. Odin then returned the original hammer, Mjolnir, to Thor. Thor, Beta Ray Bill, and the goddess Sif then left for outer space where together they battled and defeated the horde of demons pursuing Beta Ray Bill's people. Thor and Beta Ray Bill used their hammers to seal the portal from which the demons had emerged.

After Beta Ray Bill, Thor, and Sif returned to Asgard, Odin learned of Beta Ray Bill's regrets that he was trapped in a monstrous form, and transferred the enchantment that had allowed Thor to transform into mortal form and back from Mjolnir into Storm Breaker.

Now Beta Ray Bill could use the hammer to assume his original form. Accompanied by Sif, Beta Ray Bill left Asgard to return to his task of protecting his people. Odin summoned both Beta Ray Bill and Sif back to Asgard to join in the battle against Surtur's demons when the latter invaded Earth. Beta Ray Bill was made one of the commanders of the Asgardian legions during this campaign. At this time Beta Ray Bill remains on Earth, although he plans to leave eventually to help guide his people to a planet upon which they can settle.

Height: (in "Thor" form) 6' 7", (in original form) 6' 4"
Weight: (in "Thor" form) 480 lbs., (in original form) 230 lbs.
Eyes: (in "Thor" form) no visible pupils or irises
Hair: None
Strength level: In his original form, Beta Ray Bill was probably no stronger than the average male human of the same physical age, height, and build. In his bioengineered form, Beta Ray Bill was strong enough to present a threat to Thor in hand-to-hand combat, but the exact limits of Beta Ray Bill's strength were not established. In his "Thor" form, Beta Ray Bill possesses "Class 100" strength, and can lift (press) somewhere over 100 tons. His strength in this form is the equal of Thor's.
Known superhuman powers: In his "Thor" form, Beta Ray Bill possesses the same superhuman powers that Thor himself does. In addition to his superhuman strength, Beta Ray Bill is immune to all diseases, and resistant to conventional injury. Like Asgardians, Beta Ray Bill in his "Thor" form has flesh and bone that are about three times as dense as similar human tissue, contributing to his superhuman strength and weight. In his "Thor" form Beta Ray Bill also has an Asgardian metabolism which gives him far greater than human endurance at all physical activities.

The scientists who bioengineered Beta Ray Bill implanted sensors within his cyborg body that allow him to discover the location of his people's space fleet even

across vast interstellar distances.
Weapons: Beta Ray Bill carries an enchanted uru hammer called Storm Breaker which apparently possesses the same powers as Thor's uru hammer Mjolnir. The principal exception is that Odin removed the enchantment that allowed Thor to transform into mortal form from Mjolnir and transferred it into Storm Bringer. Hence, Beta Ray Bill can transform into his original non-cyborg form by stamping the hammer's head to the ground twice. The hammer then becomes a wooden cane. By stamping the cane on the ground twice, Beta Ray Bill can regain his superhumanly powerful "Thor" form, and the cane will change back into an uru hammer. It is not known whether Beta Ray Bill will revert to his original form if the hammer leaves his grasp for more than sixty Earth seconds.

Storm Breaker enables Beta Ray Bill to fly and to traverse dimensional barriers. It enables him to control the weather, and he can project energy bolts from the hammer. No unworthy living being can lift the hammer, and the hammer always returns to Beta Ray Bill's grasp after he hurls it. The hammer is two feet long and its handle is wrapped in leather which terminates in a thong; made of the mystical metal uru, the hammer is virtually indestructible.
Transportation: Beta Ray Bill, when choosing not to use his hammer to travel through space, uses an armed and armored spacecraft called Skuttlebutt. Skuttlebutt's computers give it high intelligence and a humanoid-like, apparently female personality, and Beta Ray Bill considers Skuttlebutt a partner and close friend. Skuttlebutt is heavily armored with highly destructive weaponry, can achieve faster-than-light speeds after shifting into hyperspace, and can repair itself after being damaged. Skuttlebutt's computers enable it to act independently when Beta Ray Bill is absent or otherwise engaged. ∎

SKUTTLEBUTT

BINARY

Real Name: Carol Susan Jane Danvers
Occupation: Former National Aeronautics and Space Administration security chief, former magazine editor, former freelance writer, former military intelligence agent
Legal status: Citizen of the United States with no criminal record
Identity: Secret
Former aliases: Ms. Marvel
Place of birth: Boston, Massachusetts
Marital status: Single
Known relatives: Joseph (father), Marie (mother), Steve (brother, deceased), Joseph, Jr. (brother)
Group affiliation: Former Avenger (as Ms. Marvel), companion to the X-Men (as Carol Danvers), member of the Starjammers (as Binary)
Base of operations: Outer space
First appearance: (as Carol Danvers) MARVEL SUPER HEROES #13, (as Ms. Marvel) MS. MARVEL #1, (as Binary) X-MEN #164
Origin: CAPTAIN MARVEL #18, (as Ms. Marvel) MS. MARVEL #1, 19, (as Binary) X-MEN #163, 164
History: Carol Danvers entered the Air Force at an early age and rapidly rose to become one of the leading agents in military intelligence, usually teamed with Michael Rossi, who became her lover. Upon leaving her work as a spy, she became security chief at Cape Canaveral for the National Aeronautics and Space Administration, where she met the Kree Captain Mar-Vell (see *Kree, Deceased: Captain Mar-Vell*). During a battle between Mar-Vell and his Kree foe Yon-Rogg at a hidden Kree base on Earth, Carol Danvers was accidentally irradiated by the unknown energies of the Psyche-Magnitron, a device built by the Kree. The radiation from this machine eventually augmented her entire genetic structure, giving her superhuman strength, the ability to fly and a clairvoyant "seventh sense." With these powers, she assumed the guise of Ms. Marvel and established herself as a champion of Earth. During this time she worked as a magazine editor and freelance writer in New York City. Later, in battle with the power-absorbing mutant named Rogue, Danvers lost virtually all of her Ms. Marvel abilities, leaving her with only her augmented genetic structure (see *Rogue*). Rogue also drained her of her memories, most of which, however, were restored by Professor Charles Xavier, although he could not restore to her the emotional bonds linked to those memories (see *Professor X*). Later still, Danvers was abducted by the alien Brood and subjected to an evolutionary ray which triggered the latent potential of her augmented genes (see *Alien Races: Brood*). Thus she became the cosmic-powered mutant named Binary. No longer feeling the strong emotional ties to people and places on Earth that she felt before falling victim to Rogue, Danvers decided to leave Earth and pursue adventure as a member of the spacefaring band known as the Starjammers (see *Starjammers*).
Height: 5′ 11″
Weight: 120 lbs
Eyes: Blue
Hair: Blonde
Special features: When Binary transforms into her energy-manipulating state, her skin turns red and her hair becomes a corona of cosmic flame.
Strength level: The energies that Binary

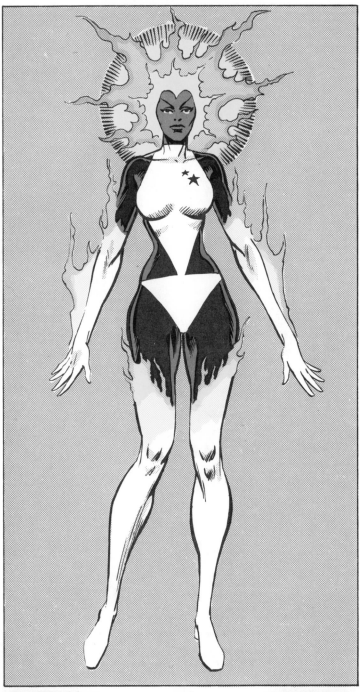

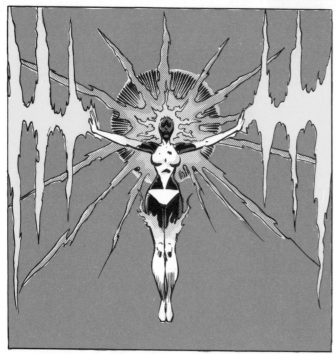

CAROL
DANVERS
AS
MS. MARVEL

taps give her Class 100 strength. She can lift (press) over 100 tons.

Known superhuman powers: Binary can tap the energy of a white hole, that region of space which is the exit-point of a point singularity's ultimate inward collapse out of this universe and into another. (A black hole is a slightly more massive star than Earth's sun that has aged to the point that its fusion reaction has burned most of its hydrogen fuel and can no longer balance the weight of its outer layers with stellar flame. When the imbalance reaches a critical point, the outer layers collapse inward, producing depending on the original mass of star, a neutron star, black hole, or point singularity. A point singularity is such an extreme distortion of the space/time fabric of our universe, that it extends into another universe. Under some circumstances, the extension is able to loop back into our space/time at some distance. This re-entrance into our universe is a white hole.) This inter-dimensional breach is the "weak" point at which Binary is able to divert small portions of cosmic energies into mentally-activated disturbances of the space/time continuum around her. She is able to shape these disturbances into various lenses that focus or diffuse these relatively vast energies for a number of star-like effects. Binary is able to radiate heat, light, and the rest of the electro-magnetic spectrum as well as gravity. Presumably the total amount of energy she can manifest is related to the cross-section, or "window" she allows to open between universes. For example, an 8-inch diameter "hole" in the surface of a point singularity would let out a torrent of various energies. Binary is apparently able to apply a mental filter to these energies, allowing only the energies she chooses to pass through.

By directing stellar energy uni-directionally, she has a means of propulsion enabling her to fly at near-light speeds. Whether she can travel unaided through inter-universe regions is not yet known. She also has a sensitivity to the flux of ambient cosmic energies, giving her certain heightened perceptions.

Binary has a steady flux of cold "pseudo flames" corruscating in small spheres around her head and hands that represent the greatest regions of her concentration.

Limitations: The limitations of Binary's physical form are not yet known. There is, however, a limit to how long she is able to remain in her Binary state. After a massive expenditure of the gamut of stellar energies, she reverts to human form, and must rest for an undisclosed length of time. Her precise limitations (how long she can remain as Binary with a moderate expenditure of energy, etc.) are not yet known. ∎

BLACK BOLT

Real Name: Blackagar Boltagon
Occupation: Monarch of the Inhumans
Legal status: Citizen of Attilan
Identity: The existence of the Inhumans is not believed by the general public of Earth.
Place of birth: Island of Attilan, Atlantic Ocean
Marital status: Married
Known relatives: Medusa (wife), Agon (father, deceased), Rynda (mother, deceased), Maximus (brother), Gorgon, Karnak, Triton (cousins)
Group affiliation: Royal Family of the Inhumans
Base of operations: Attilan, Blue Area, Earth's moon
First appearance: FANTASTIC FOUR #45
Origin: THOR #148, 149 and AVENGERS #95

History: Black Bolt was born to two of Attilan's top geneticists, Agon, head of the ruling Council of Genetics, and Rynda, director of the Prenatal Care Center (see *Attilan*). Subjected to the mutagenic Terrigen Mist while still an embryo, Bolt was born with strange powers surpassing even the Inhumans' norm (see *Inhumans*). As an infant, he demonstrated certain energy-manipulative abilities which he could not yet control, particularly that of producing quasi-sonic energy of great destructive potential. To protect the community, he was placed inside a sound-proofed chamber and given an energy-harnessing suit. There he was schooled in the art of controlling his powers until the age of nineteen, when he was permitted to enter society.

A month after being awarded his freedom, Black Bolt discovered his younger brother Maximus in the process of making a treacherous pact with emissaries of the alien Kree (see *Kree, Maximus*). Attempting to stop the Kree ship before it escaped, Bolt used the forbidden power of his quasi-sonic voice to knock the ship out of the sky. When the ship crashed to Earth, it landed on the parliament building, killing several key members of the Council of Genetics, including his parents, Agon and Rynda. The reverberations of his brother's shout affected Maximus's sanity and suppressed his nascent mental powers. Despite his guilt and silent protests, Black Bolt was obligated to accept the mantle of leadership of the Inhumans at the age of twenty.

Black Bolt's first crisis in leadership came when his cousin Triton was briefly held captive by humans. Learning of Triton's encounter upon his escape, Black Bolt decided that the Inhumans' island of Attilan was in imminent danger of discovery by humanity. Black Bolt scouted out possible sites to which to move, and settled upon the remote Himalayan mountains. After the great migration, Black Bolt faced his second great crisis when his now mad brother Maximus unleashed the Trikon, three of the Inhumans' worker drones who were transformed into energy-beings. The Trikon enabled Maximus to wrest the rule of the Inhumans from his brother and send Black Bolt and the other members of the Royal Family into exile. For the next few years, Black Bolt and his kinsmen wandered Asia, Europe, and finally America, in search of Medusa, his betrothed mate, who had been separated from the others during the battle with the Trikon (see *Medusa*). Eventually Black Bolt was reunited with Medusa and the Royal Family returned to Attilan and resumed the crown.

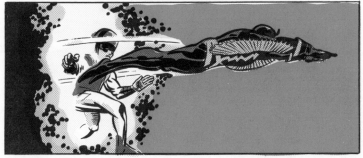

Black Bolt has led the Inhumans through some of the most turbulent times in their history, including several more attempts by Maximus to usurp the throne, revolts by the worker class, attacks by human renegades, the kidnapping of Medusa, the destruction and rebuilding of Attilan, the revelation of the Inhumans' existence to humanity, and finally the second relocation of Attilan. Recently, following the traditionally lengthy period of betrothal, Black Bolt and Medusa were wed.

Height: 6′ 2″
Weight: 210 lbs
Eyes: Blue
Hair: Black
Strength level: Black Bolt possesses superhuman strength, enabling him to lift (press) approximately 1 ton. He is stronger than the average Inhuman due to the particular way in which the mutagenic Terrigen Mist affected his genetic and physical structure. By augmenting his body with his electron power (see below), Black Bolt becomes capable of lifting approximately 60 tons under optimal conditions.
Known superhuman powers: Black Bolt possesses various superhuman powers stemming from his ability to harness free-floating electrons. The speech center of Black Bolt's brain contains an organic mechanism able to generate an as yet unknown type of particle which interacts with ambient electrons to create certain phenomena determined by mental control.

The most devastating of the effects is Black Bolt's quasi-sonic scream. Because his electron-harnessing ability is linked to the speech center of his brain, any attempt to use his vocal cords — from the merest whisper to a full scream — triggers an uncontrollable disturbance of the particle / electron interaction field. This results in a shock wave equivalent, at maximum force, to that caused by the detonation of a nuclear weapon. A whisper has generated sufficient force to rock a battleship, while a scream can reduce a mountain to rubble.

The fork-shaped antenna that Black Bolt has worn upon his brow since childhood enables him to channel his power in more directed, less destructive ways. The antenna monitors his brain's speech center activity and allows him to direct limited quantities of the unknown particle to create a number of controlled phenomena. He can channel this energy inwardly to enhance his own body's speed and strength (see above). Black Bolt is capable of channeling all available energy into one arm for one powerful punch called his Master Blow. This exertion taxes his body's ability to employ the particle / electron energy to its limit and renders him extremely vulnerable following its use.

Black Bolt is also able to direct the unknown particle outwards in ways other than by means of his vocal cords. He can rapidly route particle / electron energy through his arms to create relatively small concussive blasts. He can form a field of highly-active electrons around himself with the wave of a hand, said field being capable of deflecting projectiles up to the mass of an MX missile traveling at its maximum speed. He can create particle / electron interaction fields solid enough to be traversed upon, though this phenomenon is a particularly difficult and exhausting one. He can use these electron fields as extrasensory probes which are highly sensitive to other electromagnetic energy phenomena. He can even manipulate his electron field to jam certain electrical mechanisms.

Black Bolt can also harness the unknown particles his brain generates to interact with electrons to create anti-gravitons that enable him to defy gravity. By emitting a jet of rapidly moving particle / electron interaction by-products while enveloped by anti-gravitons, Black Bolt can fly up to 500 miles per hour for a period of 6 hours before his brain begins to tire appreciably from the effort. The anti-graviton field also serves to protect Black Bolt from the detrimental effects of rapid movement through the atmosphere.

Abilities: Like all Inhumans, Black Bolt is physically superior to normal human beings due to generations of eugenics. Attributes in which Inhumans excel over humans include reaction time, stamina, strength, resistance to injury, and speed. Humans are superior to Inhumans, however, in immunity to disease. ∎

BLACK CAT

Real Name: Felicia Hardy
Occupation: Adventurer, former burglar
Legal status: Citizen of the United States with a criminal record, granted legal amnesty
Identity: Known to legal authorities
Former aliases: Felicity Harmon
Place of birth: Queens, New York
Marital status: Single
Known relatives: Walter (father, deceased), Lydia (mother)
Group affiliation: Former partner of Spider-Man
Base of operations: New York City
First appearance: AMAZING SPIDER-MAN #194

History: Learning that her father had been an infamous cat burglar, Felicia Hardy decided to follow in his footsteps. She undertook a rigorous physical training program that increased her strength, endurance, and agility, learned such criminal skills as lockpicking and safecracking, and gained a knowledge of martial arts such as karate. Donning a costume to conceal her identity, she set out to seek her fortune as the Black Cat.

In keeping with her chosen *nom du crime*, the Black Cat decided to create the impression in her adversaries' minds that she could give them "bad luck" through some power of her own. Hence, before committing a crime in a certain area, she would carefully prepare objects in the area so that apparent "accidents" would befall any of her pursuers later on. For example, she would rig brick walls so that they would collapse, prepare ropes so that they would break, and rig fire escapes so that they would fall. Through tricks such as these, she managed to convince her principal opponent, Spider-Man, that she did indeed have the power to affect probability.

Upon finally being captured, the Black Cat feigned insanity, and some time later escaped imprisonment. She had become greatly attracted to Spider-Man, and joined him in battling criminals, thereby winning amnesty from the New York City legal authorities for her own past crimes. She sought to become the regular crimefighting partner of Spider-Man, who had by now reciprocated her love for him, going so far even as to reveal his secret identity to her. However, she revealed to him that she had no superhuman powers, and, after she was severely injured in one of his clashes with Doctor Octopus, Spider-Man considered it to be too dangerous for her to join him in fighting his superhuman adversaries.

Distraught, the Black Cat determined to gain superhuman powers by some means. Meanwhile, the Kingpin, the most powerful organized crime leader on the East Coast, sought vengeance on the Black Cat (see *Kingpin*). She had stolen a detonator for a nuclear device from him that had later fallen into the hands of Doctor Octopus. Feeling helpless to stop Octopus, the Kingpin vowed to punish the Black Cat for her theft of the detonator. Concealing his identity from her, the Kingpin offered to grant the Black Cat superhuman powers in exchange for her services. The Black Cat suspected that her unknown benefactor was a criminal, but accepted the offer, telling herself that she would turn him over to the law after fulfilling her debt to him.

The scientists in the employ of her benefactor discovered that the Black Cat had

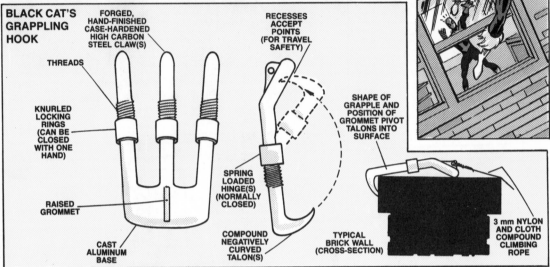

BLACK CAT'S GRAPPLING HOOK

FORGED, HAND-FINISHED CASE-HARDENED HIGH CARBON STEEL CLAW(S)

RECESSES ACCEPT POINTS (FOR TRAVEL SAFETY)

THREADS

KNURLED LOCKING RINGS (CAN BE CLOSED WITH ONE HAND)

RAISED GROMMET

CAST ALUMINUM BASE

SPRING LOADED HINGE(S) (NORMALLY CLOSED)

COMPOUND NEGATIVELY CURVED TALON(S)

SHAPE OF GRAPPLE AND POSITION OF GROMMET PIVOT TALONS INTO SURFACE

TYPICAL BRICK WALL (CROSS-SECTION)

3 mm NYLON AND CLOTH COMPOUND CLIMBING ROPE

latent abilities within her genes, and were able to activate those powers, using information from the notes of the late Dr. Farley Stillwell, who had given the Fly and the Scorpion their superhuman abilities. She now had the power to cause her adversaries "bad luck" that she had only pretended to possess before. Moreover, the Black Cat's agility and speed had also been enhanced. Only after she received these powers did the Black Cat learn that her benefactor was the Kingpin.

At first the Black Cat concealed the origin of her new powers from Spider-Man, but he eventually learned that the Kingpin was responsible for them. The Black Cat then confronted the Kingpin, who informed her that he had given her her powers in order to get revenge both on her and on Spider-Man. The Kingpin revealed to her that her powers would, in time, bring "bad luck" to anyone who was regularly in her presence. Indeed, Spider-Man had been uncharacteristically clumsy recently when near the Cat. The Kingpin said that the Cat's powers would increasingly affect Spider-Man the more time she stayed with him, and implied that the end result would be Spider-Man's death.

The Kingpin pledged to Spider-Man never again to force the Black Cat to do his bidding. The Black Cat decided that, to save Spider-Man's life, she would end her affair and partnership with him, but before she could tell him this, he put an end to them himself due to his dissatisfaction with her amorality and her disdain for his life apart from being Spider-Man.

The exact whereabouts and present ac-tivities of the Black Cat are unknown.
Height: 5′ 10″
Weight: 120 lbs.
Eyes: Green
Hair: Platinum blonde
Strength level: The Black Cat possesses the normal human strength of a woman of her age, height, and build who engages in intensive regular exercise.
Known superhuman powers: The Black Cat has certain superhuman powers which are the result of latent mutations which were activated by radiation and chemical injections.

Her principal power enables her subliminally and psionically to affect probability fields, causing improbable (but not impossible) things to occur within her line of sight. This phenomenon can cause walls and ceilings to collapse, ropes to break, machinery to explode, guns to backfire, and people to drop their weapons, or collide with each other. This talent would seem to be a natural unconsciously controlled ability to manipulate probabilities in extremely localized areas, which is triggered when she is in a stressful situation (such as fighting or escaping). Although the Black Cat cannot consciously control her ability, she can activate it by putting herself in a position in which she could be harmed. The Black Cat's powers ordinarily only cause such improbable events to befall people or objects which intend to cause her harm. However, over a period of time, her power will increasingly come to affect anyone who spends a great deal of time near her, re-gardless of that person's intentions towards her. Hence, that person will also fall victim

to those distortions of probability fields.

The Black Cat's power always adversely affects its targets; it never affects probability so as to bring them "good luck."
Abilities: The Black Cat has trained herself to be an Olympic level athlete with superb gymnastic skills. She is extremely agile, able to execute complicated flips, springs, and rolls with minimal effort. She is nimble-footed and possesses excellent reflexes. She moves with the grace and stealth of her namesake. She has been known to do standing high jumps of almost six feet and standing broad jumps of nearly ten feet. The Black Cat has a black belt in karate and judo, making her proficient in unarmed combat.
Weapons: The Black Cat sometimes car-ries a length of cable which can be strung between buildings and walked on like a tightrope, or used simply to swing on. The cable is attached to a grappling hook (see diagram above). She once used a cable which terminated in a super-adhesive ball, but has since abandoned the device for reasons undisclosed. ∎

BLACK CROW

Real name: Jesse Black Crow
Occupation: Former construction worker on workmen's compensation, mystic
Legal status: Citizen of the United States with no criminal record
Identity: Secret
Place of birth: Navajo Indian Reservation, New Mexico
Marital status: Single
Known relatives: None
Group affiliation: None
Base of operations: Queens, New York
First appearance and origin: CAPTAIN AMERICA #292
History: Jesse Black Crow is a Navajo Indian who left the reservation at the age of 18 to become a construction worker on skyscrapers in the New York area. One day some scaffolding gave way and he plunged twenty stories. Miraculously, he survived the fall, but became paralyzed from the waist down. While lying comatose in the hospital, he had a vision of the Indians' plight in America, and was transformed into a mystic warrior and protector of the Indians' dream by a "spirit of the Earth" sacred to his ancestors. Now whenever this Earth spirit has a mission for him, it causes him to lose consciousness and bodily transform into his totem, a black crow, or the mystical human warrior Black Crow. Black Crow's first mission for the Earth spirit was to challenge Captain America to a trial by combat (see *Captain America*). Black Crow told him that as a symbol of modern America, Captain America must die to balance the cosmic scales and appease his ancestral spirits. After a battle that culminated in a plunge off the Brooklyn Bridge, Captain America made a gesture of surrender to the Earth spirit, thereby ending the conflict and creating a spiritual bond between the two American champions. Weeks later, when Captain America was dying of a poison injected in him by the Red Skull (see *Deceased: Red Skull*), the Black Crow materialized minutes before he succumbed and performed a ritual which enhanced the Captain's will to live. The poison burned out of his system, Captain America awoke, with only the vaguest recollection of the Black Crow's assistance. The Black Crow has recently undertaken a mission to save Daredevil.

Height: 6′ 1″ **Eyes:** Brown
Weight: 190 lbs. **Hair:** Black
Strength level: As his crippled normal self, Jesse Black Crow's strength is below that of a man of his age, height, and build. In his mystic warrior form, Black Crow has superhuman strength, the precise extent of which is unknown.
Known superhuman powers: The Black Crow can magically transform himself into a normal-sized black crow or into a bolt of lightning. In both forms, he maintains his human intelligence. It is not known how long he can maintain these altered forms. Apparently he uses the lightning form for traveling long distances, and the crow form for reconnaissance.

He can also summon fog, but it is not known how much he can summon at once. He was able to perceive certain of Captain America's thoughts, but this may be due to the special spiritual bond between them and may not indicate general telepathic ability. The Black Crow was able to mesmerize Nomad into paralysis, but this too may not be an ability that extends over everyone (see *Nomad*).

In his warrior form, the Black Crow is superhumanly agile and a gifted unarmed combatant.

Weapons: The Black Crow carries a knife and a pouch containing various mystic herbs. He sometimes carries a longbow or a spear. ∎

BLACK KING

Real name: Sebastian Shaw

Occupation: Chief executive officer and principal shareholder in Shaw Industries, Inc.

Identity: Publicly known; however, the general public is unaware of Shaw's criminal activities

Legal status: Citizen of the United States with no criminal record

Former aliases: None

Place of birth: Pittsburgh, Pennsylvania

Marital status: Single

Known relatives: None

Group affiliation: Leader and Black King of the Hellfire Club and of its secret Inner Circle

Base of operation: Worldwide; the Inner Circle is based at the Hellfire Club mansion in Manhattan

First appearance: (voice and shadowed figure only) X-MEN #129, (fully seen) X-MEN #130

History: Sebastian Shaw was born into an impoverished family, but with his superb business skills, he became a millionaire by the age of 20. He eventually became the head of Shaw Industries, a multinational corporation which is heavily involved with United States defense contracts and the production of munitions. Shaw was invited to join the Hellfire Club, the leading organization for the elite of society (see *Hellfire Club*). Soon after joining, Shaw learned of the Club's secret Council of the Chosen, a group of members who, unknown to the others, conspired to achieve world domination through economic and political means. Through the force of his personality, Shaw became one of the leaders of the Council, rising to the rank of Black Bishop. (Members of the Inner Circle are given titles corresponding to the names of chess pieces.) The leader of the Council, a White King, had the Council give considerable financial backing to Dr. Steven Lang's attempt to create new mutant-hunting Sentinels (see *Sentinels*). Upon the collapse of Lang's enterprise, Shaw seized the opportunity to turn the White King out of office. Shaw then became Black King, leader of the Council of the Chosen (which he renamed the Inner Circle) and master of the entire Hellfire Club. As leader of the Inner Circle, Shaw works closely with another leading member of the Circle, Emma Frost, its White Queen (see *White Queen*), who like Shaw is a superhumanly powerful mutant. Recently Shaw survived an attempted challenge to his leadership of the Circle by its renegade White Bishop, Donald Pierce. Shaw is also cooperating with the United States government's covert Project: Wideawake, which is an attempt to deal with what is perceived as the possible menace presented by mutants. Shaw Industries is secretly manufacturing Sentinels for use by the Project. The government remains unaware of Shaw's criminal activities and of the fact that he himself is a superhumanly powerful mutant.

Height: 6′ 2″

Weight: 210 lbs.

Eyes: Black

Hair: Gray

Strength level: Without having absorbed additional energy, Sebastian Shaw possesses the normal human strength of a man of his age, height, and build who engages in intensive regular exercise. However, Shaw can gain superhuman levels of strength by absorbing kinetic energy, and usually takes care to absorb enough in order to keep his strength at a superhuman level throughout his waking hours: for example, upon waking he will punch walls repeatedly in order to build up his reserves of absorbed energy. There is a limit to the amount of physical strength he can achieve, but it as yet remains unknown.

Known superhuman powers: Sebastian Shaw is a mutant with the superhuman ability to absorb kinetic energy and to use it in an unknown manner to enhance his own physical strength, speed, and stamina. Shaw must be in contact with the energy in order to absorb it. If Shaw strikes a blow to someone or something, or is himself struck, he will absorb the energy of that blow. He has also been observed to be able to absorb electrical energy directed at him. Shaw's power to absorb and convert kinetic energy renders him invulnerable to various forms of attack. It is not known how long Shaw can retain the energy he absorbs. There is an upper limit to the amount of energy that Shaw can absorb and convert: once he was "overloaded" by an electrical energy discharge from the X-Man named Storm, and fell into a temporary coma. However, the exact extent of this limit remains unknown. ∎

BLACK KNIGHT

Real name: Dane Whitman
Occupation: Former scientist, former crusader, now crimefighter
Legal status: Citizen of the United States with no criminal record
Identity: Secret
Place of birth: Gloucester, Massachussetts
Marital status: Single
Known relatives: Nathan Garrett (alias the Black Knight, uncle, deceased), Sir Percy of Scandia (alias the Black Knight), Lady Rosamund, Eobar Garrington (ancestors, deceased)
Group affiliation: Current member of the East Coast Avengers
Base of operations: New York City
First appearance and origin: AVENGERS #47-48

History: The original Black Knight was Sir Percy of Scandia, a member of the Knights of the Round Table in King Arthur's Sixth Century Camelot. One of Arthur's staunchest supporters, Sir Percy adopted the guise of the Black Knight in order to serve his king in a dual capacity: as an unassuming man of the royal court and as a mysterious avenging champion. King Arthur's court magician Merlin gave the Knight the Ebony Sword, an enchanted blade constructed from a meteorite (see *Merlin*). The Black Knight's greatest foe was Mordred, "nephew" of King Arthur, and for years Percy tried to gather evidence of Mordred's treachery to no avail. Soon after the fall of Camelot, the wounded Mordred dispatched his men to kill the Black Knight, using a dagger constructed of the same meteoric ore as the Knight's Ebony Blade. The ambush succeeded, and Sir Percy was slain. Merlin, however, cast a spell upon Percy's spirit, enabling it to return to the Earthly plane when the spirit of Mordred threatened. Sir Percy's body was buried beneath his castle, and his sword interred with it (see *Deceased: Black Knight I*).

There is no record of any of Sir Percy's descendants discovering the Ebony Sword of following in his footsteps as the Black Knight until the Twelfth Century when Eobar Garrington assumed the guise of the Knight in order to fight in the Crusades. Curiously, the spirit of a Twentieth Century descendant of Garrington's, Dane Whitman, co-occupied Garrington's body during the last five years of the Crusades (as described below). Whitman possessed the body up until the time of its death. The Twelfth Century Black Knight was an ally of King Richard the Lion-Hearted.

There is no record of the activities of any of Garrington's descendants until the mid-Twentieth Century. Then British scientist Nathan Garrett discovered the tomb of Sir Percy beneath the castle he had inherited (now called Garrett Castle). Garrett saw the Ebony Blade in a scabbard near the tomb, but being unworthy to wield it, could not draw the sword. Garrett was inspired to become the new Black Knight, however, and he used his scientific genius to mutate a winged horse and to create a lance capable of discharging concussive blasts as well as other advanced weaponry (see *Appendix: Black Knight II*). Garrett used the identity of the Black Knight to commit crimes in order to finance his further scientific research. He was opposed on separate occasions by Giant-Man and Iron Man, and as a member of Baron Heinrich Zemo's original Masters of Evil, he battled the Avengers. While in

aerial combat with Iron Man, Garrett was unseated from his winged steed and was mortally wounded in the fall. He managed to contact his only living relative, his sister's son, Dane Whitman, also a scientist. On his deathbed, Garrett told Whitman he regretted the wrongs he had committed and wished for his nephew to put his discoveries to good use. Whitman decided to improve upon his uncle's work and assume the identity of the Black Knight. Using his uncle's notes, Whitman mutated a winged steed to replace his uncle's horse, who had flown away and, having been further mutated, is now in the possession of the Dreadknight (see *Dreadknight*).

Whitman first went into action as the Black Knight in order to warn the Avengers that the mutant Magneto had taken two of their members, Quicksilver and the Scarlet Witch, captive. He was mistaken for his criminal uncle, however, and after a brief skirmish parted with the Avengers on bad terms. He next appeared to warn the Avengers about a new grouping of the Masters of Evil which he had infiltrated, and succeeded in rescuing them from their clutches. Learning that he had inherited Garrett Castle, Whitman traveled to England with the intent to sell the property. However, while taking a tour of the place, Whitman stumbled upon the tomb of Sir Percy and was contacted by the ghost of his ancestor. Sir Percy explained to him the origins of his noble lineage and told him of the Ebony Sword. When Whitman tried to draw it from its scabbard, he succeeded where his uncle had failed. After successfully battling the demonic guardian of the sword, Whitman left the castle with the enchanted blade and soon found himself drawn into battle with Le Sabre, a modern day agent of Mordred. Defeating Le Sabre, the Knight resolved not to sell his castle.

Soon afterward, Whitman made the acquaintance of the occult master Dr. Strange through his neighbor, Victoria Bentley, an old friend of Strange's (see *Doctor Strange*). The Black Knight assisted Dr. Strange in his battle with the extradimensional Tiboro and the two of them joined forces with the Avengers to battle Surtur and Ymir. A short time later, the Knight helped the Avengers defeat the time master Kang and was elected to membership. He assumed reserve status, however, so he could return to his castle in England to live. He helped the Avengers battle Ares, the Olympian god of war, but later fell prey to the charms of the Asgardian Enchantress, who sought to employ him as her agent against her rival, the sorceress Casiolena (see *Enchantress*). To "reward" him for his services, the Enchantress turned the Black Knight's body to stone, and not even Dr. Strange could reverse the enchantment. (The Black Knight's winged steed Aragorn was taken into the care of the Valkyrie (see *Aragorn*).

Acquiring the Evil Eye, a mystical power object of Avalon, the realm of the Celtic gods (see *Prester John*), Dr. Strange attempted to restore the Black Knight's humanity. Instead, Strange and his fellow Defenders were transported through time to the Twelfth Century where they discovered Dane Whitman in the body of his Twelfth Century ancestor, battling the Arabs in the Crusades. The spirit of Mordred had assumed a human host, and allied himself with Prince John, King Richard's ambitious brother, and Chandu, an Arabian wizard. Whitman hoped to lend his might to that of

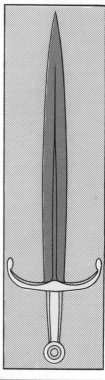

BLACK KNIGHT
WITH ARAGORN

BLACK KNIGHT
WITH VALINOR

his ancestor's and combat the evil wrought by Mordred. When the Defenders learned of Whitman's wishes, they left for their own time.

For about five years (in the Twelfth Century, but for a shorter period in the Twentieth), Dane Whitman lived in his ancestor's body in the Twelfth Century while his real body remained a stone statue in the Twentieth Century. In accounts not yet disclosed, the Black Knight defeated Mordred and his allies, and following the Crusades, met Amergin, High Druid of Avalon. Avalon was under attack by the Fomor, the ancestral enemies of the gods (see *Appendix: Fomor*), and the Black Knight offered his aid to England's ancient deities. The forces of the Fomor were too great, however, and Amergin contacted his Twentieth Century descendant, Dr. Anthony Druid, for assistance (see *Doctor Druid*). Druid dispatched the Avengers back through time to Avalon. With the Avengers' aid, the Black Knight succeeded in closing off the portal between Avalon and Earth using the Evil Eye. The process, however, destroyed the body of his Twelfth Century ancestor, Eobar Garrington. Through Amergin's magic, Dane Whitman was restored to his rightful body in the Twentieth Century, the stone having been transformed back to flesh. The Knight's Ebony Sword and his new winged steed given him by Amergin, were sent to the future with him.

Readjusting to Twentieth Century life was difficult for Whitman. After a brief adventure in which he found the amnesiac Captain Britain (see *Captain Britain*), he settled in at Garrett Castle, only to learn that its caretaker Victoria Bentley had purchased it when it was about to be seized by the

British government for non-payment of property tax. When Whitman started acting moodily, Bentley summoned Dr. Strange. Strange learned that the Ebony Sword was cursed by the blood of the victims of its original wielder, Sir Percy, and that it was this blood-curse that compelled Whitman to remain in the Twelfth Century where it could be used for more bloodshed. After convincing the Knight of the sword's malevolence, Strange instructed him to purge the Ebony Blade of its curse by plunging it into the Brazier of Truth, the mystic receptacle which was the spirit of Sir Percy's touchstone with the Earthly plane. Whitman shattered the Brazier, purging the sword of its curse, and freeing Sir Percy's spirit from all ties with the Earthly plane. The Black Knight returned to America with Dr. Strange and renewed his active membership in the Avengers.

Height: 6'
Weight: 190 lbs.
Eyes: Brown
Hair: Brown
Strength level: The Black Knight possesses the normal human strength of a man of his age, height, and weight, who engages in intensive regular exercise.
Known superhuman powers: None
Abilities: The Black Knight is an expert swordsman, horseman, and combatant. He also has considerable knowledge of advanced technology and of genetic manipulation thanks to his studies of his uncle's journals and equipment.
Weapons: The Ebony Sword, forged from a meteorite by Merlin, possesses a number of properties, some innate to the metal, and some magical enchantments. The sword is extraordinarily hard and invulnerable to all

harm. Weighing fifty pounds, the sword is capable of cleaving through any substance up to foot-thick steel. Its mystical properties include an immunity to magic. It can deflect mystical energy and shatter mystical barriers and shields. Merlin created a magical bond between the sword and its prime wielder (the Black Knight and his descendants) enabling that wielder, through arcane ritual, to magically transport himself across space and time if he should become separated from the sword.

The Ebony Sword has been purged of the blood-curse it had acquired through the deaths it had caused. Provided the Black Knight does not kill anyone with it, the sword shall remain free of the curse.

Transportation: The Black Knight has ridden two winged steeds in his career so far. The first was Aragorn, on whom Whitman had used his uncle's technique for mutating animals, to give it bird-like wings enabling it to fly. Aragorn was entrusted to the care of the Valkyrie, in whose custody it remains today. The Black Knight's second winged steed was Valinor, who possessed bat-like wings. Valinor was a gift of Amergin, High Druid of Avalon. Taking ill not long after it was transported to Twentieth Century England due to its lack of affinity for the Earth dimension, Valinor was cured by Dr. Strange's magic at the expense of its wings. The Black Knight currently employs one of the "Atomic Steeds" built and employed by the Knights of Wundagore (see *Knights of Wundagore*). ■

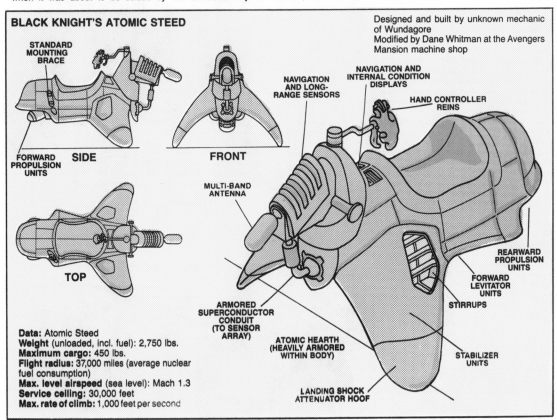

BLACK KNIGHT'S ATOMIC STEED

Designed and built by unknown mechanic of Wundagore
Modified by Dane Whitman at the Avengers Mansion machine shop

STANDARD MOUNTING BRACE

SIDE

FORWARD PROPULSION UNITS

FRONT

TOP

MULTI-BAND ANTENNA

NAVIGATION AND LONG-RANGE SENSORS

NAVIGATION AND INTERNAL CONDITION DISPLAYS

HAND CONTROLLER REINS

REARWARD PROPULSION UNITS

FORWARD LEVITATOR UNITS

STIRRUPS

ARMORED SUPERCONDUCTOR CONDUIT (TO SENSOR ARRAY)

ATOMIC HEARTH (HEAVILY ARMORED WITHIN BODY)

STABILIZER UNITS

LANDING SHOCK ATTENUATOR HOOF

Data: Atomic Steed
Weight (unloaded, incl. fuel): 2,750 lbs.
Maximum cargo: 450 lbs.
Flight radius: 37,000 miles (average nuclear fuel consumption)
Max. level airspeed (sea level): Mach 1.3
Service ceiling: 30,000 feet
Max. rate of climb: 1,000 feet per second

BLACKLASH

Real name: Mark Scarlotti
Occupation: Professional criminal, former weapons designer and special agent for the Maggia
Legal status: Citizen of the United States with a criminal record
Identity: Publicly known
Former aliases: Mark Scott
Place of birth: Cleveland, Ohio
Marital status: Single
Known relatives: Anthony (father), Barbara (mother)
Group affiliation: Former agent of the Maggia, former partner of the Melter, Man-Bull, and the Wraith, associate of Justin Hammer
Base of operations: Mobile
First appearance: (as Whiplash) TALES OF SUSPENSE #97, (as Blacklash) IRON MAN #146
History: Mark Scarlotti was contacted by the Maggia crime syndicate while working for a degree in Engineering at Rennselaer Poly-Tech (see *Maggia*). Upon graduation, he went to work for the Maggia as a weapons designer. With Maggia funds, he developed several technological weapons, the greatest among which was a steel-fiber whip capable of penetrating virtually any substance short of Adamantium. A natural athlete, Scarlotti practiced with the whip until he became an expert at it. Then, craving more excitement and money than weapons design afforded, Scarlotti asked to use his whip as a special costumed agent. He dubbed himself Whiplash and served the Maggia well, his reputation established early on by battling Iron Man to a stalemate (see *Iron Man*). Eventually, Scarlotti was assigned to go undercover for the Maggia, and under the name Mark Scott, he infiltrated Stark International's Cincinnati plant and became its head of research. There, he again encountered Iron Man and escaped from the battle unscathed.

Quitting the undercover assignment without his superiors' permission, Whiplash joined forces with the Melter and the Man-Bull to vie for the Golden Globe of Power offered by the mysterious extradimensional being, the Black Lama (see *Appendix: Black Lama*). It was then that Whiplash was decisively defeated by Iron Man for the first time, he was taken to jail, and his identity was learned by the authorities. The Maggia paid his bail and took him on once again as a contract agent. On assignment, Whiplash encountered the Wraith, whose mental powers drove Whiplash to the brink of insanity (see *Appendix: Wraith*).

Upon recovery, he was sent to Ryker's Island Prison to serve time for his various crimes. He was freed by criminal financier Justin Hammer, who was gathing a small army of costumed criminal to finance their operations in exchange for a share of the profits (see *Hammer, Justin*). Hammer provided Scarlotti with the funds and facilities to totally revamp and update his arsenal. Scarlotti renamed himself Blacklash, and went back to the Maggia as a freelance mercenary to look for an assignment. The Maggia contracted Blacklash for a job, but despite his new arsenal, Blacklash was soundly defeated by Iron Man before he could complete it. Demoralized by his recent string of defeats, troubled by family problems stemming from the public revelation of his criminal activities, and shunned by the Maggia, Blacklash has been trying to make ends

meet by taking any mercenary work that comes his way.

Height: 6′ 1″   **Eyes:** Blue
Weight: 215 lbs.   **Hair:** Blond
Strength level: Blacklash possesses the normal human strength of a man of his age, height, and build, who engages in moderate regular exercise.
Known superhuman powers: None
Abilities: Blacklash is an expert at using the whip as an offensive weapon. He is also skilled with the nunchaku, and has a fair knowledge of hand-to-hand combat.
Weapons: Blacklash wields a number of weapons, chief among which are his two cybernetically controlled whips, composed of woven boron-filament-impregnated sapphire strands plus steel braid. These whips can be snapped by a person with normal human strength with the tips reaching twice the speed of sound, whereas a normal leather whip barely reaches the speed of sound. It can be spun so fast that it deflects bullets. The tip is capable of piercing 3-inch steel.

Besides its use as a simple whip, the weapon can retract partially into its handle and be converted into a nunchaku or be extended to its full length and stiffened to become a pole for vaulting. The whip is detachable from its handle and contains a remote-controlled concussion charge. The entire whip and handle can be stored in a special sheath in Blacklash's gauntlets.

Blacklash carries a pouch with other special weaponry including a bola with discs that generate an artificial gravity field. He also wields a "necro-lash" through which he can channel all the electrical energy his gauntlets can generate.

Blacklash wears a bodysuit woven out of steel mesh and his cloak is capable of stopping medium caliber bullets. ■

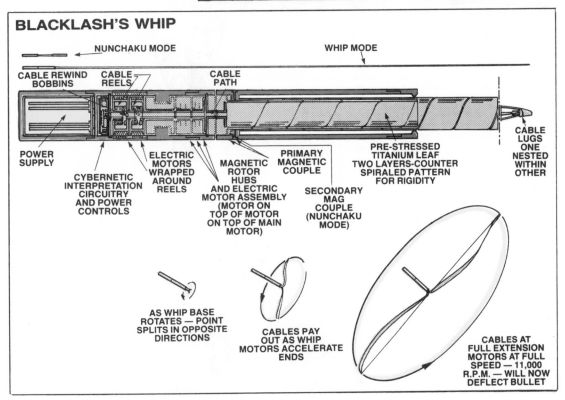

BLACKLASH'S WHIP

NUNCHAKU MODE   WHIP MODE

CABLE REWIND BOBBINS

CABLE REELS

CABLE PATH

POWER SUPPLY

CYBERNETIC INTERPRETATION CIRCUITRY AND POWER CONTROLS

ELECTRIC MOTORS WRAPPED AROUND REELS

MAGNETIC ROTOR HUBS AND ELECTRIC MOTOR ASSEMBLY (MOTOR ON TOP OF MOTOR ON TOP OF MAIN MOTOR)

PRIMARY MAGNETIC COUPLE

SECONDARY MAG COUPLE (NUNCHAKU MODE)

PRE-STRESSED TITANIUM LEAF TWO LAYERS-COUNTER SPIRALED PATTERN FOR RIGIDITY

CABLE LUGS ONE NESTED WITHIN OTHER

AS WHIP BASE ROTATES — POINT SPLITS IN OPPOSITE DIRECTIONS

CABLES PAY OUT AS WHIP MOTORS ACCELERATE ENDS

CABLES AT FULL EXTENSION MOTORS AT FULL SPEED — 11,000 R.P.M. — WILL NOW DEFLECT BULLET

BLACK MAMBA

Real Name: Tanya Sealy
Occupation: Ex-call girl, now mercenary
Legal status: Citizen of the United States with a criminal record
Identity: Known to the authorities
Former aliases: Tanya Sweet
Place of birth: Chicago, Illinois
Marital status: Single
Known relatives: None
Group affiliation: Serpent Squad II, Serpent Society
Base of operations: Mobile
First appearance: MARVEL TWO-IN-ONE #64
History: Tanya Sealy was selected by executives in the Roxxon Oil Company to be a special agent in covert operations (see *Roxxon*). At the Mutagenics Laboratory of Roxxon's subsidiary, the Brand Corporation, Sealy underwent an operation to surgically implant a special component in her forebrain, enabling her to tap her brain's energy in a unique way. Her first field mission was joining the new Serpent Squad in their attempt to retrieve the Serpent Crown. She remained with the nucleus of the group when they went freelance. Months later, she and her cohorts were invited to join the Serpent Society, an organization of mercenary costumed criminals (see *Serpent Society*). She readily accepted the invitation, savoring the prospect of steady income.
Height: 5' 7"
Weight: 115 lbs
Eyes: Green
Hair: Black
Strength level: Black Mamba possesses the normal human strength of a woman of her age, height, and build who engages in moderate regular exercise.
Known superhuman powers: Black Mamba possesses the ability to project an inky cloud of extradimensional energy known as the Darkforce. This energy is manifested by Black Mamba as a limited quantity of viscous semi-solid matter. It is not known how far Black Mamba can project this energy manifestation, but her control over it seems limited by her line of sight. It is also not known how much of it she can manipulate at once: so far she has not been observed using it against more than one person at a time. Black Mamba uses the Darkforce (a process she refers to as "shedding her skin") to surround, constrict, and suffocate her opponents. The maximum amount of pressure she can generate through her Darkforce-projection is not known. However, the superhumanly strong Thing seemed unable to break its grip when he was encompassed by it.

Black Mamba also possesses some form of hypnotic power, enabling her to mesmerize her opponents into perceiving her Darkforce projection in the image of someone they love or trust. It is not known how irresistible this ability is, but the Thing, Iron Man, and Captain America have proven susceptible to it. As part of the hypnotic illusion, her opponent imagines him or herself in the embrace of his or her self-chosen loved one, and the implausability of the loved one's sudden materialization and provocative behavior is overwhelmed by the sensation of euphoria she triggers in most human brains. If one remains in the grip of her illusory Darkforce projection for too long, he or she will succumb to suffocation. The amount of time this takes varies according to the stamina and breath control of her opponent. The victim dies, however, overwhelmed by ecstasy. Black Mamba may need to be within line of sight of her opponent not to direct the Darkforce, but to use it in conjunction with her hypnotic power.
Limitations: Besides those limits to her power described above, Black Mamba needs to concentrate in order to project her "snake-skin." Also, if her Darkforce projection is bombarded with certain powerful energies, she will feel the force of that disruption against her body. This feedback effect may cause her pain or the loss of consciousness. ∎

BLACK PANTHER

Real name: T'Challa
Occupation: King of Wakandas, scientist
Legal status: Citizen of Wakanda with no criminal record
Identity: Publicly known
Former aliases: Luke Charles
Place of birth: Wakanda, Northern Africa
Marital status: Single
Known relatives: T'Chaka (father, deceased), N'Yami (mother, deceased), Khanata, Joshua Itobo, Ishanta, Zuni (cousins), Jakarra (half brother)
Group affiliation: Reserve member of the East Coast Avengers
First Appearance: FANTASTIC FOUR #52
Origin: FANTASTIC FOUR #53
History: T'Challa is the son of T'Chaka, king of the African nation of Wakanda. When his father was slain by Ulysses Klaw, a lawless American ivory hunter who sought to possess Wakanda's Vibranium mine, the young T'Challa swore vengeance (see *Klaw, Vibranium*). The young boy succeeded in thwarting Klaw's raid. He was then sent off to be educated at the finest schools in Europe and America. T'Challa returned to his homeland, bearing a degree in Physics, to assume the mantle of leadership. He was given two tests: to triumph against six of Wakanda's greatest warriors in unarmed combat and to obtain the secret heart-shaped herb that grants great physical strength and heightened senses. T'Challa passed the tests and donned the ceremonial garb of the Black Panther, the totem of the Wakandan people. As the Black Panther, T'Challa has both protected his land from outside invaders and led his small nation into greater industrialisation and wealth. After meeting Captain America, the Panther was offered membership in the Avengers. Taking a leave of absence from his royal duties, he served with the Avengers for a lengthy interval, acquainting himself with American methods of crimefighting. Inevitably, he resumed the active kingship of the Wakandas and returned to his native land where he has ruled ever since.

Height: 6′ **Eyes:** Brown
Weight: 185 lbs. **Hair:** Black

Strength level: The Black Panther is near the pinnacle of human physical perfection, his natural strength and abilities having been heightened by the unidentified heart-shaped herb found only in Wakanda. While not superhuman, he is nearly as strong as a human being can become. He can lift (press) a maximum of 750 pounds with supreme effort.

Known superhuman powers: None
Abilities: Besides his heightened physical strength, the Black Panther possesses the speed, agility, and endurance of a gifted athlete in peak condition. He is particularly accomplished at gymnastics, acrobatics, and brachiation (swinging from one branch to another using one's arms).

The Black Panther's five senses are highly acute, although not superhumanly so like Daredevil's (see *Daredevil*). He has particularly keen eyesight and night vision. Using sight and smell, the Panther can track a quarry's trail through the jungle up to 12 hours later. In city environments, he can follow a similar trail up to 6 hours later.

The Panther is a masterful natural fighter. His fighting style does not belong to any established martial arts discipline, but incorporates acrobatics and a number of cat-like stances, moves, and blows. ∎

BLACK QUEEN

Real name: Selene
Occupation: Goddess (self-styled)
Identity: Selene's powers and history are unknown to the general public.
Legal status: Former citizen of the Roman Republic and of Nova Roma
Former aliases: The Black Priestess
Place of birth: Unknown
Marital status: Widowed
Known relatives: Marcus Domitius Gallio (husband, deceased)
Group affiliation: Inner Circle of the Hellfire Club
Base of operations: New York City
First appearance: NEW MUTANTS #9

History: Selene's origin is as yet unrevealed, but she is known to have lived for several millennia, and to have been a foe of the sorcerer Kulan Gath (see *Appendix: Kulan Gath*). In past ages she was renowned as a sorceress whose power was feared and respected by practitioners of black and white magic. She eventually came to live in the ancient Roman Republic. For unknown reasons, she accompanied the large number of Roman citizens who fled Rome in the First Century B.C. and sailed to the New World, where they founded Nova Roma ("New Rome") in a hidden section of the Amazon jungle in what is now Brazil (see *Appendix: Nova Roma*). The founders of Nova Roma fled Rome because they foresaw that its republican government would be replaced by an imperial one. For reasons that remain unknown, Selene found herself unable to leave Nova Roma, and remained there for roughly two thousand years. In Nova Roma she led the dreaded Cult of Fire as its Black Priestess.

In recent years Selene married Marcus Domitius Gallio, a senator of Nova Roma who plotted to abolish its republican government. The intervention of the New Mutants both thwarted Senator Gallio's schemes and led to Selene's apparent destruction (see *New Mutants*). However, Selene not only survived, but somehow found herself able to leave Nova Roma. She soon travelled to New York City. Over the two millennia that she was trapped in Nova Roma, a religious cult worshipping Selene as a goddess had continued to survive in the outside world. Selene made contact with a leader of the cult, Friedrich von Roehm, in New York City. Von Roehm was also a member of the Inner Circle of the Hellfire Club, an elite group secretly dedicated to achieving world domination (see *Hellfire Club*). Von Roehm successfully sponsored Selene for membership in the Inner Circle, and she rapidly rose to the high rank of Black Queen of the Inner Circle.

Height: 5' 10"
Weight: 130 lbs.
Eyes: Red
Hair: Black

Strength level: Selene possesses superhuman strength, enabling her to lift (press) about 1500 pounds under optimal conditions.

Known superhuman powers: Selene is a mutant with various superhuman attributes. She sustains herself by psionically draining the life force of other human beings into herself. Because of this, she is often referred to as a vampire, although she is not a true supernatural vampire, like Dracula (see *Deceased: Dracula, Vampires*). If she drains a person's entire life force from him or her, the victim dies and the victim's body crumbles into dust. If Selene drains only part of a victim's life force, Selene achieves a measure of psychic control over her victim's mind. Through unknown means, Selene can also cause a human being to become a psychic vampire like herself, but be subordinate to Selene's own will.

It is not known how often Selene must drain life force from another human in order to survive. It is known that great expenditure of power causes Selene to age, but she can rejuvenate herself by absorbing more life force. Selene will not age as long as she maintains her supply of absorbed life force. She is also unaffected by injuries such as knife wounds.

Selene has physical strength, stamina, speed, and reaction time that are all several times greater than those of a normal woman.

Selene possesses telekinetic abilities that give her complete psionic control over inanimate objects and fire. She can cause inanimate objects to move according to her will by projecting part of her absorbed life force into them. She can cause inanimate objects in her presence to disintegrate. She cannot, however, rearrange the atomic or molecular structure of matter.

Selene can induce a momentary hypnotic trance state in people around her. She can also momentarily move at speeds rivaling those of Quicksilver (see *Quicksilver*). She often combines these two abilities to make it seem as if she can disappear: she induces a momentary trance in witnesses, and then leaves at superhuman speed before the witnesses can recover.

Selene also possesses considerable magical abilities, having gained a great deal of mystical knowledge over the millennia. The number of magical effects that she can create has yet to be catalogued, but it is known that she can cast and counteract spells and summon demons. ∎

BLACK TALON

Real name: Unrevealed
Occupation: Houngan (voodoo priest)
Legal status: Citizen of the United States with no criminal record
Identity: Secret
Former aliases: None known
Place of birth: Unrevealed
Marital status: Unrevealed
Known relatives: None
Group affiliation: Ally of the Grim Reaper
Base of operations: New Orleans area
First appearance: (original) STRANGE TALES #173, (new) AVENGERS #152
Final appearance: TALES OF THE ZOMBIE #6
History: The first known Black Talon was millionaire Desmond Drew, who secretly led a voodoo cult that dealt in human sacrifice. As the Black Talon, Drew wore the garb of the Black Rooster, which symbolized "he who dwells in the fiery pit," and he claimed to be a "living loa," a voodoo god in human form.

In actuality Drew was a mere human being whose supernatural feats were the work of his mother, the blind houngan Mama Limbo. The Talon had his cultists kidnap young female virgins to serve supposedly as human sacrifices to the loa. However, the Talon was really carrying out the plan of his mother, who believed she had learned a means of restoring her youth, beauty, and sight by bathing in the blood of four virgins.

Learning that Drew was an imposter, the cultists beat the Black Talon to death.

Afterwards, a Creole whose true name is unknown but who possesses actual voodoo powers, took on the name and costume of the Black Talon and gathered his own group of cultists. The new Black Talon was contacted by the Grim Reaper, who wished to see his supposedly dead brother Wonder Man resurrected as a zombie (see *Grim Reaper, Wonder Man*). When the Black Talon accomplished the task, the Reaper sent his brother's body to Avengers Mansion where he hoped the zombie might wreak havoc. The Avengers subdued the zombie and then tracked down and defeated the Black Talon.

Some time later, the Grim Reaper enlisted the Black Talon in a new scheme to restore his brother to a closer semblance of what he had been. He assigned the Talon the task of creating a zombie who physically resembled his brother before becoming Wonder Man. The West Coast Avengers, the Vision, and the Scarlet Witch thwarted the Reaper's plans. The Black Talon escaped, however, and remains at large.
Height: 6′ 2″
Weight: 240 lbs.
Eyes: Brown
Hair: Black
Strength level: Black Talon possesses the normal human strength of a man of his age, height, and build who engages in regular exercise.
Known superhuman powers: The Black Talon is a true houngan, or voodoo priest, with actual supernatural abilities. Voodoo is a religion that originated in Haiti.

The Black Talon's principal power is his ability to create and control zombies. A zombie is a human corpse whose spirit has entirely left its body, but which has nevertheless been given a semblance of life and consciousness by voodoo magic. Zombies have minimal reasoning capabilities, superhuman strength, and immunity to most forms of pain. (For further information, see *Appendix: Zombie*). The Black Talon must perform a voodoo ritual in order to reanimate corpses as zombies. The Talon can give his zombies commands verbally or, when they are in his presence, by telepathy. However, the Talon cannot mentally communicate with his zombies when they are beyond his immediate vicinity. ∎

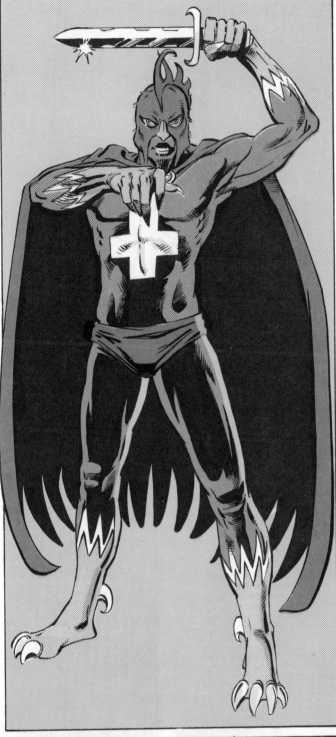

BLACK WIDOW

Real name: Natalia Alianovna Romanova ("Natasha" is the informal version of the name "Natalia," and is used by her close associates. Sometimes she has chosen to Anglicize her last name as "Romanoff." She has dropped her married name of "Shostakova.")

Occupation: Adventurer, intelligence agent, former ballerina

Legal status: Former citizen of the USSR who defected to the United States; she now lives in the United States under an extended visa authorized by SHIELD; she has a criminal record in the United States for her espionage activities for other nations, but was granted amnesty through SHIELD's intervention.

Identity: Publicly known

Place of birth: Stalingrad, Union of Soviet Socialist Republics

Marital status: Widowed

Known relatives: Alexi Shostakov (alias Red Guardian I, husband, deceased)

Group affiliation: Avengers reservist, frequent freelance agent of SHIELD, former partner of Daredevil, former member of the Champions of Los Angeles

Base of operations: Mobile, but she maintains a home in New York City

First appearance: TALES OF SUSPENSE #52

Origin: AVENGERS #44, DAREDEVIL #88

History: Natalia Romanova, a descendant of Russia's royal family, was found as a young child by a Russian soldier known as Ivan Petrovitch, who watched over her as she grew up and today works as her chauffeur. Romanova proved to be a brilliant scholar and athlete as she matured, and in her teens gained fame in the Soviet Union as a ballerina. She married the renowned Soviet test pilot Alexi Shostakov.

It was decided at the KGB, the department of the Soviet government which serves as its intelligence agency and secret police, that the Shostakovs would make good special operatives. While Alexi Shostakov was away on a mission, he was informed of the state's new plans for him, and told that from then on he could have no contact with any of his past friends and acquaintances, including even his own wife. Shostakov was then trained to become the Red Guardian, a costumed agent who was intended to act as the Soviet Union's counterpart to Captain America (see *Deceased: Red Guardian I*). Meanwhile, a Soviet official told Natalia Shostakova that her husband had died in the explosion of an experimental rocket he was testing. Distraught, Natalia Shostakova said that she wanted to do something to be worthy of the memory of her heroic husband. The KGB had anticipated her reaction, and trained her to become the spy known as the Black Widow.

At first the Black Widow did not act as a costumed agent. Her first major field assignment was to infiltrate Stark Industries in the United States and to assist her partner Boris Turgenov in the assassination of the defector Professor Anton Vanko (see *Crimson Dynamo*). The Black Widow was thwarted repeatedly by the original Iron Man in her various schemes against Stark Industries. The Black Widow used Hawkeye, who was then sought as a criminal and who found himself attracted to her, as an ally in some of her subversive activities (see *Hawkeye*). The Widow was given her

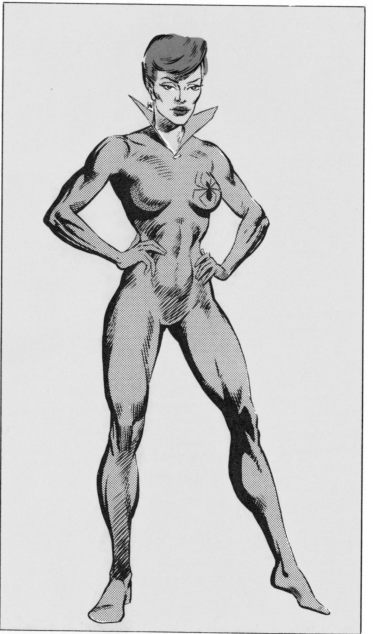

first costume in her fourth major mission in the United States. However, her growing love for Hawkeye led to a weakening of her resolve to continue her missions for the Soviets. Hawkeye refused to act as a criminal any longer, and successfully sought amnesty and Avengers membership.

The Black Widow fell into the hands of intelligence agents of the People's Republic of China, who brainwashed her into serving them. They directed her to attack the Avengers, but she freed herself from the brainwashing, was reunited with Hawkeye, and defected to the United States. She publicly revealed her true identity and offered her services to SHIELD, which has made use of them on numerous occasions.

Her romance with Hawkeye ended, as did her subsequent love affair and partnership with Daredevil, although she remains friends with both men. She was a member of the Champions of Los Angeles, and

serves from time to time as a member of the Avengers. She remains active as a freelance adventurer.

Height: 5′ 7″
Weight: 125 lbs.
Eyes: Blue
Hair: Red-auburn (formerly dyed black)
Strength level: The Black Widow possesses the normal human strength of a woman of her age, height, and build who engages in intensive regular exercise.
Known superhuman powers: None
Abilities: The Black Widow is an Olympic level athlete and gymnast, and a master of several martial arts, including karate, judo, akido, savate, and boxing. The Black Widow has had extensive training and experience in a great variety of espionage skills, and is considered to be one of the world's most effective and potentially dangerous secret agents.
Weapons: The Black Widow's uniform is

equipped with microscopic suction cups on the portions covering her fingers and feet, activated by an electro-static charge, enabling her to stick to walls and ceilings made of standard building materials.

The cartridges of her wrist-bracelets contain a spring-loaded cable capable of shooting a hooked wire a hundred feet. Called her "widow's line," the cable is primarily used for swinging from building to building. The wrist-cartridges also carry a small device capable of emitting a high frequency electrostatic charge, of a maximum distance of ten feet. This electro-blast, called her "widow's bite," is sufficient to stun a man at twenty feet. Other cartridges in her wrist-bracelets contain tear gas pellets and a radio transmitter. She also sometimes wears a belt of metallic disc-cartridges. Each of these contains a plastic explosive equivalent to 4 pounds of TNT. ∎

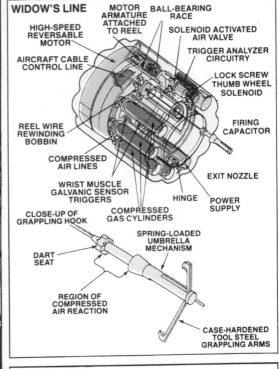

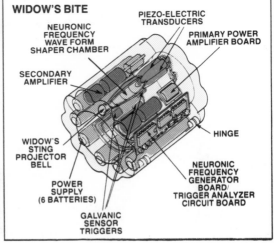

BLASTAAR

Real Name: Blastaar
Occupation: Monarch
Identity: Blastaar's existence is unknown to the general public of Earth.
Legal status: Monarch of Baluur, a planet in the Negative Zone.
Former aliases: None known
Place of birth: Baluur, Sector 56-D of the Negative Zone (as charted by Reed Richards)
Marital status: Widower
Known relatives: Nyglar (wife, deceased)
Group affiliation: Former ally of the Sandman and Annihilus
Base of operations: Baluur
First appearance: FANTASTIC FOUR #62
Origin: MARVEL TWO-IN-ONE #75
History: Blastaar is the king of the planet Baluur in the anti-matter universe called the Negative Zone (see *Appendix: Other Dimensions*). He ruled ruthlessly for years until many of his subjects rose against him and imprisoned him in an adhesion suit set adrift in outer space in the Negative Zone. Blastaar eventually broke free and sighted Reed Richards of the Fantastic Four and Triton of the Inhumans, who were returning to Earth from the Negative Zone. Blastaar followed them back to Earth through the interdimensional portal that Richards had opened into the Zone. The Fantastic Four drove Blastaar back into the Zone, but he subsequently has returned to Earth several times, hoping to conquer it. Each time Blastaar has been defeated and ultimately deported to the Negative Zone. Eventually public sentiment on Baluur shifted, and Blastaar not only reclaimed his throne there, but also led Baluur's forces in carving out an interplanetary empire in the Negative Zone. He remains a deadly threat to Earth as well.
Height: 6′ 6″
Weight: 520 lbs.
Eyes: Gray
Hair: Gray
Skin: Gray
Strength level: Blastaar possesses superhuman strength, enabling him to lift (press) approximately 50 tons under optimal conditions.

Known superhuman powers: Blastaar's principal power is the ability to generate an unknown type of highly concussive kinetic force which he can then release at will through his fingertips. He can release sufficient force to penetrate 6 inch thick titanium-overlayed steel from a distance of 25 feet. The maximum range of his blasting power, limited by his inability to finely focus his beams of energy, is about 1,000 feet.

By carefully releasing a steady stream of blasts from his fingertips, Blastaar can propel himself through the air in the manner of a nuclear-engined rocket. He is able to generate sufficient propulsion to reach Earth's escape velocity (25,000 miles per hour), and can remain in flight almost indefinitely.

Blastaar has superhuman strength, endurance, and resilience. He is virtually tireless. His body can withstand extreme variations in temperature (from 200° below zero to 11,000° Fahrenheit) and pressure (from 0 to 10 Earth atmospheres). His skin is strong enough to withstand the impact of up to .30 caliber armor-piercing machine gun bullets. He can survive for weeks without nourishment and can survive in airless space for months by willing himself into a state of hibernation. ∎

BLAZE, JOHNNY

Real name: John "Johnny" Blaze
Occupation: Former stunt motorcyclist
Legal status: American citizen with no criminal record
Identity: Johnny Blaze's former identity as the demonic Ghost Rider is unknown to the general public.
Former aliases: The Ghost Rider
Place of birth: Waukegan, Illinois
Marital status: Single
Known relatives: Barton (father, deceased), Clara (mother, deceased), Craig "Crash" Simpson (stepfather, deceased), Mona Simpson (stepmother, deceased), Roxanne Simpson (stepsister)
Group affiliation: Former member of the Champions of Los Angeles
First appearance and origin: MARVEL SPOTLIGHT #5
Final appearance (as Ghost Rider): GHOST RIDER #81
History: Johnny Blaze was the son of stunt motorcyclist Barton Blaze, the top attraction at Crash Simpson's Daredevil Cycle Show. The elder Blaze was killed performing a dangerous stunt, and Johnny, now an orphan (his mother Clara having died shortly after his birth), was adopted by Crash Simpson and his wife Mona. At first frightened of motorcycles, Blaze soon conquered his fear and became an accomplished amateur motorcyclist. Blaze practiced stuntriding on his own, and became romantically involved with his stepsister Roxanne Simpson.

Blaze also began to take an interest in the occult. Just when the Simpson Cycle Show was about to get its chance at fame with a booking at New York City's Madison Square Garden, Crash Simpson learned that he was dying of a rare blood disease. Desperate to save his stepfather, Blaze performed a ritual to summon up the "devil," whom Blaze believed to be the Biblical Satan but was actually the demon lord Mephisto (see *Demons, Mephisto*). Mephisto agreed to save Simpson from his fatal disease in return for Blaze's soul.

At Madison Square Garden, Crash Simpson performed the greatest stunt of his career, a cycle jump over 22 car widths, and crashed to his death. Blaze was shocked, since he believed the "devil" would protect his stepfather. When Mephisto appeared to collect Blaze's soul, the demon explained that he only promised to save Simpson from the disease, and nothing more. However, before Mephisto could take Blaze's soul, Roxanne Simpson arrived and recited a spell of banishment she had read in one of Blaze's occult books. Mephisto was forced to leave without Blaze's soul, but was able to graft the essence of the demon Zarathos to Blaze's body (see *Appendix: Zarathos*).

Zarathos was a demon who attacked human souls. In order to capture Zarathos, many centuries ago Mephisto stole the soul of an American Indian now known as Centurious (see *Appendix: Centurious*). When Zarathos' attack on Centurious therefore proved ineffective, the demon's followers lost faith in him. Mephisto then stole the living flame that was Zarathos' soul. Over the centuries Mephisto amused himself by placing the essence of Zarathos within various human hosts. Johnny Blaze was the latest of these.

Blaze was unaware of the seperate consciousness of the being that dwelled within him, and believed that the demonic personality was a sinister side of his own personality. At first the demon manifested itself every nightfall, mystically burning Blaze's flesh to become a fiery skeletal being. Using his demonic hellfire to create a fiery motorcycle to ride, the composite Zarathos/Blaze entity became publicly known as the Ghost Rider. Whenever the Ghost Rider returned to human form, Blaze's flesh would be immediately restored.

At first Johnny Blaze dominated the Ghost Rider's personality. After a few months, Blaze's automatic transformations at nightfall ended. He then became the Ghost Rider whenever he mystically sensed "evil" in his vicinity. Later, Blaze was able to control his transformations as well as the actions of the demon when it manifested itself. It was during this period that the Ghost Rider became a member of the Champions of Los Angeles, a short-lived group of superhuman adventurers (see *Appendix: Champions of Los Angeles*). But the more Blaze became the Ghost Rider, the stronger the demon became. Eventu-ally Zarathos tried to take control of their composite form. Blaze no longer summoned the demon within him to help him accomplish his ends, such as fighting crime. Instead, Blaze valiantly struggled to prevent Zarathos from taking control and wreaking havoc.

Centurious still lived and sought vengeance on Zarathos for being the reason why he lost his soul. Centurious entrapped Blaze's soul within his "crystal of souls" and then defeated Zarathos. Zarathos cracked open the crystal, releasing Blaze's soul and many others, and entrapping Centurious within the crystal when it mystically resealed. An associate of Centurious offered to send Zarathos into the crystal to take vengeance, and the demon agreed. Zarathos' essence was sucked out of Blaze's body into the crystal, where Zarathos grapples eternally with Centurious, neither able to defeat the other.

Johnny Blaze had thus been permanently freed from his bond to Zarathos. Since then, Blaze and Roxanne Simpson have been travelling through America together by motorcycle.
Height: 5' 10"
Weight: 180 lbs.
Eyes: Blue
Hair: Reddish blond
Strength level: Johnny Blaze possesses the normal human strength of a man of his age, height, and build, who engages in moderate regular exercise.
Known superhuman powers: None
Other abilities: Johnny Blaze is one of the greatest living stunt motorcyclists. He has some knowledge of the occult, but has forsworn using it.
Former superhuman powers: As the Ghost Rider, Blaze possessed superhuman strength, enabling him to lift (press) about 5 tons, and immunity to most forms of conventional injury. He could create "hellfire" that could harm or traumatize a human soul, and with which he created the fiery motorcycles he rode. Blaze possessed none of these powers in human form. ∎

BLOB

Real Name: Fred J. Dukes
Occupation: Ex-circus performer, now professional criminal
Legal status: Citizen of the United States with a criminal record
Identity: Publicly known
Place of birth: Lubbock, Texas
Marital status: Single
Known relatives: None
Group affiliation: Former member of both the original and new Brotherhood of Evil Mutants, former member of Factor Three, frequent partner of Unus, member of Freedom Force
Base of operations: Mobile
First appearance: X-MEN #3
History: The Blob is a mutant whose latent superhuman powers became manifest when he reached puberty. Thinking of himself as no more than, in his own words, "an extra-strong freak," the Blob used his superhuman powers as a performer in a carnival. The original X-Men came to the carnival in their everyday identities to invite him to meet with their mentor, Professor Charles Xavier (see *Professor X, X-Men*). Attracted to the beautiful young X-Man Jean Grey, the Blob accepted, and went with the X-Men to Xavier's mansion. There Xavier asked the Blob to join the X-Men, but the Blob arrogantly refused. Xavier then knew he had to use his mental powers to erase the Blob's knowledge of the X-Men's true identities. But the Blob had no intention of letting this happen, and after fighting the X-Men, escaped back to the carnival.

The Blob had learned through meeting Xavier and the X-Men that he himself was a superhumanly powerful mutant. Believing himself therefore to be superior to normal people, the Blob took over the carnival. Knowing that the X-Men considered him dangerous because he knew who they really were, the Blob decided to strike out at them first. He led the other members of the carnival in an attack on Xavier's mansion. The Blob hoped to steal whatever scientific discoveries and special weapons that the X-Men might possess and use them against ordinary humans. However, the X-Men defeated the Blob and his allies, and

Xavier wiped out their memories of the X-Men.

Later, Magneto attempted to recruit the Blob for his Brotherhood of Evil Mutants (see *Magneto; Appendix: Brotherhood of Evil Mutants*). A severe blow to the head restored the Blob's memory of the X-Men, and he joined Magneto's Brotherhood in an attack on them. In the midst of battle Magneto launched powerful torpedoes at the X-Men, not caring that the Blob was in the way. Torpedoes struck the Blob but did not seriously injure him. The Brotherhood escaped, and the Blob, feeling betrayed, swore never to trust anyone again and returned to his job with the carnival.

Months later the Blob met another superhumanly powerful mutant, Unus the Untouchable, and the two of them attempted to frame their mutual enemies, the X-Men, as thieves (see *Unus*). This was the start of the Blob's long and close friendship with Unus, which ended only recently with Unus's apparent death. The two mutants next joined Factor Three, an organization of superhumanly powerful mutants that attempted world conquest (see *Appendix: Factor Three*). Unus and the Blob teamed up with other mutants, including Magneto, for other criminal activites, although they were continually thwarted by superhumanly powerful crimefighters.

Eventually the Blob was recruited by Mystique for her new Brotherhood of Evil Mutants (see *Mystique*). Although the Blob has sometimes operated independently of Mystique's organization since then, he continues to act as one of its members. Recently, aware of the United States govern-ment's increasing anti-mutant activity, Mystique renamed the Brotherhood "Freedom Force" and offered its services to the government (see *Freedom Force*). The Blob participated in Freedom Force's first mission for the government: the capture of Magneto, his former leader in the original Brotherhood.

Height: 5′ 10″
Weight: 510 lbs
Eyes: Brown
Hair: Brown
Strength level: The Blob does not truly possess superhuman strength, but his enormous size gives him considerably greater strength than a man of the same age and height with a normal build.
Known superhuman powers: The Blob's mutant powers relate to the mass, strength, resilience and indestructibility of his obese body. His primary ability is to become virtually immovable at will as long as he is in contact with the ground. He does this by bonding himself to the earth beneath him by force of will, which in effect creates a monodirectional increase of gravity beneath him. This gravity field extends about five feet in radius from his center of balance. Thus if there is sufficient power to uproot him, it would take the ground beneath his feet in an area corresponding to the radius of the field. Through intense concentration, the Blob is able to extend the gravity field beneath him farther than five feet.

The Blob's body has several unusual properties in itself. The first is its superhuman resistance to injury. The fat tissues that comprise the Blob's epidermis are able to absorb the impact of rifle bullets, cannon-balls, bazooka shells, and even torpedoes. The larger of these projectiles recoil from his body at one half the force of impact. The smaller ones imbed themselves in his layers of fat tissue, enabling him to eject them by merely flexing his muscles. The Blob's nerve endings do not relay any tactile perceptions to his brain which are near the threshold of pain. The fat tissue of his epidermis is resilient enough to revert to its normal shape within seconds after deformation caused by impact. It is virtually impervious to physical injury. The Blob's skin cannot be punctured, lacerated, frostbitten, or ravaged by any skin disease, due in part to the skin's great elasticity and toughness and in part to the highly accelerated rate at which his skin cells grow and replace themselves. His skin is somewhat less resistant to burning.

It is not yet known if there is an upper limit to the Blob's ability to absorb impact. While he could easily survive a head-on collision with a bus traveling at a hundred miles an hour, and even a highly ferrous meteorite fifty feet in diameter at terminal velocity, it is not known whether he could survive a collision with an object travelling at near light speed. Further, it is not known whether his skin's imperviousness to heat could survive the 11,000,000 degree heat at ground zero of a multi-megaton atomic blast. Although the Blob's skin is virtually invulnerable, his eyes, nose, mouth and ears are probably not. Thus if a projectile impacted with the surface of his eye or penetrated his nostrils, opened mouth, or inner ear, he would suffer injury. ∎

BOOMERANG

Real Name: Fred Myers
Occupation: Ex-baseball pitcher, now freelance assassin
Legal status: Naturalized American citizen with a criminal record
Identity: Secret
Other aliases: Fred Slade
Place of birth: Alice Springs, Northern Territory, Australia
Marital status: Single
Known relatives: None
Group affiliation: Former employee of the Secret Empire, former ally of Viper II and the Silver Samurai, former employee of the Kingpin
Base of operations: Mobile
First appearance and origin: TALES TO ASTONISH #81
History: Fred Myers was born in Australia but moved to America when he was a small child. In America, his great love was baseball and he developed an extraordinary pitching arm. He became a professional baseball player in the minor leagues after graduating high school, and a few years later entered the major leagues. Within a year he was suspended for accepting bribes. Embittered, he was eventually contacted by the subversive criminal organization, the Secret Empire, and offered employment (see *Secret Empire*). They designed special weaponry for him to exploit his pitching ability and he became their special operative, code-named Boomerang. When the Empire crumbled, Boomerang went to Australia to hide out and recuperate. There he incessantly practiced the art of throwing a boomerang and decided to become a freelance assassin. Obtaining a new arsenal of weapons designed and financed by underworld financier Justin Hammer, Boomerang came back to America to pursue his criminal ambitions (see *Hammer, Justin*). He has since taken various freelance assignments, notably for the Kingpin.
Height: 5′ 11″
Weight: 175 lbs
Eyes: Brown
Hair: Brown
Strength level: Boomerang possesses the normal human strength of a man of his age, height, and build who engages in intensive regular exercise.
Known superhuman powers: None
Abilities: Boomerang is an expert pitcher whose accuracy has few rivals.
Weapons: Boomerang's primary weapons are the boomerangs which he wears on his uniform. There are seven boomerangs attached in plain sight, each of which is rigged with special gimmicks. He carries "shatterangs" which detonate at impact with the explosive power of twenty hand grenades. A single shatterang can totally demolish an automobile. He also carries "gasarangs" which release highly-concentrated tear gas upon impact. His razor-edged "razorang" is capable of slicing through a gun barrel. Boomerang has also employed sonic-blasting "screamerangs," and whirling "bladerangs" which cut like buzzsaw blades. Boomerang is constantly diverting a percentage of his earnings to modify and replenish his arsenal of modified boomerangs.
Paraphernalia: Boomerang can fly by means of his boot-jets. Controlled by mental command through cybernetic circuitry in his cowl, the boot-jets generate a fine spray of two unusually potent hypergolic (exploding on contact) chemicals which act like a jet exhaust. Because of the small quantities used in the reaction, the boot-jets are capable of keeping him aloft at an average speed of 30 miles per hour for up to two hours, before refueling. The maximum speed at which Boomerang can fly by means of his boot-jets is 60 miles per hour, which will deplete his fuel supply in about 45 minutes. The boot-jets are powerful enough to support Boomerang's weight plus about one hundred pounds. More weight than that will cause the jets to lose altitude and eventually be grounded. The boot-jets are extremely maneuverable, allowing Boomerang to change direction and speed at mental command. They can also be used as an offensive weapon when Boomerang stands firmly on the ground or braces himself against some object and fires them at an enemy at close range. ∎

BOX

Real Name: I: Roger Bochs II: Jerome "Jerry" Jaxon III: Walter Langkowski

Occupation: I: Engineer, mechanic II: Executive vice-president of Am-Can Petroleum, later of Roxxon Oil III: Former physics professor, adventurer

Identity: Secret, known to certain members of the Canadian government

Legal status: Citizens of Canada with no criminal records

Former aliases: I, II: None III: Sasquatch

Place of birth: I: Moosejaw, Saskatchewan II: Red Deer, Alberta III: Vancouver, British Columbia

Place of death: II: New York City III: Vancouver, British Columbia

Marital status: I: Single II: Divorced III: Single

Known relatives: I: None II: Unnamed wife, children, father-in-law III: Lillian von Loont (alias Gilded Lily, great-aunt, deceased)

Group affiliation: I, III: Alpha Flight II: Omega Flight

Base of operations: I: Tamarind Island off British Columbia II: New York City III: Mobile

First appearance: I: (as Box) ALPHA FLIGHT #1, (as Bochs) ALPHA FLIGHT #11 II: (as Jaxon) ALPHA FLIGHT #3, (as Box) ALPHA FLIGHT #12 III: (as Langkowski) X-MEN #120, (as Box) ALPHA FLIGHT #24

Final appearance: II: ALPHA FLIGHT #12 III: (death) ALPHA FLIGHT #23, (as Box) INCREDIBLE HULK #313

History: Roger Bochs is a brilliant engineer and mechanic who, for unrevealed reasons, is missing both his legs. He invented a large humanoid robot, which he called "Box" in a pun on his name. James McDonald Hudson, the leader of Alpha Flight, helped Bochs perfect Box, and recruited him as a candidate to join Alpha Flight (see *Alpha Flight: Deceased: Guardian*). Bochs entered the initial training program for recruits, Gamma Flight, and had graduated into the next level, Beta Flight, when the Canadian government disbanded Department H, which supported Alpha Flight and the two

training groups. Bochs returned to his ordinary life in Saskatchewan. Alpha Flight continued to operate independently of the Canadian government.

Sometime later, Bochs was recruited by Delphine Courtney, the robotic assistant to Jerome Jaxon, to join his new group of superhuman operatives, Omega Flight (see *Omega Flight*). Ten years before, Jaxon had been Hudson's superior at the Am-Can Petroleum Company in Canada, and had insisted that the special suit Hudson had designed for geological exploration be turned over to the American military. Hudson thereupon stole the psycho-cybernetic helmet that made the suit work, and destroyed Am-Can's plans for the helmet and suit. As a result, Jaxon's career was ruined. Years later, Jaxon discovered that Guardian was Hudson, took a position with Roxxon Oil, and organized Omega Flight to destroy Guardian and Alpha Flight in revenge. Bochs, who was loyal to Hudson, joined Omega Flight only to sabotage it from within. Jaxon realized Bochs' intentions, and seized control of Box himself. Controlling Box through Bochs' helmet, Jaxon sent it into battle against Guardian. Guardian destroyed Box with an electronic blast from his power pack, causing feedback that killed Jaxon. However, Guardian's power pack then blew up, killing Hudson.

Six weeks later, Bochs met with a man named Jeffries, whom Guardian had called a transmutator. Jeffries can levitate any mechanical part made of metal, plastic, or glass, and can reshape and organize such parts into analogues to portions of his body. Together Bochs and Jeffries created a new, bigger, and stronger Box, which Bochs could control from inside by "phasing" into the robot's body (see Known superhuman powers). Bochs felt responsible for Guardian's death since he had invented the original Box, with which Jaxon had indirectly caused Hudson's death. Bochs intended to use Box to hunt down Jaxon, if he still lived, and Courtney.

Later, Snowbird discovered the truth behind her Alpha Flight teammate Walter Langkowski's transformations into the beastlike Sasquatch (see *Snowbird; Deceased: Sasquatch*). Langkowski thought that he could turn into Sasquatch as the result of gamma radiation effects similar to those that created the Hulk (see *Hulk*). However, he had actually accidentally created a magical link with the other-dimensional mystical beast Tanaraq. Each time that Langkowski became Sasquatch, Tanaraq's control over him grew. Finally, when Tanaraq had taken full control of Sasquatch, Snowbird killed Sasquatch's physical form. Several members of Alpha Flight traveled into the beasts' dimension, where one member, Shaman, recovered Langkowski's soul. Unable to return the soul to Langkowski's body, which mystic forces had caused to crumble into dust, Shaman, with Bochs' consent, instead projected it into Box.

While Langkowski's spirit animated Box, Bochs searched for a living form for Langkowski to inhabit. He finally discovered such a form at an interdimensional nexus, and drew it to Earth. The being turned out to be the Hulk, and Bochs' plan to transfer Langkowski's spirit into him failed. Langkowski's spirit finally departed Box permanently, and Bochs now controls it once more, and has become an official member of Alpha Flight.

Height: (Box) 7′, (Bochs) 4′, (Jaxon) 6′ 1″, (Langkowski) 6′ 4″

Weight: (Box) (originally) 326 lbs., (current) 465 lbs., (Bochs) 140 lbs., (Jaxon) 175 lbs., (Langkowski) 245 lbs.

Eyes: (Bochs) Blue, (Jaxon) Blue, (Langkowski) Blue

Hair: (Bochs) Red, (Jaxon) Sandy blond, later white, (Langkowski) Blond

Strength level: The Box robot possesses great superhuman strength, and can lift (press) roughly 85 tons. The original Box could lift (press) 40 tons.

Known superhuman powers: The original Box robot was made primarily of steel, had vast strength and was highly resistant to damage. It was mentally controlled from outside by a person wearing a psycho-cybernetic helmet. The helmet transformed psions from the wearer's mind into electrical impulses which it then broadcast to Box. The wearer needed only to will Box to perform an action in order to cause Box to do it. Moreover, the helmet allowed its wearer to perceive mentally the sensory data registered by Box: the wearer "saw" and "heard" what Box perceived.

The new Box is constructed principally of an unidentified "living metal." Through an act of will, Roger Bochs can "phase into" Box's body in order to control it from within. This is to say that Bochs can cause his own body to pass into Box's form without damaging either, and to somehow fuse with Box's form. It is not known how Bochs became able to perform this feat. Bochs has indicated that only he can physically enter into and control Box in this way.

The new Box has greater strength than the previous one, and has a greater resistance to damage. Powerful jets in the soles of its feet enable the robot to fly. Box also contains many different devices, among which are ones enabling it to tap into computers and to receive or jam radio signals. Box contains special tracking equipment, and it can see in all areas of the electromagnetic spectrum. Other devices can also be installed within Box if the need arises.

Roger Bochs mentally controls Box from within its body, and he can perceive whatever it perceives. However, although Bochs can not actually feel physical pain while within Box, his psychic link with Box is so strong that he can feel psychic pain if enough force is inflicted upon Box. Moreover, the longer that Bochs stays within Box, the greater becomes the danger that he will become unable to leave it, and, indeed, psychologically incapable of leaving it. So far, Bochs has spent no more than a few hours at a time within Box. ∎

BROTHERS GRIMM

Real names: Percy and Barton Grimes
Occupations: Realtors
Identities: Known to American legal authorities
Legal status: Citizens of the United States with criminal records
Other known aliases: None
Place of birth: Fresno, California
Marital status: Single
Known relatives: None
Group affiliation: None
Base of operations: Los Angeles, California
First appearance: (originals) SPIDER-WOMAN #3, (current) IRON MAN #188

History: The original Brothers Grimm were two life-sized mannikins garbed in death-headed costumes who were animated by magic. Doll collector Nathan Dolly (who had once battled Iron Man as Mister Doll) acquired two 12-inch wooden figures from a dollmaker on Wundagore Mountain, a mountain in the Balkans of Central Europe where the Earthly essence of the demon Chthon was imprisoned (see *Chthon*). Chthon had infused the entire mountain and all that was on it with his mystical might. Thus the wood from which the dolls had been carved possessed magical potential. The dollmaker showed Dolly how he could animate the figures by projecting his life essence (astral form) into it. Nathan Dolly made the fatal error of trying to animate both dolls at once, and in succeeding to do so left his human body lifeless. His consciousness trapped in the twin figures, Dolly managed to mail himself to his wife Priscilla in America. There Dolly researched the occult until he discovered a way to transfer his life essense from the dolls to full-sized mannikins. The mannikins, whom he named the Brothers Grimm, possessed certain powers of prestidigitation, such as the conjuring of lethal substances in the form of novelty items. Dolly used his two surrogate bodies to commit crimes and acts of mayhem. Eventually Dolly desired to possess a real human body rather than exceedingly lifelike mannikins. With his wife's help, Nathan Dolly coerced the sorcerer Magnus into performing a magical rite of transference for him (see *Appendix: Magnus*). However, at the last minute, Magnus prevented Dolly's spirit from taking possession of the human body he sought to inhabit and blocked his spirit's return to the mannikins. Consequently, Nathan Dolly's life essence had nowhere to go and presumably passed from the Earthly plane.

Months later, two brothers acquired the run-down theater where the magical ceremony had taken place. Discovering the full-sized mannikins of the Brothers Grimm, Percy and Barton Grimes felt compelled to try the Brothers Grimm costumes on. Doing so, they discovered they possessed the same powers of prestidigitation that the original Brothers Grimm mannikins had. They used these powers to take revenge on a business rival, and were opposed by Iron Man II. Percy and Barton Grimes were taken into police custody for their crimes and are currently out on bail. It is not yet known how they gained the power of the Brothers Grimm: whether Nathan Dolly's abilities were conferred upon the costumes at his demise, or whether Dolly's life essence in some way possesses the costumes.

Height: (both) 5′ 10″ **Eyes:** (Percy) Blue, (Barton) Green
Weight: (both) 210 lbs. **Hair:** (Percy) Black, (Barton) Brown
Strength level: Each of the Brothers Grimm possesses the normal human strength of men of their age, height, and build, who engage in minimal regular exercise.
Known superhuman powers: The Brothers Grimm possess the magical ability to conjure seemingly from somewhere in their costumes a variety of novelty items with special offensive capabilities. The objects appear as if by sleight of hand, and seem to be limited to a size that can be held with one hand. Apparently, the Brothers can conjure whatever novelty items they can imagine. The limit to the number of items they can conjure in rapid succession is not yet known. Among the items they have produced are long strands of nearly unbreakable golden thread, corrosive-filled eggs, pies filled with blackbirds, paralytic "stardust," and amazingly fast-growing bean seeds.
Transportation: The Brothers Grimm employ floating five-pointed "stars" to perch upon and a small bank of clouds which is somehow solid enough to stand on. Where these vehicles come from is unknown. ∎

BROTHER VOODOO

Real Name: Jericho Drumm
Occupation: Ex-psychologist (M.D.), houngan (voodoo priest)
Legal status: Citizen of Haiti with no criminal record
Identity: Publicly known
Place of birth: Port-au-Prince, Haiti
Marital status: Single
Known relatives: Matilda (aunt), Daniel (brother, deceased)
Group affiliation: None
Base of operations: Port-au-Prince, Haiti
First appearance and origin: STRANGE TALES #169

History: When Jericho Drumm returned to his native Haiti after twelve years of education and practice in America, he discovered that his brother Daniel, the local houngan, was dying, a victim of the magic of a bokor (voodoo sorcerer) who claimed to be possessed by the spirit of Damballah, the serpent-god. Just before he died, Daniel made his brother vow to visit Papa Jambo, the man who taught him the arts of the houngan. Jericho Drumm did so, and after studying under the aged houngan for several weeks, gained a greater mastery of voodoo practices than his own brother. To augment his might still further, Papa Jambo performed a rite that summoned Daniel Drumm's spirit back from the dead and joined it with Jericho's own. Having fashioned a worthy successor, Papa Jambo died. As Brother Voodoo, Jericho Drumm challenged Damballah and his cult and vanquished them. He then established himself as Haiti's houngan supreme and champion of the land.

Height: 6′
Weight: 220 lbs
Eyes: Brown
Hair: Brown

Strength level: Unless augmented by his brother's spirit (see Known superhuman powers) Brother Voodoo possesses the normal human strength of a man of his age, height, and build who engages in moderate regular exercise.

Known superhuman powers: Brother Voodoo possesses numerous mystical and quasi-physical powers derived from the *loa*, the spirit-gods of voodoo, a faith originated and practiced in Haiti. Brother Voodoo can effortlessly enter a trance-like state in which he is immune to fire. Not only does he not feel the heat of the flame, but also his skin becomes mystically impervious to burning. Brother Voodoo cannot create flame, but he can control it. He can, for example, cause a matchstick to blaze like a bonfire or douse a raging wall of flame simply by concentrating on it.

Brother Voodoo can mystically create smoke at will. This smoke serves to cover his movements, and is always accompanied by the sound of voodoo drums. He can mystically see through smoke as if it were not there. The incessant pounding of the voodoo drums has a disorienting, unnerving effect on those who hear it.

Brother Voodoo also has the ability to command certain living things by a mystic sort of hypnotism. His degree of control over a creature is determined by the creature's level of intelligence. Human beings are least affected by his mystical hypnotism. Generally, he cannot command them to do much more than to stop what they are doing. He has greatest control over animals: snakes, dogs, birds, frogs and so

forth, will do his bidding within the parameters of their own physical and mental capacities. Even plants will obey his mystic coercion, although their immobility tends to limit their usefulness. The two major limitations on this power are that the being under control must be alive (zombies and rocks are unaffected by his power), and he can only command one creature at a time (if he were attacked by a pack of dogs, he would have to order them to back off one at a time). Unless Brother Voodoo keeps asserting control over a given creature, it will revert to its prior frame of mind immediately upon completion of its appointed task.

Brother Voodoo's most unusual talent is the ability to summon the specter of his deceased brother Daniel from its dwelling place within his own body. By calling upon his brother's spirit, he is able to double his physical strength, making him strong enough to lift approximately 500 pounds. He is able to send his brother's spirit forth to temporarily "possess" other people's bodies and totally control their actions. Though somewhat similar to his mystic-hypnotic control over people, spiritual possession is far more effective. Through his hypnotic power, he can influence a person to perform but one simple act before relinquishing control. Through possession, the person's body and mind is a virtual slave, capable of performing any number of complex activities for the duration of the possession. The only major limitation of the power is that the person possessed must be alive and cannot already be possessed by a foreign spirit. Once Brother Voodoo sends forth his brother's spirit to possess someone, the spirit becomes autonomous enough in its activity that Brother Voodoo does not have to consciously exert control over his second self. The spirit of Daniel Drumm becomes an invisible accomplice attuned to his brother's intents and needs. As yet, there is no known limit to the time in which Daniel can remain outside his brother's host-body. When Daniel ceases possession of a person, the dispossessed generally suffers disorientation, nausea or even trauma.

■

BUSHMASTER

Real name: Unknown
Occupation: Professional criminal
Identity: Secret
Legal status: Unknown
Other known aliases: None
Place of birth: Unknown
Marital status: Unknown
Known relatives: None
Group affiliation: Member of the Serpent Society
Base of operations: Mobile
First appearance: CAPTAIN AMERICA #310
History: A quadriplegic (either since birth or by accident), the man who became Bushmaster had bionic arms attached to his shoulders and a snakelike tail to his lower torso an undisclosed time ago by par-

ties unrevealed. Little else is known about him except that he accepted Sidewinder's invitation to join the Serpent Society and has been an active member since (see *Serpent Society*). While in battle with Modok, Bushmaster had his artificial arms severed, but they have since been reattached.
Height: 18½ feet (from head to tail)
Weight: Unknown
Eyes: Brown
Hair: Black
Unusual features: Bushmaster has no legs.
Strength level: Unknown.
Known superhuman powers: Bushmaster possesses a long snake-like tail that enables him to move and strike at superhuman speed. The tail, which extends ap-

proximately 14 feet from his lower abdomen, is permanently attached to his body. By rapid muscular contractions along the length of his tail, Bushmaster can move at speeds up to 40 miles per hour under optimal conditions. By wrapping his tail into a tight coil, and making a sudden lunging motion, he can move 18½ feet (his length from head to tail) in under 2 seconds. His tail has sufficient strength to deform a steel pipe 6 inches thick.
Weapons: Bushmaster wields two 6-inch "fangs" strapped to the back of each of his hands. The fangs are needle-sharp at their tips, and contain a fast-acting poison derived from snake venom.

■

CALIBAN

Real name: Unrevealed
Occupation: Locator of mutants for the Morlocks
Identity: Caliban's existence is unknown to the general public.
Legal status: Unknown
Former aliases: None
Place of birth: Unrevealed, presumably in New York City area
Marital status: Single
Known relatives: None
Group affiliation: Morlocks
First appearance: X-MEN #148
History: Caliban was born with a freakish appearance, which caused his father to name him (or possibly only nickname him) after the grotesque being in William Shakespeare's *The Tempest*. At some point Caliban was recruited by the mutant Callisto to use his power to find other mutants for her, whom she organized into the underground community known as the Morlocks (see *Callisto, Morlocks*). Caliban lived beneath the Manhattan streets with them, but felt lonely even among his fellow mutant outcasts.

One evening Caliban sensed the presence of mutants in a New York City nightclub. He entered only to find himself in conflict with the mutants Dazzler, Storm, and Ariel (now called Shadowcat), as well as the original Spider-Woman. The battle ended peacefully, with the four women allowing the pathetic Caliban, who only sought friendship, to return to his underground home.

Sometime later, the X-Men, the team of mutant adventurers to which Shadowcat belonged, found itself in conflict with the Morlocks. Shadowcat, suffering from fever, was held captive by Caliban, who had fallen in love with her. Intent on helping her teammates and escaping, Shadowcat promised to stay with Caliban forever if he would help the X-Men against his fellow Morlocks. Caliban agreed, and carried out his part of the bargain, but Shadowcat did not keep her promise. Weeks later the Morlocks kidnapped Shadowcat on orders from the vengeful Callisto, and attempted to force her to keep her word by marrying Caliban. Guilt-ridden, Shadowcat finally agreed to marry him, but Caliban, realizing that she did not truly wish to live with him, released her from her promise. Since then Caliban and Shadowcat have been friends.

Height: 5′ 8″
Weight: 150 lbs.
Eyes: Black pupils against yellow (no apparent irises)
Hair: None
Skin: Chalk white
Strength level: Caliban possesses the normal human strength of a man of his age, height, and build who engages in minimal exercise. However, a fear-induced surge of adrenalin can cause Caliban to become temporarily superhumanly strong. The limits of this superhuman strength are unknown, but he has proved to be nearly a match for the original Spider-Woman, who could lift (press) about 7 tons.
Known superhuman powers: Caliban is a mutant who can psychically sense the presence of other superhumanly powerful mutants within a radius of 25 miles. When Caliban is panic-stricken, adrenalin is released in his body which temporarily gives him two more superhuman powers. One is superhuman strength; the other is the ability to absorb the psionic energy in the fear radiated by humans around him and to turn it against them so as to overpower them. ∎

CALLISTO

Real name: Unrevealed
Occupation: Former leader of the Morlocks, who still leads them in the absence of their current leader, Storm
Identity: Callisto's present identity is unknown to the general public.
Legal status: Presumably a citizen of the United States, criminal record unknown
Former aliases: None known
Place of birth: Unrevealed
Marital status: Single; her past marital status is unrevealed
Known relatives: None
Group affiliation: Morlocks
First appearance: X-MEN #169
History: Very little is known about Callisto's past. She was once a beautiful young woman; it is not known how she lost her right eye or gained the scar on her face. Callisto came to think of herself as a mutant outcast from society and a rebel against it. She discovered the "Alley," a huge tunnel built underneath Manhattan in the 1950s as part of a network of tunnels for use by the United States government and military in case of nuclear war, but since abandoned. Callisto made her home in the "Alley," and then found another mutant, Caliban, who had the psychic ability to locate other superhumanly powerful mutants (see *Caliban*). Using Caliban's power, Callisto gathered together a large community of mutants who considered themselves social outcasts, and who came to live under her leadership in the network of tunnels. Callisto named these mutants the Morlocks after the subterranean race depicted by H.G. Wells in his science fiction novel *The Time Machine* (see *Morlocks*).

Eventually Callisto had the Morlocks kidnap the mutant known as the Angel, whom she intended to force to become her mate (see *Angel*). Several of the Angel's former teammates in the X-Men came to his rescue but were taken prisoner themselves (see *X-Men*). Finally, one of the X-Men, Storm, fought a trial by combat with Callisto and won (see *Storm*). Storm thereupon became Callisto's successor as leader of the Morlocks, and so the X-Men went free. Callisto subsequently clashed with the X-Men when she attempted to force one of their members, Shadowcat, to marry Caliban. Since then, however, the Morlocks have obeyed Storm's orders, and Callisto and the X-Men have become uneasy allies. Although Storm has lost her mutant powers, Callisto has not challenged her to another duel over the leadership of the Morlocks, preferring to wait until Storm regains her powers.

Height: 5' 9" **Eyes:** Blue
Weight: 130 lbs. **Hair:** Black
Strength level: Callisto possesses the normal human strength of a woman of her age, height, and build who engages in intensive regular exercise.
Known superhuman powers: Callisto is a mutant with superhumanly sharp senses of sight, hearing, smell, touch, and taste. The limits of these sense are as yet unknown. It is known that she has particularly good night vision, enabling her to see better in dark underground tunnels than an ordinary human could. Callisto's sharp senses enable her to track down people and animals with far greater skill than a normal human being who was a hunter could. ∎

CANNONBALL

Real Name: Samuel Guthrie
Occupation: Student, former coal miner
Legal status: American citizen with no criminal record, still a minor
Identity: Secret
Place of birth: Cumberland, Kentucky
Marital status: Single
Known relatives: Father (name unrevealed, deceased), mother (name unrevealed), Josh, Jedediah (brothers), another brother and two sisters (names unrevealed)
Group affiliation: New Mutants
Base of operations: Professor Xavier's School for Gifted Youngsters, Salem Center, New York
First appearance and origin: MARVEL GRAPHIC NOVEL #4
History: Sam Guthrie is a mutant whose latent superhuman abilities first manifested themselves when he was trapped with co-workers in a coal mine. The stress of trying to save his partner and himself triggered his propulsive power and enabled them to escape. Donald Pierce, a renegade member of the Inner Circle of the Hellfire Club (see *Hellfire Club*), located Guthrie and learned of his superhuman powers by means of a machine the Hellfire Club had built by adapting plans they had stolen for Professor Xavier's Cerebro device (see *X-Men*). Pierce recruited Guthrie to be one of his operatives, and sent him into battle against Xavier and his newly organized group, the New Mutants (see *New Mutants, Professor X*). However, during the battle, he refused to obey Pierce's order to kill the New Mutants, and Pierce attempted to kill Guthrie in retaliation. Xavier, however, saved Guthrie's life by defeating Pierce. Realizing that Guthrie was not an evil person, Xavier invited him to join the New Mutants, and Cannonball has risen to become one of the New Mutants' leaders.

Height: 6'   **Eyes:** Blue-grey
Weight: 150 lbs   **Hair:** Blond
Strength level: Cannonball possesses the normal human strength of a young man of his age, height, and build. However, when he uses his powers to apply thrust beneath him, the force thus generated has enabled him so far to bear aloft over a ton of weight in addition to his own.
Known superhuman powers: Cannonball possesses the ability to bodily generate thermo-chemical energy and release it from his skin. This energy, released by an act of will, is accompanied by smoke, flame and condensation, much like the exhaust of a rocket engine. At his present level of experience, he can only release this energy in one direction, beneath him. The equal and opposite reaction to this thrust causes his body to be propelled into the air like a human rocket. At first, he could not stop his propulsion until his immediate store of energy was depleted or until he hit an obstruction of sufficient mass to stop him. However, recently he has learned how to cut off his propulsive power at will.

As a side effect of forming the thermo-chemical energies over the surface of his body, Cannonball becomes virtually invulnerable. Accompanying the release of energy is a half-inch thick field which channels the explosion and protects his skin from the direct effects of the blast. It also negates momentum and related energy effects which cushions his entire body from any impact up to a half-minute from the depletion of his energy. Not only is he protected from rough landings, but he is also protected from nearly all types of injury while in flight. The protective field also protects any person or object with which he is in physical contact.
Limitations: At present there is no known upper limit to the range that Cannonball can travel while using his powers or to the velocity he can achieve. He has yet to be observed to travel as fast as the speed of sound. ∎

CAPTAIN AMERICA

Real Name: Steve Rogers
Occupation: Freelance artist, crimefighter
Legal status: Citizen of the United States with no criminal record
Identity: Secret
Former aliases: Nomad
Place of birth: New York City
Marital status: Single
Known relatives: Joseph (father, deceased), Sarah (mother, deceased)
Group affiliation: Former member of the Invaders, former partner to Bucky, the Falcon, and Nomad, current member of the East Coast Avengers
Base of operations: Mobile
First modern appearance: AVENGERS #4
Origin: CAPTAIN AMERICA #255
History: Steve Rogers was born during the Depression and grew up a frail youth in a poor family. His father died when he was a child, his mother when he was in his late teens. Horrified by newsreel footage of the Nazis in Europe, Rogers was inspired to try to enlist in the army. However, because of his frailty and sickness, he was rejected. Overhearing the boy's earnest plea to be accepted, General Chester Phillips of the U.S. Army offered Rogers the opportunity to take part in a special experiment called Operation: Rebirth. Rogers agreed and was taken to a secret laboratory in Washington, D.C. where he was introduced to Dr. Abraham Erskine (code named: Prof. Reinstein), the creator of the Super-Soldier formula.

After weeks of tests, Rogers was at last administered the Super-Soldier serum. Given part of the compound intravenously and another part orally, Rogers was then bombarded by "vita-rays," a special combination of exotic (in 1941) wavelengths of radiation designed to accelerate and stabilize the serum's effect on his body. Steve Rogers emerged from the vita-ray chamber with a body as perfect as a body can be and still be human. A Nazi spy who observed the experiment murdered Dr. Erskine mere minutes after its conclusion. Erskine died without fully committing the Super-Soldier formula to paper, leaving Steve Rogers the sole beneficiary of his genius.

Rogers was then put through an intensive physical and tactical training program, teaching him gymnastics, hand to hand combat and military strategy. Three months later, he was given his first assignment, to stop the Nazi agent called the Red Skull (see *Deceased: Red Skull*). To help him become a symbolic counterpoint to the Red Skull, Rogers was given the red, white and blue costume of Captain America.

All during the war, he served as both a symbol of freedom and America's most effective special operative. Then, during the final days of the war, he was trying to stop a bomb-loaded drone-plane launched by Nazi technician Baron Heinrich Zemo when the plane exploded, killing his partner Bucky; and throwing him unhurt into the icy Arctic waters. The Super-Soldier formula prevented crystallization of Captain America's bodily fluids, allowing him to enter a state of suspended animation. Decades later, he was rescued by the newly-formed Avengers and became a cornerstone of the team. His might undiminished, Captain America remains a symbol of liberty and justice.

Height: 6' 2" **Eyes:** Blue
Weight: 240 lbs **Hair:** Blond

Strength level: Captain America represents the pinnacle of human physical perfection. While not superhuman, he is as strong as a human being can be. He can lift (press) a maximum of 800 pounds with supreme effort.

Known superhuman powers: None

Abilities: Captain America has agility, strength, speed, endurance, and reaction time superior to any Olympic athlete who ever competed. The Super-Soldier formula that he has metabolized has enhanced all of his bodily functions to the peak of human efficiency. Notably, his body eliminates the excessive build-up of fatigue-producing poisons in his muscles, granting him phenomenal endurance.

Captain America has mastered the martial arts of American-style boxing and judo, and has combined these disciplines with his own unique acrobatic hand-to-hand style of combat. He engages in a daily regimen of rigorous exercise (including aerobics, weight-lifting, gymnastics, and simulated combat) to keep himself in peak condition. Captain America is one of the finest human combatants Earth has ever known.

Limitations: Captain America is subject to all human vulnerabilities, although his immunity to diseases is extraordinary.

Weapons: Captain America's only weapon is his shield, a concave disk 2.5 feet in diameter, weighing 12 pounds. It is made of a unique Vibranium-Adamantium alloy that has never been duplicated (see *Adamantium, Vibranium*). The shield was cast by American metallurgist Dr. Myron MacLain, who was contracted by the U.S. government to create an impenetrable substance to use for tanks during World War II. During his experiments, MacLain combined Vibranium with an Adamantium-steel alloy he was working with and created the disc-shaped shield. MacLain was never able to duplicate the process due to his inability to identify a still unknown factor that played a role in it. The shield was awarded to Captain America by the government several months after the beginning of his career.

The shield has great aerodynamic properties: it is able to slice through the air with minimal wind resistance and deflection of path. Its great overall resilience, combined with its natural concentric stiffness, enables it to rebound from solid objects with minimal loss of angular momentum. It is virtually indestructible: it is resistant to penetration, temperature extremes, and the entire electromagnetic spectrum of radiation. The only way it can be damaged in any way is by tampering with its molecular bonding. ■

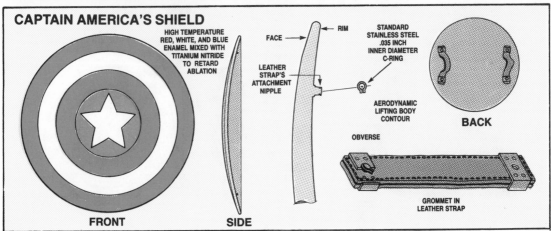

CAPTAIN AMERICA'S SHIELD

HIGH TEMPERATURE RED, WHITE, AND BLUE ENAMEL MIXED WITH TITANIUM NITRIDE TO RETARD ABLATION

FACE

RIM

LEATHER STRAP'S ATTACHMENT NIPPLE

STANDARD STAINLESS STEEL .035 INCH INNER DIAMETER C-RING

AERODYNAMIC LIFTING BODY CONTOUR

BACK

OBVERSE

GROMMET IN LEATHER STRAP

FRONT

SIDE

CAPTAIN AMERICA'S HOTLINE

Captain America's Hotline is a nationwide telephone service enabling American citizens to directly contact Captain America with information pertaining to national security or crises beyond the scope of conventional authorities. Captain America established the tollfree hotline using funds he obtained from the U.S. government as his back pay since World War II. The Hotline is headquartered in a nondescript building in Brooklyn Heights, New York, and is fully computer-automated so it requires no personnel. Incoming calls are recorded, transferred to printed text, and transmitted by computer to Captain America's portable briefcase terminal. All messages are simultaneously sent to the Stars and Stripes, an independent nationwide network of computer enthusiasts who have volunteered to assist Captain America in his data-processing. The volunteers scan all messages and correlate them as to duplication, urgency, and location. This information extract is then forwarded by computer through telephone lines to Captain America. As Captain America roves the country, he has constant access to information regarding his mission to serve the nation.

First appearance: CAPTAIN AMERICA #312.

HOTLINE HEADQUARTERS

BRIEFCASE TERMINAL

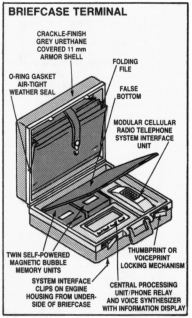

CRACKLE-FINISH GREY URETHANE COVERED 11 mm ARMOR SHELL

FOLDING FILE

O-RING GASKET AIR-TIGHT WEATHER SEAL

FALSE BOTTOM

MODULAR CELLULAR RADIO TELEPHONE SYSTEM INTERFACE UNIT

TWIN SELF-POWERED MAGNETIC BUBBLE MEMORY UNITS

THUMBPRINT OR VOICEPRINT LOCKING MECHANISM

SYSTEM INTERFACE CLIPS ON ENGINE HOUSING FROM UNDER-SIDE OF BRIEFCASE

CENTRAL PROCESSING UNIT/PHONE RELAY AND VOICE SYNTHESIZER WITH INFORMATION DISPLAY

CAPTAIN AMERICA'S MOTORCYCLE

Captain America rides a Harley-Davidson custom special motorcycle, custom built for him by young motorcycle mechanic Jonathan Coulson of Queens, New York. Coulson modified the bike for the Captain in repayment for the Avenger's help in reconciling the youth with his father. Captain America then took it to SHIELD, where it was further modified. While living in Brooklyn Heights, Captain America stored the motorcycle in a service garage operated by Richard Dumbrowski. Captain America now keeps his motorcycle in his van and takes it wherever he travels (see *Captain America's Van*).

First appearance: CAPTAIN AMERICA #259.

Data: Captain America's Motorcycle
Make and model: Harley-Davidson Custom Special
Engine: 700 cc HV V-twin in-line 4 stroke engine
Curb weight, full tank: 480 lbs.
Seat height: 32 inches
Cruising range: 340 miles
Performance:
Standing start 1/4 mile: 11.5 sec. @ 122 miles per hour
Engine RPM at 60 mph top gear: 3850

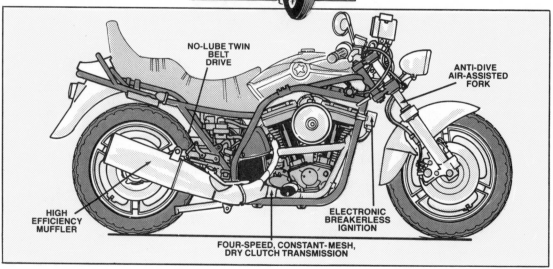

NO-LUBE TWIN BELT DRIVE

ANTI-DIVE AIR-ASSISTED FORK

HIGH EFFICIENCY MUFFLER

ELECTRONIC BREAKERLESS IGNITION

FOUR-SPEED, CONSTANT-MESH, DRY CLUTCH TRANSMISSION

CAPTAIN AMERICA'S VAN

Captain America travels in a custom-built Chevrolet van whose nondescript outward appearance allows him to travel incognito. The van was outfitted by the Wakanda Design Group, the same company who services the Avengers' Quinjets and automobiles (see *Avengers Quinjets*). The van's interior contains a mount for Captain America's motorcycle and a built-in cot for sleeping. Built into the engine housing is a computer interface cradle designed to work in conjunction with Captain America's briefcase modem-computer system to enable him to receive messages from his hotline service (see *Captain America's Hotline*). First appearance: CAPTAIN AMERICA #318.

Data: Captain America's Van
Curb weight: 5,900 lbs.
Engine: Chevrolet turbo-charged electronically fuel-injected V-8 290 cubic inch 210 horsepower
Overall length: 162″
Wheel base: 82″
Steering radius, 80° turn: 66″
Range at 6,300 lbs. (140 gallons @ 30 miles per gallon at 55 miles per hour): 4,200 miles

Performance:
0–400 mph acceleration: 4.2 sec.
0–60 mph acceleration: 7.5 sec.
0–100 mph acceleration: 11.5 sec.
Special features: Alternating license plates. Multilayered skin includes epitaxial tomographically aligned crystal film that allows vehicle to change color.

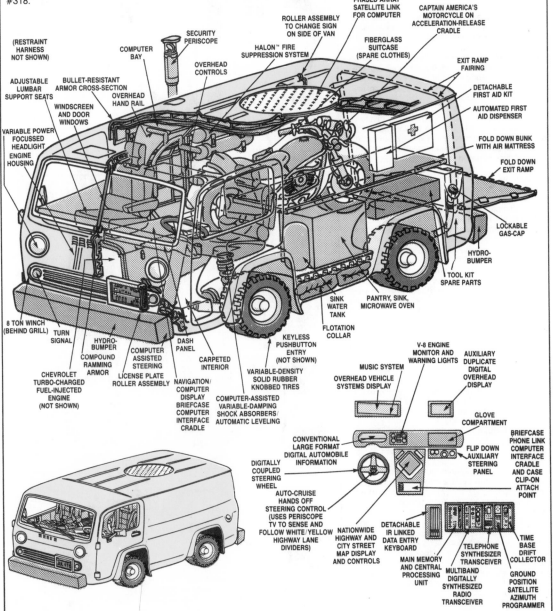

113

CAPTAIN BRITAIN

Real Name: Brian Braddock
Occupation: Physics student at Thames University in London
Legal status: Citizen of the United Kingdom with no criminal record
Identity: Secret
Place of birth: Malden, England
Marital status: Single
Known relatives: None
Group affiliation: None
Base of operations: London, England
First American appearance: MARVEL TEAM-UP #65, (in new uniform) CAPTAIN AMERICA #305
History: Brian Braddock was employed as a student research assistant at the Darkmoor Research Centre when the criminal Reaver attacked the base with the intent to steal its secrets. In his attempt to escape, Braddock ran his motorcycle off a cliff and lay near death. In a vision, Merlin the Magician and the Goddess of the Northern Skies appeared to him and bade him to choose one of the mystic objects before him: the amulet of right or the sword of might (see *Merlin*). Braddock chose the amulet of right and was instantly bombarded with mystical energy that endowed him with superhuman strength and stamina. The patron spirits decreed that he shall be Britain's champion and garbed him in a symbolic costume and gave him a mystic star-sceptre to enhance his fighting ability.

Captain Britain battled various criminals and superhuman menaces for a time, then mysteriously dropped out of sight. He was found some time later by the Black Knight, a victim of amnesia. Captain Britain accompanied the Black Knight, who had just returned from the Crusades on a quest to save Camelot (see *Black Knight*). This adventure took them to various alternate dimensions. While away, Captain Britain's memory returned. At the quest's end, Captain Britain and his elfin companion Jackdaw were sent by Merlin back to Earth. En route, Merlin transformed Captain Britain's amulet and star-sceptre into a lattice of mystical "micro-circuitry" duplicating all the properties of his old weaponry. Eventually arriving on Earth, Captain Britain became engaged in combatting the machinations of an extradimensional madman, during the course of which Jackdaw was killed. Captain Britain emerged victorious, saving the world in the process, and is currently England's foremost champion.

Height: 5' 11"
Weight: 180 lbs
Eyes: Blue
Hair: Blond
Strength level: When not clad in his strength-augmenting uniform, Captain Britain possesses the normal human strength of a man of his age, height, and weight, who engages in regular exercise. With his strength augmented by his uniform, Captain Britain can lift (press) approximately 2 tons under optimal conditions.
Known superhuman conditions: Captain Britain possesses a number of superhuman powers derived from his mystically enhanced uniform. First, the uniform enhances his strength (see Strength level). Second, the uniform enables him to fly. Captain Britain can fly at a maximum speed just under the speed of sound (770 miles per hour) for prolonged periods of time (until bodily fatigue requires him to rest). Third, the uniform can erect mystical force fields at Captain Britain's mental command. This force field is employed to protect him from atmospheric conditions while flying. It is strong enough to deflect a bazooka shell without deforming or rendering its wielder unconscious from the concussion. (Repeated blasts would weaken the field considerably, and eventually penetrate it.) The uniform also enhances Captain Britain's stamina and reflexes to superhuman levels. ∎

CAPTAIN MARVEL

Real name: Monica Rambeau
Occupation: Former harbor patroller, now professional adventurer
Legal status: Citizen of the United States with no criminal record
Identity: Secret
Former aliases: None
Place of birth: New Orleans, Louisiana
Marital status: Single
Known relatives: Frank (father), Maria (mother)
Group affiliation: East Coast Avengers
Base of operations: New Orleans, Louisiana
First appearance: AMAZING SPIDER-MAN ANNUAL #16

History: Monica Rambeau was a lieutenant in the New Orleans harbor patrol when a friend of her grandfather, physicist Andre LeClare, came to her for help. LeClare had discovered a means to draw energy from another dimension, while working under the auspices of South American dictator Ernesto Ramirez. Learning that Generalissimo Ramirez intended to use his discovery to make a weapon, LeClare journeyed to the United States to enlist Rambeau's aid. Rambeau agreed to investigate his claim and accompanied LeClare to an oil rig where the dictator had assembled his energy disruptor weapon. While attempting to destroy the weapon, Rambeau was bombarded by its extradimensional energies and converted into living energy. Materializing in physical form back in New Orleans, Rambeau contacted the navy, then put together an identity-concealing costume out of Mardi Gras outfits. Instinctively reassuming her energy-state, she flew back to the oil rig to witness LeClare getting shot by the scientist who designed the disruptor and to discover that the damaged weapon had created a growing interdimensional breech. Rambeau was sucked into the breech where she managed to seal the hole with her body's own energies. She then saved LeClare from a second bullet and overpowered the gunman, leaving him to the authorities. Days later, the convalescing Professor LeClare visited Rambeau and presented her with a costume based on the one she had worn, only composed of unstable molecules. LeClare explained to the woman the theoretical extent of her new powers and suggested that she use them for the public good. He showed her a newspaper account of her first exploit wherein she was dubbed "Captain Marvel."

Rambeau decided the professor's suggestion had merit, and resigned from the harbor partrol so she could devote more time to it. Soon discovering that the extra energy she had absorbed from the interdimensional breech was building up incontrollably, Rambeau traveled to New York City to enlist the aid of Reed Richards of the Fantastic Four. When she found Richards was not home, she went to the Avengers where Iron Man, with the aid of the passing Spider-Man, managed to siphon off the excess energy. As Captain Marvel, Rambeau accepted the Wasp's offer to become an Avenger-in-training. In a short time, Captain Marvel was awarded full membership in the Avengers, and she has been active ever since.

Recently Captain Marvel revealed to her parents her secret identity. She was also abducted to the Skrull Galaxy recently by a band of space pirates led by Nebula (see

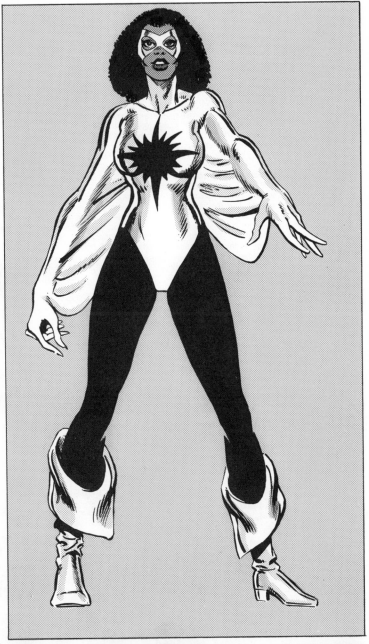

Nebula). After spending several weeks in outer space, she found that she had lost a noticeable amount of weight by the time she returned to Earth.

Height: 5' 10"
Weight: 130 lbs.
Eyes: Brown
Hair: Black
Strength level: Captain Marvel possesses the normal human strength of a woman of her age, height and build, who engages in moderate regular exercise.

Known superhuman powers: Captain Marvel possesses the power to transform her body into any form of energy in the electromagnetic spectrum, from radio waves to x-rays and every wavelength in between, simply by willing it. She apparently accomplishes this transformation by mentally shunting the matter of her body into the dimension from which she draws her energy and replacing it with a corresponding amount of energy. Her mind remains in this dimension to control the energy-parcel that has taken the place of her body. By assuming an energy-form, she gains all of the properties of that energy.

For instance, if she becomes light, she is blindingly bright. Some of her energy-forms permit her to pass through solid objects. All of her energy-forms enable her to fly. In all energy-forms except visible light, she is invisible. The electromagnetic spectrum is comprised of cosmic-ray photons, gamma rays, X-rays, ultraviolet radiation, visible light, infrared radiation, microwaves, and radio waves.

Besides being able to totally exchange her matter for energy, Captain Marvel can direct relatively small amounts of the energies she employs through her hands or presumably any other area of her body. She apparently does this by creating small interfaces with the dimension from which she derives her powers, and letting the designated energy pass through. She mentally controls both the type and quantity of energy she wishes to transmit. It is not known the maximum amount of energy she can transmit at a given time.

Captain Marvel can use her light-energies to create convincing three-dimensional holographic images of herself. Other than the fact that they cast no shadows, they are extremely lifelike.

In some as yet unknown manner, Captain Marvel can travel slower than the speed of light (186,274 miles per second) in her various energy forms. She may accomplish this by retaining a few molecules of matter interspersed with her energy-form, sufficient to create a "dragging" effect.

Limitations: Captain Marvel is apparently unlimited by the amount of time that she can remain in her energy-form. She apparently only transform herself into one wavelength of energy at a time, but she can transform between one energy-state and another in a fraction of a second. As noted above, the amount of energy she can transmit through her body at a given time is not known. Extensive energy transformation and manipulation can be physically taxing once she reassumes her physical form.

Note: Captain Marvel is not related in any way to the Kree Captain Mar-Vell, who was also called Captain Marvel by the inhabitants of Earth (see *Deceased: Captain Mar-Vell*). ∎

CAPTAIN ULTRA

Real name: Unrevealed
Occupation: Plumber, adventurer
Identity: Secret
Legal status: Citizen of the United States with no criminal record
Other known aliases: None
Place of birth: Unknown
Marital status: Unknown
Known relatives: None
Group affiliation: None
Base of operations: Chicago, Illinois
First appearance: FANTASTIC FOUR #177

History: Very little is known about the background of Captain Ultra. He was first glimpsed in the New York area when he answered a newspaper advertisement placed by the Wizard to recruit a new fourth member for the Frightful Four (see *Wizard*). Although the Wizard deemed Ultra's superhuman powers a worthy addition to the team, he soon rejected the applicant for fainting in the presence of a lit match. Captain Ultra was next glimpsed at the mass meeting for "super heroes" at the Richmond Riding Academy on Long Island prompted by an unauthorized television program revealing the existence of the Defenders. Among the twenty costumed crimefighters who investigated the spurious open invitation, Ultra accompanied a small band of them into New York City to stop a crime spree. Like the rest of the ersatz Defenders, Captain Ultra became disenchanted with the team and never petitioned the core members of the Defenders for acceptance into their ranks. Captain Ultra was most recently seen in Chicago, where in his civilian identity he relocated, when he stumbled into the thunder god Thor during the Asgardian's brief residency there. Captain Ultra's current activities are unknown.

Height: 5′ 11″
Weight: 175 lbs.
Eyes: Unknown
Hair: Unknown
Strength level: Captain Ultra possesses superhuman strength enabling him to lift (press) approximately 9 tons under optimal conditions.
Known superhuman powers: Besides superhuman strength, Captain Ultra possesses the ability to fly (presumably this is a natural ability and not a property of his costume) and the ability to see through solid objects (also presumably natural). Ultra can fly at speeds up to 60 miles per hour, the maximum rate of speed at which he can still breathe. He can see through substances up to 18 inches in thickness, at a maximum distance of 20 feet.
Limitations: Captain Ultra cannot tolerate fire, even the minutest flame. Whether this is a physical vulnerability or a psychological aberration is not known. ∎

CAPTAIN UNIVERSE

Captain Universe is the generic name for the recipient of the Uni-Power, a special kind of energy that endows an individual with a host of superhuman powers. The Uni-Power is a manifestation of the Enigma Force, an extradimensional energy originating in the subatomic realm called the Microverse, wielded by the ethereal Time Travelers (see *Appendix: Other Dimensions*). The Uni-Power appears to be a floating globule of luminescent energy that appears seemingly from out of nowhere to engulf an individual, conferring upon him or her the costume, powers and knowledge of Captain Universe. The Uni-Power only manifests itself at a time of crisis — be it personal or worldwide — and withdraws when the crisis has abated. How it chooses the individual who gets full possession of the Uni-Power to solve his or her crisis is not yet known. The Uni-Power does not remain un-manifested for very long. It transfers from one person to another across the face of the world with no perceptible time lapse between. At all times somewhere on Earth there is a Captain Universe (once, a pair of twins were Captain Universe simultaneously).

The Uni-Power can be manipulated by each Captain Universe in a variety of ways, dependent upon each recipient's imagination and strength. The Uni-Power amplifies strength about fifty times. Thus if a person can normally lift (press) 150 pounds, he or she would now be able to lift approximately 7,500 pounds. Each Captain Universe is also granted the ability to fly by harnessing the Uni-Power's energy to generate anti-gravitons. The Uni-Power also grants the ability to manipulate the molecular structure of objects, changing one shape into another, or even transmuting the elements of an object from one substance to another. This power of molecular manipulation extends to both organic and inorganic matter. Thus the Uni-Power can be used to heal wounds by rearranging the molecules of flesh, tissues or organs, or it can be used to alter the physical characteristics of a person (enlarging the hands or changing their features). The Uni-Power can also be wielded like an energy-beam, generating a luminous burst of energy with a concussive force determined to an extent by the user's ability. The Uni-Power also grants each Captain Universe Uni-Vision which enables the user to see the molecular structure of an object, to see through walls, or to see long distances away. The Uni-Vision is emitted by Captain Universe's eyes and produces a visible beam of energy. This energy has certain hypnotic side-effects: a skillful wielder of the Uni-Vision can use it to hypnotize people into telling the truth.

So far, the identities and exploits of but a handful of Captain Universes have been disclosed. The first was ex-astronaut Ray Coffin (MICRONAUTS #8) who wielded the Uni-Power to help battle the Microversian tyrant Baron Karza. Other recipients have been Steve Coffin, the son of the original Captain Universe (MARVEL SPOTLIGHT #9), the twins Clare and Ann Dodgson (MARVEL SPOTLIGHT #10), the cat burglar Monty Walsh (MARVEL SPOTLIGHT #11), the Hulk's alter ego Bruce Banner (HULK ANNUAL #10) and the sorcerer supreme Doctor Strange (MICRONAUTS #35). ∎

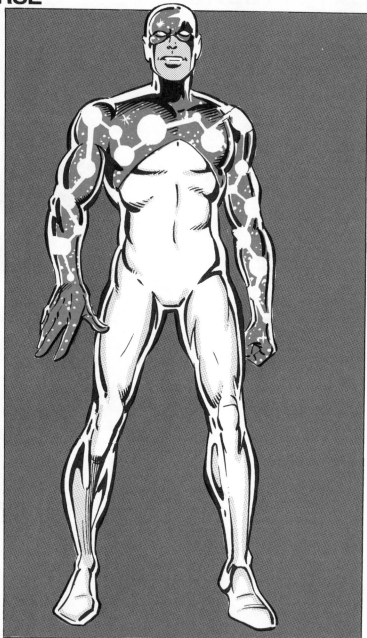

CASSIDY, BLACK TOM

Real Name: Thomas Samuel Eamon Cassidy
Occupation: Professional criminal
Identity: Publicly known
Legal status: Citizen of Ireland with an international criminal record
Former aliases: None
Place of birth: Dublin, Ireland
Marital status: Single
Known relatives: Sean Cassidy (alias Banshee, cousin), Theresa Rourke (alias Siryn, cousin), Maeve Rourke Cassidy (cousin by marriage, deceased)
Group affiliation: Frequent partner of the Juggernaut
Base of operations: Mobile
First appearance: X-MEN #99 (in shadow), #101 (fully seen)
History: Thomas "Black Tom" Cassidy was the heir to his family fortune and estate of Cassidy Keep in Ireland. However, he wagered both the fortune and estate on a throw of dice, and thereby lost them to his younger cousin, Sean Cassidy. Black Tom and Sean Cassidy were rivals for the love of Maeve Rourke, and Sean eventually prevailed and married her (see *Cassidy, Sean*).

While still a young man, Black Tom Cassidy turned to crime as a way of seeking thrills. Discovering how much he liked it, Black Tom decided to make crime his profession. At first he masked his criminal activities under the guise of being a soldier of fortune. As such, he roamed the world offering his services as a gun for hire, while pursuing his criminal activities as well. While imprisoned in a Third World jail for acting as a mercenary for revolutionary forces that were defeated, Black Tom Cassidy met a fellow mercenary, Cain Marko. Cassidy and Marko struck up a friendship, and Cassidy used his own mutant power, which he had already discovered, to enable both of them to escape jail.

Sean Cassidy was assigned by Interpol to a top secret mission which required that he stay out of touch with his family for a considerable length of time. When he left on his mission, his wife Maeve was in her first month of pregnancy, although neither Sean nor Maeve knew it at the time. Their daughter, Theresa, was born during Sean's absence. Maeve took the infant Theresa with her on a visit to her relatives in Armagh in Northern Ireland. While she was there, Maeve, an innocent bystander, was killed by an explosion caused by terrorists. No trace of Theresa was found by the authorities, and it was assumed that she too had been killed. However, Black Tom Cassidy had been present at the scene of the explosion and had secretly carried Theresa off with him. Knowing of his own and Sean's mutant powers (Sean Cassidy is the former X-Man known as the Banshee), Black Tom suspected that Theresa might herself develop superhuman powers as she grew older. Moreover, Black Tom saw Theresa as the daughter he wished that he and Maeve could have had together. So Black Tom decided to raise Theresa himself secretly. Those who knew that Theresa had been born decided not to inform Sean Cassidy that Maeve had had a daughter in order to spare him additional grief when he returned and learned of Maeve's death.

Eventually Black Tom Cassidy was reunited with his friend Cain Marko, who had become the superhumanly powerful Juggernaut (see *Juggernaut*). Cassidy suggested they form a partnership for criminal activities, and this partnership has proved profitable to both ever since. Cassidy forced Theresa, who had grown into adolescence and developed superhuman powers, to help them in their cimes, but her heart was never in a life of crime (see *Siryn*). While briefly in the custody of legal authorites, Black Tom gentlemanly exonerated Theresa of responsbility for her crimes, and wrote a letter to Sean explaining who Theresa was. Black Tom escaped and Sean and Theresa were joyfully reunited. Today Black Tom Cassidy and the Juggernaut both remain at large.
Height: 6'
Weight: 200 lbs.
Eyes: Dark blue
Hair: Black
Strength level: Black Tom Cassidy possesses the normal human strength of a man of his age, height, and build who engages in moderate regular exercise.
Known superhuman powers: Black Tom Cassidy is a mutant with the superhuman power to generate blasts of force or heat. He uses a wooden shillelagh (a kind of Irish cane) to help him project the blasts, since wood acts as a focus for his power. It is not known whether there is anything unusual about his shillelagh, or how well, if at all, he can use his power without focusing it through wood. No upper limit has yet been observed as to the power of the energy blasts he can project. He can wreak considerable damage with the force blasts, and can melt metal with focused heat blasts. ■

CASSIDY, SEAN

Real Name: Sean Cassidy
Occupation: Former Interpol agent, former adventurer, now a retired gentleman of leisure
Identity: Secret
Legal status: Citizen of the Republic of Ireland with no criminal record
Former aliases: The Banshee
Place of birth: Cassidy Keep, Ireland
Marital status: Widower
Known relatives: Maeve (wife, deceased), Thomas (known as "Black Tom," cousin), Theresa Rourke (alias Siryn, daughter)
Group affiliation: Former member of Factor Three, former member of the X-Men
Base of operations: Cassidy Keep, Ireland and Muir Island, off the coast of Scotland
First appearance: X-MEN #28
Final appearance (as Banshee): X-MEN #129

History: Sean Cassidy was born as the heir to the castle and estate of Cassidy Keep, Ireland, as well as a small fortune. After graduating from Trinity College, Dublin, with the degree of Bachelor of Science, Cassidy became a detective at Interpol, the international law enforcement organization. By the time he married Maeve Rourke, Cassidy had risen to achieve the rank of inspector at Interpol. Although Cassidy had discovered his mutant powers in his adolescence, he kept them secret, even from the rest of Interpol.

However, Cassidy's powers were known to his disreputable cousin Black Tom Cassidy, who had discovered that he himself was a superhumanly powerful mutant (see *Cassidy, Black Tom*). Sean and Black Tom had long been rivals, especially over the love of Maeve Rourke before she finally married Sean.

Sean Cassidy was assigned by Interpol to a top secret mission which required that he stay out of touch with his family for a considerable length of time. When he left on the mission, Maeve was in her first month of pregnancy, although neither Sean nor Maeve knew it at the time. Their daughter, Theresa, was born during Sean's absence. Maeve took the infant Theresa with her on a visit to her relatives in Armagh in Northern Ireland. While she was there, Maeve, an innocent bystander, was killed by an explosion caused by terrorists. No trace of Theresa was found by the authorities, and they and Maeve's relatives assumed that Theresa had also been killed in the explosion. In fact, however, Black Tom Cassidy had been present at the scene of the explosion and had secretly carried Theresa off with him. Black Tom suspected that Theresa might develop superhuman mutant powers as she grew older, and therefore he intended to raise her secretly so that he might exploit her powers himself.

On returning from his mission Cassidy was informed that his wife was dead. Those who knew that Theresa had been born decided not to inform Sean Cassidy that Maeve had had a daughter in order to spare him further grief. At first Cassidy attempted to escape his despair over this news by throwing himself into his work at Interpol. Eventually, however, the still melancholy Cassidy left Interpol to become a freelance operative, and as time went on, he even found himself engaged in criminal activities. The legal authorities never discovered that Cassidy was guilty of crimes,

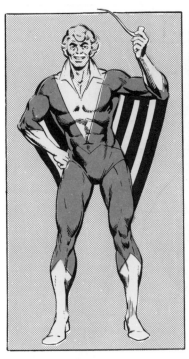

but the mutant known as the Changeling did, thanks to the technology of the subversive organization of superhumanly powerful mutants and their underlings known as Factor Three (see *Changeling, Appendix: Factor Three*). The Changeling contacted Cassidy, whom Factor Three's technology had also identified as a superhumanly powerful mutant, and invited him to join the organization. Cassidy was appalled upon learning of Factor Three's goals and adamantly refused. However, the Changeling and his superior, the so-called Mutant Master, agreed that Cassidy's powers and knowledge of the workings of law enforcement agencies were too valuable for Factor Three to lose, and so they sent their agents to capture Cassidy. Factor Three had a headband containing explosives placed around Cassidy's head. If Cassidy defied their orders, the headband could be detonated by remote control; it would also detonate if Cassidy attempted to remove the headband himself. Furthermore, Factor Three put Cassidy, who went by the code name of the Banshee, under the supervision of one of their trusted human agents, the Ogre. The Banshee thus felt forced to obey Factor Three's commands, and, accompanied by the Ogre, performed various criminal missions for the organization.

While in New York City on a mission for Factor Three, the Banshee clashed with the original X-Men, who captured both him and the Ogre (see *X-Men*). The X-Men's leader, Professor Charles Xavier, used a psionic "mental bolt" on the Banshee's headband which prevented the detonation mechanism from functioning so that the Banshee could remove it. Once freed of the headband, the Banshee told the X-Men all that he knew about Factor Three. Later, the Banshee discovered Factor Three's secret European headquarters, only to be recaptured. But the Banshee participated in the X-Men's battle with the Mutant Master, and it was the Banshee's powers which exposed the Mutant Master as an extraterrestrial.

The Banshee returned to an honest life, and time passed without major incidents for him, except for his brief captivities by the Sentinels and by the second Secret Empire. Professor Xavier later invited the Banshee to join the X-Men when he was recruiting new members to battle the menace of Krakoa (see *Appendix: Krakoa*). The Banshee remained in the X-Men for some time. It was during this time that he met Xavier's silent partner, the Scots geneticist Moira MacTaggert. Cassidy and MacTaggert soon fell in love with each other, but while Cassidy was based at Xavier's mansion, MacTaggert was based at her mutant research center on Muir Island off the coast of Scotland.

While in Japan the X-Men found themselves in battle with Moses Magnum, a criminal mastermind who had been endowed with the psionic power to cause earthquakes (see *Appendix: Magnum, Moses*). Magnum unleashed tremendous psionic energy in an attempt to create seismic waves great enough to cause a chain reaction that would destroy Japan. The Banshee simultaneously used his powers to create waves of vibratory force that would cancel out the waves of force that Magnum was creating. The Banshee succeeded to the extent that only small uninhabited islands in the vicinity of Magnum's base were destroyed. However, the tremendous strain that the Banshee had placed upon his powers in performing this heroic feat seriously damaged his vocal cords. Cassidy soon regained his ability to speak, but his superhuman sonic powers, which were dependent on his vocal cords, have to this day not returned.

Cassidy accompanied the X-Men to Muir Island where they battled the menace of Proteus, Moira MacTaggert's mutant son, who at one point took his mother prisoner. Proteus was defeated, and the experience of seeing the woman he loved in danger made Cassidy realize that he wanted to stay by her side. Therefore, Cassidy retired

from the X-Men, and he and Moira MacTaggert now principally divide their time between Cassidy Keep and Muir Island. Cassidy briefly returned to aid the X-Men against operatives of Arcade during an emergency situation when most of the X-Men were simultaneously engaged in conflict with an android which Doctor Doom had created in his own image (see *Arcade, Doctor Doom*).

Later, the X-Men battled Black Tom Cassidy, his partner the Juggernaut, and Theresa, who had developed sonic powers of her own, which she used under the alias of Siryn (see *Siryn*). Theresa felt obliged by her duty towards Black Tom, the man who had raised her (and whom she called "uncle" out of respect, although they are actually cousins), to assist him in his crimes. After they were defeated by the X-Men, Black Tom gave Theresa a letter to Sean, explaining that she was the daughter he had thought was dead. Sean and Theresa were joyfully united at Xavier's mansion, and Theresa now lives with Sean and Moira MacTaggert.

Height: 6′   **Eyes:** Blue-green
Weight: 170 lbs.   **Hair:** Reddish-blond
Strength level: Sean Cassidy possesses the normal human strength of a man of his age, height, and weight who engages in regular exercise.

Former superhuman powers: Sean Cassidy is a mutant who had the same powers that his daughter Siryn has, but who could not use them in as many ways as she can. His powers functioned in the same way that hers do: basically he could create powerful sonic waves with his voice with which he could achieve various effects, often with the assistance of limited psionic abilities which functioned only in unison with his sonic power. The Banshee could use his sonic powers to propel himself through the air in flight, to shatter solid objects, to place human beings temporarily into a hypnotic trance, or to cause human beings to fall temporarily unconscious. ∎

CELESTIALS

The Celestials are a star-faring race of humanoid aliens who possess untold cosmic power. Standing two thousand feet tall, the Celestials are clad in full body armor. No Earth being has ever seen what they look like beneath their armor or knows their origin.

What is known is that they have visited the Earth at four different periods in the Earth's past, each time altering the course of history. The First Celestial Host came to Earth approximately one million years ago to perform genetic tests and experimentation on Earth's highest lifeform, the nascent human being. Testing the versatility of human genes, the First Host created two sub-species of humanity, the Eternals and the Deviants (see *Deviants, Eternals*). Their sole legacy to the mainstream human race was the implantation of a dormant DNA complex which would one day permit benevolent mutations.

The Second Celestial Host came to Earth approximately twenty-five thousand years ago to inspect the results of their first visit. Finding the direction of Deviant technology counter-productive, the Celestials destroyed the Deviants' major stronghold, Lemuria. Repercussions of that destruction caused tectonic plate shifting that eventually contributed to the sinking of the continent of Atlantis (see *Atlantis*).

The Third Celestial Host arrived on Earth one thousand years ago to inspect the progress of the human race. Their landing site was arranged by the Eternals working in conjunction with the Incas of Peru. The Third Host was met by a contingent of Earth's mythological gods, including Odin of the Asgardians and Zeus of the Olympians, who challenged the Celestials' right to interfere in Earth's affairs. The outcome of that encounter was that all of the major races of gods swore to forego their active involvement in the destiny of mankind.

The Fourth Celestial Host arrived in recent years in order to judge mankind's worthiness now that the dormant DNA complex for benevolent mutations had become activated by the worldwide increase in radiation levels. The Celestials deemed humanity fit to survive. A group of twelve human beings representing the great accomplishments of mankind accompanied the Celestials when they left Earth (see *Appendix: Young Gods*).

It is not known how many Celestials there are in existence. Even the number of Celestials on Earth in the Fourth Host is a mystery. Nine were known by name and function, others were glimpsed but not identified. The Fourth Host was led by the Celestial known only as The One Above All, who remained aboard the orbiting mothership during the entire stay on Earth. The head of the landing party was Arishem.

However, it is known that the Celestials have visited many other worlds in order to perform genetic experimentation. For example, the Skrulls are known to be a result of Celestial experimentation (see *Skrulls*). The Celestials have returned to judge many of these worlds, and Earth is apparently the only one of these that they judged favorably and hence did not destroy for posing a potential menace to the universe.

There have only been indications of the full scope of the Celestials' power. Each member of the Fourth Host withstood a full frontal attack by the collective power of the Eternals and the Asgardians. Arishem has been shown to have sufficient power to permanently seal dimensional portals to the godly realms. The Celestials are not indestructible, however. During the Third Host, the Celestials used their combined might to slay one of their brethren for breach of conduct.

Another indication of the Celestials' power is that when the Fourth Host left Earth, they eradicated all evidence of their recent and past presence from the minds and records of mortal men. Only the Eternals, Deviants, dimensional gods of Earth, and a handful of human beings are now aware of their existence and remember the nature of their visits.
brethren for breach of conduct.

Another indication of the Celestials' power is that when the Fourth Host left Earth, they eradicated all evidence of their recent and past presence from the minds and records of mortal men. Only the Eternals, Deviants, dimensional gods of Earth, and a handful of human beings are now aware of their existence and remember the nature of their visits. ∎

ARISHEM THE JUDGE
First appeared in ETERNALS #2

GAMMENON THE GATHERER
First appeared in ETERNALS #4

JEMIAH THE ANALYZER
First appeared in ETERNALS #7

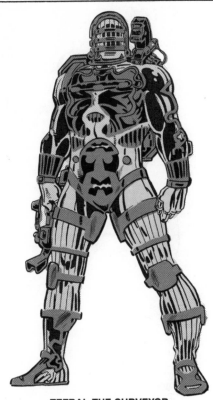

TEFRAL THE SURVEYOR
First appeared in ETERNALS #7

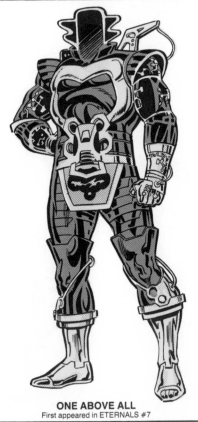

ONE ABOVE ALL
First appeared in ETERNALS #7

NEZARR THE CALCULATOR
First appeared in ETERNALS #9

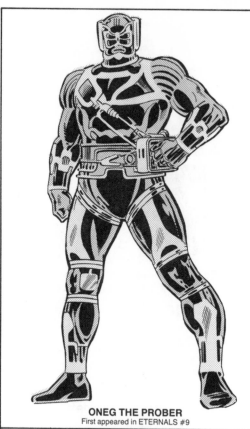

ONEG THE PROBER
First appeared in ETERNALS #9

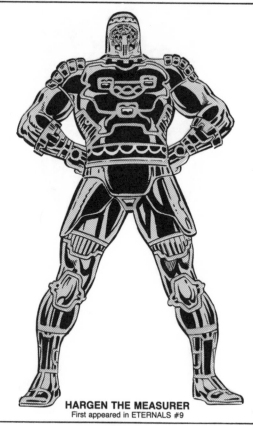

HARGEN THE MEASURER
First appeared in ETERNALS #9

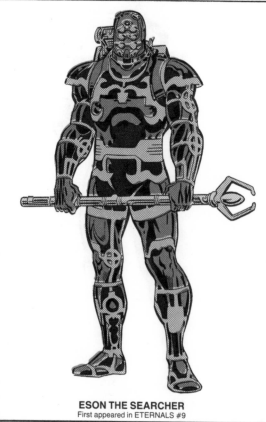

ESON THE SEARCHER
First appeared in ETERNALS #9

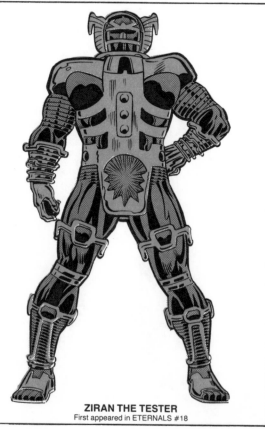

ZIRAN THE TESTER
First appeared in ETERNALS #18

CHIEF EXAMINER

Real Name: Unknown
Occupation: Examiner, analyzer, and duplicator of the powers of various superhuman beings of Earth
Identity: Secret
Legal status: Apparently a citizen of a distant planet whose name has not yet been revealed
Place of birth: Presumably the aforementioned unnamed planet
Marital status: Unknown
Known relatives: None
Group affiliation: None
Base of operations: The aforementioned unnamed planet
First appearance: QUESTPROBE #1
History: On a planet in another galaxy, the leaders of a peaceful humanoid race watched in horror as the invading Black Fleet of starships destroyed world after world, moving towards the humanoids' own solar system. The leaders of the humanoid race did not know how to cope with the approaching invaders, for their race had been pacifists for centuries. Not only had the race no weaponry for defense, but its members were so dedicated to their pacifist philosophy that they found the very idea of warring against the invaders abhorrent. Among the leaders only Durgan the Philosopher sought a means of fighting back against the Black Fleet. He had used the race's advanced technology to observe the superhumanly powerful beings of Earth, and wondered if somehow their powers could be turned to the service of his race.

Sometime later, a helmeted, robed figure calling himself the Chief Examiner began to appear from time to time on Earth. The Chief Examiner would observe superhumanly powerful beings in action, and attempt to lure them through a strange, floating black portal. Once inside the portal, the superhumanly powerful being would be examined and analyzed by an alien technology. The superhumanly powerful being would also temporarily lose his or her powers to some extent. The superhumanly powerful being would then emerge from the portal back upon Earth. The entire process takes no more than moments. The superhumanly powerful being soon thereafter would again reach his normal power level. However, the Chief Examiner could now duplicate that being's powers for his own uses with his technology, having analyzed and drained part of them.

It is known that the Chief Examiner was sent to Earth by Durgan. However, the Chief Examiner's identity remains unknown.

Height: 7' 6" **Eyes:** Unknown
Weight: Unknown **Hair:** Unknown
Strength level: Unknown

Known superhuman abilities: The Chief Examiner can levitate himself, and also appear from seemingly nowhere and disappear. This latter power may be a form of invisibility rather than an indication of a self-teleportation power, since it has been observed that the Chief Examiner, when pinned by rocks at one time, could not use his disappearing power to escape. However, at other times the Chief Examiner has seemed to be intangible, except for his cloak and helmet or able to become intangible. The Chief Examiner can also somehow reprogram computers by touching them. It is not clear whether the Chief Examiner's powers are natural or are the result of the use of advanced technology.

Paraphernalia: The Chief Examiner carries a small device which apparently allows him to analyze the biological structure of living beings to some extent. Possibly it also allows him to monitor the more complete analyses conducted within the portal, and it may possibly also contain the energy drained from the superhumanly powerful beings who pass through the portal.

The Chief Examiner is accompanied by a strange black rectangular portal which floats in the air and which he can somehow cause to follow him about, and to appear and disappear as he himself does. Possibly the portal is a gateway into a tiny pocket dimension. Beings lured within the portal are analyzed by an unknown technology, which also drains part of whatever superhuman energies they possess, so as to enable the Chief Examiner to use his technology to duplicate them. All of the being's memories are laid open to examination in the analysis process. The analysis process takes mere moments, and so a being who enters the portal from Earth will pass through it and return to Earth almost immediately. Passage through the portal significantly diminishes the momentum of the being or object moving through it. Most of the kinetic energy that may be directed against the portal will be absorbed or dissipated by the portal; thus, the portal can resist virtually any attack made against it.

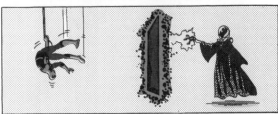

■

CHTHON

Real name: Chthon
Occupation: Inapplicable
Identity: Inapplicable. Chthon's existence is unknown to most inhabitants of Earth.
Legal status: Inapplicable
Other aliases: The Other, Demon of the Darkhold
Place of birth: Earth
Marital status: Inapplicable
Known relatives: Gaea ("sister")
Group affiliation: Inapplicable
Base of operations: An unknown extra-dimensional realm
First appearance: (as The Other) MARVEL CHILLERS #1, (in human host) AVENGERS #185, (true appearance) AVENGERS #187
Origin: THOR ANNUAL #10
History: Chthon is one of the major Elder Gods who first materialized in Earth's biosphere shortly before mankind appeared on Earth. He and his sister god Gaea were among those who inhabited the land masses of the Earth (as opposed to the sea or skies), and may have had something to do with forming certain geological patterns (see *Gaea*). When Gaea gave birth to the first of the newer gods, Chthon perceived that his sister's progeny would eventually supplant the Elder Gods. A scholar by nature, Chthon inscribed a parchment with the mystical knowledge of the world he had thus amassed. This parchment would later be known as the Darkhold. Chthon intended the Darkhold to be his touchstone with the Earthly dimension. As he surmised, Gaea's son Atum was a god-slayer, dedicated to the consumption and elimination of the evil which the Elder Gods had wrought in their degradation into demons (see *Demons*). Chthon managed to escape to a nether dimension before Atum could slay him. When the Darkhold passed into the hands of intelligent beings at some later date, Chthon would have an indestructible medium through which to manipulate Earthly pawns as well as a talisman that could one day be turned into a dimensional portal for his return to Earth.

The Darkhold was first discovered by human sorcerers of pre-Cataclysmic Atlantis who managed to remove it from the doomed island-city before it sank (see *Atlantis*). They founded a cult called the Darkholders and used the spells contained in the book to create vampires (see *Deceased: Vampires*). The book passed through a succession of hands through the next millennia, including Babylonian savants, Egyptian priests, and Hebrew scholars. Whoever employed the knowledge contained within did so at the cost of the corruption of their "soul." This earned the Darkhold the name "Book of Sins."

In the Sixth Century A.D., the parchments found their way to Britain where the sorceress Morgan Le Fey had them bound into book form for the first time (see *Morgan Le Fey*). Morgan used the book to summon Chthon to the Earthly plane for the first time, but discovered Chthon was far too powerful to do her bidding. It took the sorcerous might of Morgan and her new band of Darkholders to repel Chthon from the mortal plane. A renegade Darkholder named Magnus stole the Darkhold, placed it in a tower and wove an intricate spell whereby no one of evil intent could enter (see *Appendix: Magnus*). An apprentice sorcerer named Modred misguidedly en-tered the Tower and had his soul corrupted by Chthon (see *Modred the Mystic*). Centuries later he would serve as Chthon's agent.

Eventually the Irish monk St. Brendan removed the Darkhold from the Tower, believing it to be a temptation to evil, and scattered the various indestructible pages throughout Europe. In the Twelfth Century, a corrupt Spanish monk named Aelfric used occult means to reassemble the scattered pages of the Darkhold. The parchments continued to pass through various hands, although few were skilled enough to employ the spells within to real effect. Transylvanian scholar Baron Gregor Russoff bound the parchments back into book form and used the blank pages he placed in the back as a diary for his occult experiences. The possession of the Darkhold triggered Russoff's hereditary tendency toward lycanthropy and turned him into a werewolf (see *Werewolf*).

Russoff had inadvertently brought the Book close to where the Earthly essence of its demonic author had been imprisoned, Wundagore Mountain. Chthon made his second major bid to return to the Earthly plane, but was repulsed by the forces of the High Evolutionary and the spirit of the Sixth Century sorcerer Magnus (see *High Evolutionary*). When Russoff died, an American named Miles Blackgar bought his estate and acquired the Darkhold. Aware of the danger inherent in the book, Russoff's son Jacob stole it and entrusted it to the care of Father Joaquez, a priest.

From there, it came into the temporary possession of Dracula, Lord of the Vampires, who was looking for a means to restore his flagging powers (see *Deceased: Dracula*). The spirit of Morgan Le Fey also renewed her interest in the Darkhold, and gained as a mortal enemy the original Spider-Woman, who had been befriended by the ghost of Morgan's former colleague Magnus (see *Drew, Jessica*). Morgan once used her magic to simulate the aspect of Chthon in an attempt to defeat the Spider-Woman. When Modred the Mystic was released from suspended animation, Chthon commanded him to fetch the Darkhold so he could be released on Earth. In an elaborate scheme, Chthon took demonic possession of the mutant Scarlet Witch, who had been born atop Wundagore Mountain (see *Scarlet Witch*). The Avengers managed to dispossess the Scarlet Witch and imprison Chthon's earthly essence in Wundagore Mountain.

Finally, Dracula sought the Darkhold once more, realizing that the spell to destroy all vampires was contained within. Earth's sorcerer supreme Doctor Strange managed to use the Darkhold to destroy all vampires on Earth and create a spell by which vampires could no longer exist on Earth (see *Doctor Strange*). Due to his vast power, Strange was the only person to ever use the Darkhold without forfeiting his soul to Chthon. The Darkhold is currently in the custody of Doctor Strange. Chthon is still in his nether dimension, patiently awaiting a fourth attempt to return to Earth.

Height: Unknown **Eyes:** Red
Weight: Unknown **Hair:** None
Strength level: Unknown
Known superhuman powers: Chthon possesses a mastery of the forces of magic on a scale that defies description. In the dimension where he resides he has absolute control over every aspect of that dimension's reality. His major limitation is that he cannot freely teleport between dimensions because it takes such an enormous rift to accomodate the massive magical force that dwells within him. He cannot travel to Earth without the most elaborate of preparations due to the exhaustive magical screens around Earth first erected by his sister Gaea and reinforced by Earth's multitude of sorcerers over the millennia. It is far easier for Chthon to take mortal host-bodies on Earth than to manifest himself in his psychophysical entirety. Even so, it appears that Chthon cannot easily (if at all) transfer his entire power into such host-bodies. ∎

CIRCUS OF CRIME

The Circus of Crime is a traveling band of circus performers, usually led by Maynard Tiboldt, better known as the Ringmaster, who use their special skills to rob their audiences (see *Ringmaster*).

The Circus of Crime was originally Tiboldt's Circus, a small Austrian traveling circus managed for generations by members of the Tiboldt family. In the 1930s Fritz Tiboldt, then the manager and ringmaster of the circus, became active in Nazi party activities. After World War II began, he was asked by German intelligence to take his circus to America, supposedly just to give performances in major cities, but actually in order to use the talents of the Nazi sympathizers among his performers to murder high government officials. However, Tiboldt, who came to be known as the "Ringmaster of Death," was captured by Captain America, and both Tiboldt and the members of his circus who had aided him in his subversive activities were deported (see *Captain America*).

Fritz Tiboldt and his wife Lola continued to manage Tiboldt's Circus after the war. Eventually Fritz and Lola Tiboldt were murdered by Nazis who had escaped capture in vengeance for their cooperation with the Allies. Fritz's son, Maynard Tiboldt, thereupon succeeded him as leader and ringmaster of the circus, and decided to move it to America, far from the scene of Hitler's rise to power and his parents' deaths.

But once in America, Tiboldt's Circus proved incapable of competing successfully with larger American circuses. Blaming Americans not only for ignoring his circus, but also for his father's humiliating capture in America years before, Tiboldt decided to turn to crime. If Americans would not enrich him and his performers willingly, they would be forced to do so. Tiboldt outlined his plans to the members of his troupe, a number of whom had accompanied him from Europe, and others of whom had joined the troupe after it came to America. A good percentage of the troupe quit, refusing to turn to a life of crime. However, a surprising number of the circus members eagerly agreed to join Tiboldt in his criminal endeavors, and they became the first members of what is now known as the Circus of Crime.

The Circus of Crime's usual modus operandi is the following. They will give a performance before a large audience. At some point the Ringmaster will use the powerful mind-control device concealed in his hat to put the audience into a trance. The Circus members then rob the audience, who remember nothing about the thefts when the Ringmaster releases them from the trance and the performance continues. The Circus of Crime performs under different names so that audiences will not suspect they are the Circus of Crime.

Over the years the membership of the Circus of Crime has varied, although there is a core group that has participated in most of its criminal ventures. The Ringmaster and his accomplices have been imprisoned by the law numerous times, but rarely for long, given the difficulties of proving the charges against them, since their victims usually have no memory of being robbed by them. Occasionally the Circus of Crime has operated without the Ringmaster, either because he is in prison, or because some have become dissatisfied with his leadership. However, he has always returned as their leader.

First modern appearance: HULK #3.

Other sometime members of the Circus of Crime include:

RAJAH (Kabir Mahadevu) An Indian elephant trainer and rider. He first performed with the troupe during a stay of theirs in Europe, and recently rejoined them in the United States. First appearance: SUPER-VILLAIN TEAM-UP #8.

TEENA THE FAT LADY (Mary Stensen) An American sideshow performer. She left the Circus in the hope of marrying and raising a family, but has recently returned to it. She is more agile than she seems and can use her vast bulk as a weapon against opponents. First appearance: HULK #3.

BLACKWING (Joseph Manfredi, alias Joe Silvermane). The son of Maggia family leader Silvio "Silvermane" Manfredi, Joseph Manfredi joined the Circus in the guise of Blackwing while he and his father were secretly associated with HYDRA so that they might observe the Circus's criminal activities (see *HYDRA, Deceased: Silvermane*). HYDRA scientists supplied Blackwing with special devices which enabled him to control bats psionically, and he used bats to steal for the circus. First appearance: DAREDEVIL #118. ∎

STRONGMAN

Real Name: Bruce "Bruto" Olafsen
Occupation: Circus strongman and weight-lifter
Identity: Publicly known
Legal status: Former Swedish citizen, now naturalized American citizen with a criminal record
Place of birth: Stockholm, Sweden
Marital status: Single
Known relatives: None
First appearance: HULK #3
Height: 6' 4"
Weight: 280 lbs.
Eyes: Brown
Hair: Brown
Abilities: Bruto has particularly strong biceps and teeth, although his strength is not at superhuman level.

THE CLOWN

Real Name: Eliot "Crafty" Franklin
Occupation: Circus clown
Identity: Publicly known
Legal status: American citizen with a criminal record
Place of birth: Orlando, Florida
Marital status: Single
Known relatives: Corky (father)
First appearance: HULK #3
History: The Clown has twice been leader of the Circus of Crime for brief periods, and once attempted to have the Circus members captured by the law. However, since then, apparently because he feels he has nowhere else to go, the Clown has rejoined the Circus of Crime.
Height: 5' 8"
Weight: 175 lbs.
Eyes: Brown
Hair: Brown
Abilities: The Clown is a skilled comedian, juggler, and unicyclist.
Weapons: The Clown uses a trick cane and juggler's balls as weapons.

FIRE-EATER

Real Name: Tomas Ramirez
Occupation: Circus fire-eater
Identity: Publicly known
Legal status: Former Spanish citizen, now naturalized American citizen with a criminal record
Place of birth: Madrid, Spain
Marital status: Single
Known relatives: None
First appearance: GHOST RIDER #72
Height: 6' 1"
Weight: 200 lbs.
Eyes: Brown
Hair: Bald
Abilities: Using the traditional methods of circus fire-eaters, Fire-Eater can consume flame within his mouth and then project it from his mouth without suffering injury.
Weapons: Fire-Eater uses incendiary "inferno discs" designed by himself and the Clown.

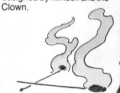

GREAT GAMBONNOS

Real Names: Ernesto and Luigi Gambonno
Occupation: Acrobats and aerialists
Identity: Publicly known
Legal status: Former Italian citizens, now naturalized American citizens with criminal records
Place of birth: Milan, Italy
Marital status: Single
Known relatives: None
First appearance: AMAZING SPIDER-MAN #16
Unusual physical characteristics: Ernesto and Luigi Gambonno are identical twins. Hence, the specifications below apply to both.
Height: 5' 10"
Weight: 195 lbs.
Eyes: Blue
Hair: Black
Abilities: The Gambonnos are superb aerialists and acrobats.

HUMAN CANNONBALL

Real Name: Jack Pulver
Occupation: Human cannonball, acrobat
Identity: Publicly known
Legal status: American citizen with a criminal record
Place of birth: Burbank, California
Marital status: Single
Known relatives: None
First appearance: HULK #3
Height: 5' 8"
Weight: 180 lbs.
Eyes: Blue
Hair: Brown
Abilities: The Human Cannonball is a skilled acrobat.
Paraphernalia: The Human Cannonball's helmet and costume protect him from injury.

LIVE WIRE

Real Name: Rance Preston
Occupation: Performer of rope tricks, former cowboy
Identity: Publicly known
Legal status: American citizen with a criminal record
Place of birth: Houston, Texas
Marital status: Divorced
Known relatives: None
First appearance: FANTASTIC FOUR ANNUAL #5, (as a member of Circus of Crime) POWER MAN #24
History: Before joining the Circus of Crime, Live Wire worked as an agent of the Psycho-Man (see *Psycho-Man*).
Height: 6' 1"
Weight: 200 lbs.
Eyes: Blue
Hair: Brown
Abilities: Live Wire is a master at handling the lariat. He also has various skills that he learned working on a ranch as a cowboy, such as horseback riding.
Weapons: Live Wire uses an electrified lariat. Special insulation in his gloves and clothing protect him from electrical shock.